France in Focus

France in Focus

Film and National Identity

Edited by
Elizabeth Ezra and Sue Harris

Oxford • New York

First published in 2000 by
Berg
Editorial offices:
150 Cowley Road, Oxford OX4 1JJ, UK
838 Broadway, Third Floor, New York, NY 10003-4812, USA

Berg is the imprint of Oxford International Publishers Ltd.

Library of Congress Cataloging-in-Publication Data

A catalogue record for this book is available from the Library of Congress.

British Library Cataloguing-in-Publication Data

A catalogue record for this book is available from the British Library.

ISBN 1 85973 363 8 (Cloth)
ISBN 1 85973 368 9 (Paper)

Typeset by JS Typesetting, Wellingborough, Northants.
Printed in the United Kingdom by Biddles Ltd, Guildford and King's Lynn.

Contents

Contents

Preface

The origins of this book can be traced to an international conference organized by the editors in the University of Stirling French Department. The conference, 'Visual Culture and French National Identity', was a broad-based interdisciplinary event, which examined questions of how national identity is articulated through the range of forms of representation that surround us in our daily lives. We would like to extend our thanks to those scholars who presented erudite papers on French advertising, television, art and film, and to all the conference participants who made such a valuable contribution to the generation of ideas that has inspired this book.

Taking up where the conference left off, this volume brings together a selection of the original papers on French film, reworked in the light of the conference debates, and combines them with a number of subsequently commissioned papers that further address the complexities of the visual mediation of national identity. That the questions raised here are fundamental to our understanding of both the French film industry and French identity itself is underlined in the trajectory of some of the original companion pieces, which have recently been published in *French Cultural Studies, French Cinema in the 1990s* (Powrie, Oxford University Press, 1999), and *Space in European Cinema* (Konstantorakos, Intellect Press, 1998).

We are grateful to the following people for their kind support: to Oron Joffe, Suzanne Ramage, and Marilyn Scott for their advice and, at times, heroic interventions, on the computing front; to Eileen Kelly and Alison Cooper for their assistance with organizational matters; and to Philippa Caine for her work translating the essay by Jean-Pierre Jeancolas. We would also like to convey our personal thanks to Neil and Euan Harris, and Paul Jackson, respectively, for bearing with our divided attentions for the duration of this project.

On an institutional level, we wish to express our gratitude to the School of Modern Languages at Queen Mary and Westfield College for funding the photographs in this volume, to the Museum of Modern Art Film Stills Archive and the British Film Institute for providing the photographs, and

Preface

to Manchester University Press for permission to include the chapters 'Framing Dreyfus' and 'Heritage, Nostalgia and the Woman's Film: the Case of Diane Kurys', which appear in revised form in *Georges Méliès: The Birth of the Auteur* (2000) and *Diane Kurys* (1999).

Elizabeth Ezra and Sue Harris

Notes on Contributors

Martine Beugnet, formerly a visual art curator at the Institut français d'Ecosse, is currently working as a lecturer in film studies at the University of Edinburgh. She is the author of a book on contemporary French cinema entitled *Sexualité, marginalité, et représentation dans le cinéma français contemporain* (l'Harmattan, 2000).

Philippa Caine is completing a doctoral thesis in the Department of French at the University of Stirling on contemporary French women's writing.

Elizabeth Ezra lectures in French studies at the University of Stirling. She is the author of *The Colonial Unconscious: Race and Culture in Interwar France* (Cornell University Press, 2000) and *Georges Méliès: The Birth of the Auteur* (Manchester University Press, 2000).

Sue Harris lectures in the French Department at Queen Mary and Westfield College, University of London. She is the author of *Bertrand Blier* (Manchester University Press, forthcoming), as well as a number of articles and book chapters on contemporary French cinema.

Susan Hayward is the Chair of French at Exeter University. She is the author of *French National Cinema* and the General Editor for the Routledge Series on National Cinemas; she is also the author of *Cinema Studies: Key Concepts* (Routledge, 2000) and *Luc Besson* (Manchester University Press, 1998). Currently, she is writing a book on Simone Signoret.

John Izod is Professor of Screen Analysis in the department of Film and Media Studies at the University of Stirling, where he has taught since 1978. He is the author of a number of Jungian studies of cinema, including *The Films of Nicolas Roeg: Myth and Mind* (Macmillan, 1992).

Jean-Pierre Jeancolas is a founding member of the Association française de Recherche sur l'histoire du cinéma, a regular contributor to the film journal *Positif*, and the author of, among other books, *Le Cinéma des Français: la Vᵉ République* (Stock Cinéma, 1979), *15 ans d'années trente* (1983) and *Histoire du cinéma français* (Nathan, 1995).

Russell King, who teaches in the Department of French at the University of Nottingham, has written extensively on nineteenth-century French poetry, especially Baudelaire and Verlaine, and on Truffaut and Blier. He organized the first UK French Cinema conference in December 1994.

Laurent Marie lectures in French at University College Dublin. He has recently completed a Ph.D. in Film Studies at the University of Warwick on the relationship between the French Communist Party and French cinema since 1944. He has published articles on Claude Berri's *Germinal*, Bruno Dumont's *La Vie de Jésus*, Jean Grémillon's *L'Amour d'une femme*, Hervé Le Roux's *Reprise*, and Jacques Tati's *Play Time*.

Martin O'Shaughnessy is subject leader in French at Nottingham Trent University and specializes in French cinema. He is the author of *Jean Renoir* (Manchester University Press, 2000) and has also published a number of articles and chapters on French colonial cinema, gender in popular cinema and representations of war and nation.

Simon P. Sibelman is Associate Professor of French at the University of Wisconsin-Oshkosh. He is the author of *Silence in the Novels of Elie Wiesel* (St Martin's Press, 1995), as well as a number of articles on French cinema, French-Jewish identity and Holocaust literature.

Louise Strode recently completed doctoral research at Loughborough University. Her thesis examined the relationship between French policy on language, culture and national identity in the 1990s. Her contribution to this collection is based on some of the findings of this research in the area of audiovisual policy.

Carrie Tarr is a Research Fellow at Kingston University (UK). She has published widely on gender and ethnicity in French cinema, including *Diane Kurys* (Manchester University Press, 1999), and has co-edited *Women, Immigration and Identities in France* (Berg, 2000). She is currently preparing a book on twenty years of women's film-making in France.

Florianne Wild is a visiting assistant professor at the State University of West Georgia. She has written on Agnès Varda's *cinécriture* in *L'Esprit*

Créateur, Jewishness and scapegoating in Duviver's *Panique* for *Identity Papers: Contested Nationhood in Twentieth Century France* (University of Minnesota Press, 1996) and Renoir's *La Bête Humaine* in *Film/Literature Quarterly* (forthcoming). She has also edited a special issue of *Contemporary French Civilization*, 'French Film of the 1990s' (Summer/Fall 1998).

Michael Witt teaches French cinema at the University of Surrey Roehampton, and is the author of a doctoral thesis on the film and television work of Anne-Marie Miéville and Jean-Luc Godard. He is currently co-editing (with Michael Temple) *The French Cinema Book* for the BFI and preparing a study of Godard's *Histoire(s) du cinéma*.

Introduction: The French Exception
Sue Harris and Elizabeth Ezra

The term 'l'exception française', which emerged in the wake of the 1993 GATT agreements, signals an attempt to carve out a distinctive role for French culture in a changing world, in the face of both continuing Americanization and encroaching Europeanization. The influence of American culture in France, which dates from at least the end of the First World War, when domination of the world film market shifted from France to the United States, continues unabated. The Liberation of 1944 has given way to the Disneyfication of the *fin de siècle*, in everything from music, food, and consumer habits to film (American films routinely outnumbering French productions on French screens). Meanwhile, for the first time in history, French fiscal autonomy is itself threatened by the implementation, albeit long desired, of a single European currency.

French reaction to these cultural invasions has taken two forms, which reflect apparently conflicting, but actually complementary, notions of fear and desire of 'the foreign'. One form has involved absorbing the 'alien' culture and co-opting, or Gallicizing it: witness French hamburger chains, French rap, French talk shows, French action films. The other reaction, more resistant, has been for France to counter current American cultural hegemony and the threat of European absorption by looking to its own past distinction. At the beginning of the twenty-first century, there remains little doubt that the urge, indeed the need, to communicate to the outside world a sense of the legitimacy of the now recognized 'exception française' has transformed French production. The end of the twentieth century saw the emergence of profoundly nostalgic cinematic genres, such as the heritage film and the literary adaptation, which spoke to a wider world of an authentic and cherished collective identity, founded on long-standing intellectual and literary traditions. These projections of nationhood as inherent and coherent were powerfully supplemented by the emerging 'cinéma du look', a form of cinema that confirmed and renewed accepted notions of French culture as stylish and visually sophisticated. Thus, films like *La Gloire de mon père* (Robert, 1991), *Germinal* (Berri, 1992), *Nikita* (Besson, 1989) and *La Haine* (Kassovitz,

1995) not only achieved high levels of success on the domestic front, but quickly assumed ambassadorial status for French cinema on the world stage. As the mythologies of the past fused with those of the present, so French cinema seemed to affirm in practice what the GATT talks had proved on paper: that the solidity and distinctiveness of French national culture was enough to protect it from the contemporary impulse towards globalization. French fears that transnational integration in the economic and political spheres would inevitably lead to national disintegration in the cultural domain had won the day, but had left many important questions unanswered. Was this mythologizing process, for example, a genuine attempt to rehistoricize French culture in the face of late capitalism's flattening out of history, or was it merely a flat and empty substitute for that history, a simulacrum? Was the 'heritage industry', that powerful vehicle of France's cultural distinctiveness, ultimately no more than a subsidiary of the culture industry, a kind of temporal tourism?

What is certain is that the French recognized earlier than most the importance of cultivating a national image – 'une certaine idée de la France', as de Gaulle famously put it; and they also recognized the central role of cinema in constructing and disseminating this image. This recognition is visible in the governmental policies in place since the end of the Second World War, which allowed France to rebuild its film industry after the Occupation, and which continue to contribute to its relative prosperity today. One of the key factors in the success of such policies has been their emphasis on the distinction between products of the culture industry and other commodities.

Because of the money involved, and because of its necessarily collaborative means of production (which would not be disputed by even the most insistent *auteur* theory of individual genius), cinema is a profoundly industrial art, one of the first new art forms to be born in the age of mechanical reproduction. But an industrial art is an art nonetheless. In carving out a distinctive role for artistic and cultural products within industry, France has acknowledged the need for a new conception of art in the (post)industrial age.

This new conception of art, however, is not without its complexities. Scholars have wrestled with the question of whether an art that might seek to transcend the limitations of national identity is the expression of a new, postnational vision of a global community, or simply the cultural manifestation of late capitalism's multinational corporatism. The chapters here do not formalise this question as such, but agree that one thing is certainly clear: the traditional base-superstructure model of art as a perfunctory and transparent medium for a political message has been replaced by the recognition of a more interactive relation between art and politics. And cinema, as one of the most popular and populist art forms, *is* in many ways the new politics. This fact is viewed by many film-makers and critics in different ways. Some film-makers (such as Godard) worry that simulacra such as television and mass-market films are replacing political engagement, lulling and distracting audiences from pressing social concerns; but for Jean-Pierre Jeancolas, one of France's foremost film critics and historians, cinema is a political and politicizing force capable of giving rise to actions such as the protest against the treatment of immigrants led by young French film-makers in the spring of 1997. There are signs that film-makers in France are assuming the functions of public discourse formerly filled by intellectuals, philosophers and novelists – those who work with the written word. Conversely, there has also been movement in the other direction, as some established literary figures and philosophers (one thinks of Marguerite Duras and Bernard-Henri Lévy) have tried their hand at film-making, with varying results.

These exchanges confirm cinema's role as possibly the single most important medium for the transmission of French cultural values and identity in the twentieth and twenty-first centuries. The cinema both constructs and disseminates France's cultural heritage, and remains the vehicle by which the nation conveys an image of itself abroad, thereby reinforcing its projected (or desired) identity, both industrially and artistically. As a 1959 government report noted, 'France's genius may be recognized in the face that its films give it' (cited by Jeancolas). It is the contours of this 'face of France' that are traced in this volume. The pieces collected here provide an assessment of a dominant art form's engagement with expressions of national identity at key moments in French (cinematic) history: from the birth of cinema in the nineteenth century, to the inter-war period, through the Occupation and post-Liberation period, to the New Wave and contemporary film. The chapters share a concern with the concept of marginality in national identity, focusing variously on representations of the 'exotic', the continuing importance of industrial institutions established in the post-war period, and the evolution of French approaches to film-making and criticism in terms of profoundly French political traditions.

Despite the plurality of themes, genres, and approaches represented in this volume, the chapters collected here coalesce into three general rubrics. The first, entitled 'An Archeology of French Cinema', examines the historical origins of the status of film today in France. Jean-Pierre Jeancolas traces the vibrancy of contemporary French film-making to measures put in place in the wake of the Second World War that enabled the modern domestic industry to flourish. His description of the depleted and derelict cinema of a newly liberated France in 1944 helps us to understand the rationale for the implementation of protectionist policies, which has been fiercely defended in France ever since. Aside from their obvious financial impact, we learn that these measures were intrinsic to the foundation in France of a culture of cinephilia, and we learn the extent to which, more than in any other European country, the French film-going public has come to identify with the products of its visual culture industry. The recognition of this identification outside of France in the GATT agreements has, Jeancolas suggests, provided a strong foundation for the industry's contemporary descendants.

The next chapter of this section examines the ideological positions of one of the most influential theorist-practitioners of a whole generation, who has contributed to an enduring view of French cinema as introspectively avant-garde. Michael Witt's chapter charts the vicissitudes of Jean-Luc Godard's pronouncements on the function and status of cinema as a barometer of social, political and cultural transformation. Like Jeancolas, Godard views the Second World War as a turning-point in film history, but in the service of a somewhat different conclusion: the war precipitated the end of cinema, by pointing up the failure of the medium adequately to represent the unthinkable. But Michael Witt argues that, despite his oft-cited lament of the death of cinema, Godard allows for, and indeed insists on, certain exceptions to this pronouncement, including, to a certain extent, the movement with which his own films have come to be identified, the French New Wave. As Witt makes clear from his reading of Godard's theoretical writings, nation, history and cinema are unstable concepts, but are nevertheless complementary, interacting and mutually realigning in relation to one another: any construction of nationhood is inextricably bound up with the negotiation of these elements.

In the next chapter, Laurent Marie documents and analyses the ideological rift that coloured debates about the role and value of art, especially cinema, in the French Communist Party during and after the New Wave, and which paved the way for a new kind of militant, marginal cinema that gained ascendancy in the wake of May 1968. Marie's paper underscores the Party's growing recognition of the role and importance of style in debates about artistic creation, which was coming to be perceived no longer simply as a manifestation of a particular political ideology. The ensuing debate revolved increasingly around aesthetics, questions not only of what, but of *how* film could represent. The innovations introduced by the New Wave, Marie argues, ultimately prompted

the PCF to acknowledge the creative independence of artists and intellectuals, even if they could still be criticized on ideological grounds.

Finally, Louise Strode brings this section full circle in taking up the
paradox, outlined by Jeancolas, of French protectionist policy-making
within a European context of integration and construction. By looking at
the cross-party consensus that prevails in the French fear of global cultural
uniformity, Strode's chapter on the debates surrounding the political
acknowledgement of the French 'exception culturelle' takes us in more
precise detail into the ways in which France's self-image and its sense of
national identity are built into its visual culture industries.

The notion of 'heritage' discussed earlier, which is central to the
construction of national identity, raises a troubling and crucial question:
of whose heritage, exactly, are we speaking? The term 'exception
française', in the context of this question, also signifies the many instances
of setting apart, of casting out, that have made it possible to conceive of
such a thing as French culture in the first place. Accordingly, the second
section of this volume, entitled 'French Civilization and its Discontents',
addresses some of the exclusions that have been carried out in order to
foster the illusion of a unified heritage, especially in the contexts of
ethnicity and gender. Simon Sibelman's chapter concentrates on Julien
Duvivier's little-studied 'Jewish films', examining the disturbing stereotypes disseminated within them. Sibelman considers the extent to which
representations of Jews in French cinema in the 1930s fanned the flames
of a climate of rabid anti-Semitism that was to reach its apogee in the
Vichy years. Using the example of Duvivier, widely acknowledged as
one of the major talents of the French cinematic golden age, but whose
'Jewish films' have been largely overlooked by film scholars, Sibelman
analyses the power of cinema to confirm myth as reality, and highlights
the danger of the abdication of artistic and moral responsibility in
constructing images that purport to reflect society. Although Duvivier
apparently made no claim to an anti-Semitic stance in either his work or
his personal or political life, Sibelman reveals how the film language
employed in three of his films works to legitimize a menacing depiction
of the 'stranger within' French society. This formulaic representation
based in anti-Semitic antecedents prevalent in the culture at large was to
endure in French cinema, fuelling debates around other depictions of the
'outsider' in French film.

Susan Hayward also takes up the question of alterity in her chapter for
this volume. Charting the development of European film industries first
through an economic lens, and then through the construction of national
cinemas, Hayward argues here that a national cinema functions doubly.

First, cinema serves as an agent of self-delusion, a screen on to which a nation projects its own idealized images, and which serves to suppress both those deemed different and the very fact of differentiation itself. But national cinemas also provide a site of contestation in which the appearance of a homogeneous national identity is exposed as a sum of scattered subjectivities. Cinema, in other words, promotes the illusion of a cohesive identity, but also points to its own status as illusion. This it does by means of representations of the gendered human body. The disavowal of difference privileged in psychoanalytic theories of gender distinctions not only structures individual films that fetishise women's bodies, but also serves as a model of the suppression of difference within nationalist discourse. Hayward advocates an aesthetics and a politics of sexual border-crossing as a strategy for undermining the hierarchies that this disavowal engenders.

Until fairly recently, most heritage films have glossed over women's contributions to French history, literally writing them out of the picture. But Carrie Tarr shows how one film-maker, Diane Kurys, subverts the heritage genre, so successful at the end of the twentieth century, by reinserting female agency into the French national image, which has risked being subsumed in the parade of shrinking violets, silently suffering matriarchs, and frolicking nymphs found in many instantly consumable and enduringly popular French exports. Despite their attention to period detail and scenic display (a feature they share with more conventional heritage films), Kurys's films do not subsume their gendered political content within the visual pleasures they undoubtedly provide, but instead allow narrative and spectacle to reinforce one another. This formal interplay is mirrored on a thematic level in Kurys's treatment of the relationship between her characters' individual lives and the larger socio-historical context in which these unfold. By showing the extent to which key moments in history are experienced through the domestic intricacies of everyday life, Tarr reveals the imbrication of the personal and the political for women in post-war France.

Martin O'Shaughnessy pursues this line of inquiry into the relation between gender and history by demonstrating how, in Jean Renoir's films, pivotal narratives of nationhood and access to the space in which they are enacted are profoundly gendered. Reading Renoir's famed humanism as somewhat less all-encompassing than previous criticism has allowed, O'Shaughnessy reveals that concepts of community and fraternity are in fact highly exclusive in Renoir, privileging a virile community of active men and relegating the potentially destabilizing female presence to the domestic sphere. In films from 1926–1964, Renoir's narratives engage with moments of crisis in which the national myths of Frenchness are called into question. Thus the collapse of the values of civilization implicit in the barbarism of the First World War, the decadence and xenophobia of the 1930s and the impact of rapid industrialization during *les trente glorieuses* (from the mid-1940s to the mid-1970s) are all represented, according to O'Shaugnessy, as moments in which French national identity must be reinvented. That the moment that brings the community together should exclude at least half of it points to an unresolved contradiction at the heart of the work of one of the most important and well-respected French directors of all time, and thus of the legacy of French film history itself.

The final section of this volume, 'Cinematic Communities', examines films that question traditional notions of community. The first two essays in this section address the function of filmic conceptions of history – of the role of history itself – in the construction of cultural self-definitions. Going back to the very beginnings of cinema, Elizabeth Ezra's chapter, 'Framing Dreyfus', examines *L'Affaire Dreyfus* (1899), the film series (the first of its kind) made by Georges Méliès about the Dreyfus Affair as it was unfolding. France has traditionally accorded a preponderant significance to literature and the written document in shaping its historical identity – its conception of history and its place in it – but in the twentieth century, cinema came to challenge the dominance of the written word. In his well-known book *Imagined Communities*, Benedict Anderson links the construction of 'imagined communities' to the rise and spread of print journalism; it is doubtless no accident that the scope of Anderson's study terminates at the end of the nineteenth century, when the advent of cinema would effect a lasting change in the forms that these imagined communities would take, and on the means by which they would be created. In creating a filmic testimony of a historical event, Méliès was challenging the hegemony of the document, thereby inventing a new genre, the documentary film, and in the process changing the face of history. Méliès's series thus prompted a redefinition of the limits of *l'histoire*, as both history and storytelling.

According to Florianne Wild, Jacques Becker's *Goupi Mains-Rouges* (1943) has a similar metahistorical function. Rather than an allegory in the reflective mode pertaining to a specific historical era, Wild reads *Goupi* as an allegory of history itself, as much a testimony to earlier historical events as to the period during which it was made (the Occupation). Such a reading, in which a film is examined transversally through its historical allusions, enables us to detect the points at which it is shot through with the unresolved tensions of other eras: in other words, the ways in which it is historically overdetermined. Specifically, Wild focuses on the dynastic imagery that inflects the film's depiction of the Goupi family, which reveals the imperialist legacy informing the construction of French national identity at the end of the Third Republic.

Russell King also examines the use of a familial allegory, in the work and interviews of one of French cinema's most influential ambassadors, François Truffaut. Truffaut was the key figure of New Wave cinema and criticism, leading the attack on the so-called 'cinéma de papa', and its long-standing French bourgeois traditions of performance and *mise-en-scène*. Like his peers in the movement, the director sought to replace what he perceived as an outmoded and nationally insular mode of film-making with a new contemporaneity in subject-matter and style, drawing on exposure to international, as well as French, traditions of film-making. King argues that Truffaut's denial of a clear socio-political significance to his films (despite the fact that his early film-making, like that of other New Wave directors, took place against the background of colonial wars in Algeria and Vietnam) points to a refusal to accept that the work of an artist inevitably constitutes a reflection of his political, cultural and social environment. King's analysis posits Truffaut's attention to language as an expression of his Frenchness, and argues that a sense of an authentic auteurist identity emerges through an emphasis on units of collaboration and social cohesion that, perhaps utopically, attempt to transcend France and all things French by creating a filmic family, a cinematic community, both within and beyond the boundaries of national identity.

In the penultimate chapter in this volume, John Izod presents a provocative analysis of Jean-Jacques Beineix's *Diva* (1981), which has become, for a whole generation of cinema audiences, an integral part of France's heritage, a defining point of reference in the shared repository of cultural experience. Following a Jungian trajectory that has been eclipsed in film studies in favour of a the more predictable Freudian analysis-by-numbers, Izod argues that the film's use of archetypal images and motifs reveals a renewed engagement with traditional and specifically French notions of the mythic, which enable it to challenge the wider cultural assumptions of modern French film-making. The quest for self-knowledge that, according to Izod, structures the film's narrative and explains the motivation of the principal protagonists, is here representative of new exploratory strategies in filmic aesthetics, which use symbolism to uncover the unconscious processes of national self-definition.

Finally, Martine Beugnet also examines the thriller genre, but from a social and moral perspective. Recent crime films, she argues, while appearing to confine representations of evil to exceptional acts of horror, actually identify what Hannah Arendt termed its 'banality'. Analysis reveals that evil is not a function of singular acts of abnormality, but rather of the dangers inherent in the conformity of the plural, in other words, in the construction of collective identities. Examining *Dr Petiot* (Christian de Challonges, 1991), *J'ai pas sommeil* (Claire Denis, 1994), and *La Cérémonie* (Claude Chabrol, 1995), Beugnet contends that these films depict modern-day evil not as a departure from the norms of the community, but as the very adherence to those norms. Whereas this volume began by investigating the notion of the 'exception française', or France's desire to differentiate itself from rival cultural discourses, it concludes with Beugnet's demonstration that what might initially seem to be exceptional, a display of exclusiveness and singularity, is in fact the flipside of conformity and therefore, by (a not-so-great) extension, of the mechanism that underwrites constructions of national identity.

It will have become apparent that virtually all the chapters in this volume go against the grain in their attempts to construct an alternative history of French cinema, whether by bringing to light overlooked films or by re-examining well-known, indeed possibly even 'over-exposed', films or film-makers in a new light. In doing so, they attempt to read between the lines of the well-rehearsed story of French national identity, to reveal the structure of 'l'exception française', in which France makes an exception for itself by suppressing alterity within it. French film and national identity have been inextricably bound up together at least since 1891, when Georges Demeny, an anatomist, used Étienne-Jules Marey's serial camera (an immediate precursor of the *cinématographe*) to film a continuous sequence of individual shots of himself uttering the syllables 'Vi-ve la Fran-ce'. It is our hope that, as we begin a new century of cinema, this book will bring France into better focus by showing that national identity is more than the sum of its parts.

Part I
An Archaeology of French Cinema

—1—

The Reconstruction of French Cinema
Jean-Pierre Jeancolas

This chapter will endeavour to answer two questions at once. The first is historical: how was it that French cinema, in a critical condition in the summer of 1944, recovered its vitality in the five years that followed? The other question, often heard in relation to French cinema in European circles, is more journalistic: why is it that French cinema at the beginning of the twenty-first century is still alive and kicking, while old-style continental film-making – Italian or German – is undergoing an economic and artistic crisis that has persisted for two decades?

All of this implies an assertion that must be substantiated: that of a continuity between French cinema as brought back to life by the 'doctors' of the post-war period, and cinema as it is, at its most contemporary. This, in turn, takes us to the roots of the cultural specificity, or *exception culturelle*, so frequently discussed in 1993, at the renegotiations – in Brussels and then in Geneva – of the GATT Agreements.

First of all, the term 'reconstruction' must here be re-inscribed with the specific meaning it had in the France of the late 1940s. In November 1945, a 'Ministry of Reconstruction' appeared in de Gaulle's interim government. It was to remain part of practically every government of the Fourth Republic (with the position being held for five years and seven governments by the same man, Eugène Claudius-Petit), and was later to become the 'Ministry of Construction' under the first government of the Fifth Republic. The reconstruction of the cinema was only very marginally a matter for this *ad hoc* ministry, whose remit was limited to the actual physical rebuilding of the cinemas that had been destroyed during the war. Indeed, the reconstruction of cinema in France had very specific requirements, which were more than just a question of money and of industrial concern. Beyond the studios, the cinemas, and the factories producing film stock, the most pressing concern was to revive an ethos of creation, as much a matter of public morale – and thus of politics – as of aesthetics.

In the newly-liberated Paris of September 1944, cinematic activity was non-existent: auditoriums were closed, studios destroyed or closed. This was the autumn before the industry began to come back to life, and then only in extremely precarious conditions. Power cuts, a shortage of film stock, and the scarcity of actual movies made activity in all branches of the profession terribly uncertain; Jean Cocteau's production diary for *La Belle et la bête*, filmed one year on, between August 1945 and January 1946, gives a clear idea of those difficulties. These material circumstances were matched by important institutional concerns. Between 1940 and 1944, the Vichy government had taken control of the film industry, placing it under the administrative jurisdiction of an Organizational Committee that conformed to the corporate discourse of the regime. It was to the credit of this committee (the *Comité d'Organisation de l'Industrie Cinématographique*) that it imposed certain new and austere reforms. The implementation of these measures, frequently debated in the pre-war years, was now facilitated by the military-technocratic authoritarianism of the regime, and by the quasi-autarchy in which French cinema, protected by the German forces from American competition, was to live and prosper. And yet, even before the Normandy landings on 3 June 1944, the *Comité français de libération nationale*, which paved the way for the interim government, had declared null and void those cinematic texts that had been produced by 'the *de facto* authority calling itself The French State'. It was therefore the very status of cinema in France that was ripe for reconstruction.

Ten years earlier, the question had already been asked. Then too, economic crisis had damaged the large corporations of the sector (Pathé and Gaumont), and had brought the powers that be face to face with their responsibilities. The cinema could not be left at the mercy of unchecked liberalism and abandoned to wheeling and dealing. Two contradictory reports were drawn up in 1935 and 1936: one proposed interventionism and the supervision of the profession; the other proposed a liberal solution, involving informed and responsible corporate authorities. The problem reappeared in 1945 in a power balance upset by the war. The post-liberation politicians were, on the whole, in favour of increased direct state intervention. Thus, de Gaulle, pressurized by a strong left-wing majority, nationalized some major sectors of the economy, including utility services, leading banks and the automobile manufacturer Renault. Throughout the whole of 1945 rumours circulated about the possible nationalization of the cinema.

On 25 October 1946, the government legislated to create the *Centre national de la cinématographie* (National Centre of Cinematography),

Figure 1. *Hiroshima mon amour* (1958), Alain Resnais. Courtesy Museum of Modern Art, New York.

the CNC, which, more than fifty years later, still plays the leading role in all cinematographic activity in France. It is what French administrative law calls a 'Public Corporation', and was initially attached to the Ministry of Information, which dealt with matters relating to the cinema. The CNC was created to provide a legislative and financial structure for the cinema, and to aid in the production and distribution of films. It was placed under the authority of a director, a position held between 1947 and 1952 by Michel Fourré-Cormeray, a senior Gaullist civil servant, who had already been put in charge of cinematic affairs in 1945. He was undoubtedly one of the principal protagonists in setting up the new structures.

The CNC was a shell, and in 1946 that shell was empty. Industrial regulations consisted of long-standing but often outdated directives (a number of measures taken by the Vichy government were provisionally retained), which were often badly administered. The profession was, as ever, divided. Production had certainly started up again, in some quite adventurous conditions. The profession (especially the employers) feared state intervention and made no secret of this. And yet interventionism triumphed with the *Loi d'aide* passed on 23 September 1948, which enshrined both a principle and a space – that space being the one in which, and thanks to which, French cinema has thrived ever since. The law created a source of financial aid (said at the time to be 'temporary', it was to be reviewed and replenished regularly) available to the industry, to producers, and to those showing the films. This assistance was funded by taxes levied on box office sales, regardless of the provenance of the film being shown; thus the success of a British or American film in France automatically benefited the creation and exhibition of French films, and this still holds true at the beginning of the twenty-first century. The law came into its own in 1949, when French film production finally returned to pre-war levels. The aid fund guaranteed fresh finance for the production of films, and financed the reconstruction and refurbishment of the auditoriums. To put it plainly, the success of *Gone With The Wind*, shown to a French public for the first time in May 1950, contributed to the production of films by directors such as Christian Jacque and Jacques Tati, just as it contributed to the physical reconstruction of the small-town cinema halls.

The law was intended to last for five years. In 1953, a second *loi d'aide* was adopted, which both maintained automatic entitlement to financial aid for production and exhibition and, what is more, made provision for contributions to cultural innovations such as Henri Langlois' *Cinéma-thèque*, *Ciné-Club* federations and the IDHEC (*Institut des hautes études cinematogaphiques*). Discreetly then, the law took account of an evolution in the social status of the cinema, and France began to embrace *la cinéphilie*, to which we shall return below.

In June 1959 France had just changed constitutions, and André Malraux was appointed to head the brand-new Ministry of Culture. It was as such that he was to sign the decree of 19 June that formed a third *loi d'aide*. The *fonds d'aide* (aid fund) now became the *fonds de soutien* (support fund); this was intended principally to facilitate production, through the creation of a selective system of advances. The mechanism of the *avance sur recettes* (advance against takings, a grant given to film-makers by the government), still a determinant factor today for new cinema, was already implicitly present in the *décret Malraux* of June 1959, which was itself preceded by a report that defined the role of French cinema, and its specificity:

> The intervention of the state in the film industry finds its primary justification in the concern to provide the economy of this sector with the means to withstand, free of difficulties, the constraints of an art. However, as much as being the creative instrument of an art, the cinema must also be the creative instrument of a culture. [. . .] The intervention of the State in this domain

thus fulfils a function of another kind, which is that of ensuring, by channelling financial resources, that France's genius may be recognized in the face that its films give it.

In its time this text gave cause for concern. One could reasonably read into it the threat of an outright seizure of control, the threat of cinema turning into an 'official' or 'sovereign' form of art. With hindsight, it is possible to find an echo of this emphasis in François Mitterrand's speech at Gdansk on 21 September 1993, at the very height of the GATT battle:

> Creations of the spirit are not mere merchandise, cultural services are not simple commercial concerns. Defending the pluralism of works of art and of the public's freedom to choose is a duty. At stake here is the cultural identity of our nations, the right of each people to its own culture, the freedom to choose our own images. A society that abandons to others its means of representation, that is to say its means of expressing its own sense of self, is an enslaved society.

From one pole of official society to the other, the speeches bounced off one another: the cinema escaped the status of merchandise. Cinema was deemed to fall within the province of 'artistry', and as such to hold a representational value that justifies the intervention of the state in the areas of both production and distribution.

Returning to the post-war period, the reconstruction of the French cinema after the war also flowed through two further channels. First, the concept of *droit d'auteur*, or royalties, was to be given a revised modern definition. The question of who exactly is the 'author' of a film, of who has the right to the royalties, has been contentious since the 1920s. Wholly in keeping with its industrial line of logic, occupied France tried in 1943 to insist upon the primacy of the producer. But this legislation was abrogated after the Liberation. The debate was thus taken up once again by the profession, resulting in a global review of the concept of copyright as enshrined in French laws dating from 1791 and 1793, laws that were evidently ill-adapted to the unstable *mélange* of industry and personal creation known as the 'seventh art'. Twelve years' work culminated in the law of 11 March 1957, which classed film among the *œuvres de l'esprit*, or 'imaginative works', officially recognizing as authors of the film the director, composer, and all those involved in writing the film, to the detriment of the producer, now excluded from all royalty rights. Modified in 1985 to accommodate advances in technology and to pay heed to the common practice that deems the director the privileged *auteur* of the film, the law of 1957 had been a decisive step for the recognition of film 'ownership' – in line with the evolution of French society and the growing trend towards cinephilia – but at odds with the American conception of industrial copyright, which deems the production company sole author and beneficiary of the film.

Second, fifty years ahead of contemporary concerns over the prospect of globalization, this period witnessed a desire to address the question of defining geographic and economic space. This occurred in two stages, the first of which was the key agreement with the United States, shrewdly negotiated in Washington as early as Spring 1946 (before the CNC had even been created) and signed on 28 May within the framework of the Blum–Byrnes agreements. It was a matter of great urgency: in 1946, after the Liberation of France, American cinema represented both a formidable temptation for the French film-goer, deprived of these films since 1940, and a major threat to the security of the domestic industry. Hollywood could flood the French market with between one and two thousand films – films that had already broken even on home ground – and thereby put paid to all efforts to reconstruct a viable national cinema. The Blum–Byrnes agreement, judged harshly by artistic and industrial professionals alike, at least had the merit of defining and protecting a space for the distribution of French films over a period of two years. Effectively, this space served as a shield, providing the shelter in which a non-competitive industry began its renaissance. Two years later, a new agreement signed in Paris widened this space. The main danger had been overcome.

The next step was the establishment of good-neighbourly relations (that is to say co-production agreements) with the other European film-making industries, and in particular, with Italy. The two first co-production agreements between France and Italy were signed between 1946 and 1949. The number of films resulting from their co-production grew from six in 1949 to thirty-six in 1953. Similar agreements were also concluded with other partners: Franco's Spain, the former Federal Republic of Germany, the UK, Canada, Austria, and the former Soviet Union. Co-production places heavy demands on the financial resources of films: the more substantial the budget, the greater the potential for loss. The film industry does very well out of co-production; artistic expression, however, fares less well. The co-production of films has its own particular requirements (the mix of production teams, the inclusion of Italian actors in French films and vice versa), but this hasn't stopped the system from functioning to this day: as late as 1996, sixteen French–Italian co-productions were made.

Again, with hindsight, we might take account of a less quantifiable element, one that caught the attention of commentators during cinema's centenary celebrations, that of cinephilia, or a passion for the cinema. The development of the *ciné-club* (film society), and of new expressions of curiosity about film, together with the establishment of cinema as a legitimate cultural phenomenon (for example, in *lycées* during the 1950s, where rudimentary but highly influential *ciné-clubs* were being run) – all this came about in a climate of state voluntarism, which was itself inspired by the ideas generated within the Resistance movements during the war. Cinema journals multiplied (and fragmented); meetings and debates forged a new public with its own particular demands. Cinephilia set in motion a demand within society that, from the mid-1950s onwards, was to place productive pressure on creativity: it was the *ciné-clubs* that lent their support to *l'Ecole nationale de court-métrage* (the French School of Short Films), and that were to establish the likes of Alain Resnais, Agnès Varda, and Georges Franju. The great upheaval of French cinema around 1960 was not the doing of new prodigal *auteurs*. It was the happy encounter of apprentice *auteurs*, animated by a passion for the cinema acquired in the *ciné-clubs* or at the Henri Langlois *Cinémathèque*, with an eager and appreciative public ready to welcome with enthusiasm films as diverse as *Hiroshima mon amour* (Resnais, 1958), *A bout de souffle* (Godard, 1959) and *Le joli mai* (Marker, 1963).

To summarise, French cinema was reconstructed by the state. Significantly, though, all those involved in the cinema, from film-makers to technicians, from audiences to critics, essayists and intellectuals such as Edgar Morin and Gilles Deleuze, all knew how to use to their full potential the tools that power had made available to them; their common interest in the 'seventh art' served also to legitimize it. The state, however, has been guilty of ambiguity, of duplicity. While Malraux, as Minister of Culture, defined a state that was to be protector of the Arts, of Literature, and of the Cinema, making it clear that this state would have the authority to 'ensure that France's *génie* [genius, spirit] may be recognized in the face that its films will give it', other ministers were busy controlling and censoring the very same films. For half a century now, relations between tutelary public powers and artists have been neither easy nor harmonious. The 'creative space' defined by the *lois d'aide* and their avatars has always been a minefield of conflict. Nonetheless, the fact remains – and this is what is important in this context – that the existence of this creative space has never been called into question.

French cinema has thus thrived, and still does today, in a protected space. The continuity of film creation in France may be explained by the production structures widely available to young film-makers (over the period 1987 to 1996, 312 film-makers made their first film, of which thirty-seven were made in 1996, and of those 312 first films, 148 benefited from an *avance sur recette*), as well as at the other end of the commercial 'chain', structures for exploiting the films produced, namely the construction, renovation, and transformation of a significant number of cinemas (4,365 cinemas were in use in France at the end of 1995). The lack of these structures in neighbouring countries, in particular in Germany and Italy, contributes to the double crisis – economic, no doubt, but above all else, artistic – being experienced elsewhere in Europe. It is the administrative safety barrier in France, of which the first elements were established over fifty years ago, that founded the vitality of the French film industry, which is, in every respect, quite unique.

It would be logical to conclude at this point, on the fragility of this unique situation within France, which one could refer to as the mode of production *à la française*. This fragility was at the heart of the GATT negotiations in December 1993, which, although settled in an apparent victory for France, amount to little more than a provisional agreement. However, we should not underestimate the importance of the outcome: that with the backing of the European Community, the French obtained recognition of their cultural specificity. For the time being at least, cinema is not to be a commodity like any other: films are not simply put into circulation, they are not merely fabricated like sausages or Coca-Cola.

However, in the wake of this key moment in French cultural history, it may be possible to draw another, more open conclusion, the pertinence of which will only become apparent in the years ahead. In order to analyse this possibility we must return to 1997, and to a series of events in cinema circles that had the potential to change the image, and beyond that, the status, of the filmic *auteur*.

On 12 February 1997, the daily newspaper *Le Monde* published on its front page an appeal signed by fifty-nine directors, belonging, for the most part, to what is known as *le jeune cinéma français*, or 'young French cinema' (film-makers under thirty-five, and who made their first film sometime during the last ten years). The article focused not on the cinema, but rather on the need to adopt a collective stance in a debate that was stirring up society as a whole, that of the legal status of foreigners living in France in what was deemed an 'irregular situation', those referred to as the *sans papiers* because they do not possess valid legal documents. At the time, the French parliament was putting the finishing touches to a law that was both restrictive and inhumane, and the appeal by the film-makers was a reasoned call to disobey the law. In just a few days their appeal had set in motion a wider movement of petitioners and demonstrators, and had reanimated debate in the media, in the street, among the political parties and in parliament, first regarding the status of these foreigners, and then more generally on the 'correct practice' of citizenship.

Acting together, young directors and then film-makers of all generations (a second appeal was circulated in several hundred cinemas across France at the end of March 1997) served as cultural sparks, prompting a reawakening of the notion of the 'citizen', the consequences of which are still immeasurable. One can only take note and attempt to understand. There was, on the part of these film-makers, an acceptance of responsibility and the awareness that it was possible and necessary to act as a driving force in order to mobilise public opinion. There was, in the space of a few days, a display of collective engagement and of determination to enter into the political arena. There was also, at the outset, a very real element of risk-taking: it is uncommon, within the French democratic tradition, to appeal to people actively to disobey the law.

The film-makers thus took over the role of agitators, a role that in preceding generations had been played by the great intellectuals, by Sartre, Breton, Leiris, Nadeau, who adopted stances against the Algerian War that were every bit as transgressive. All of which prompts an inevitable question. Why film-makers? Why those particular film-makers? Why not philosophers, academics, writers? Indeed, as the question was asked, it in turn called into question the status of the intellectual in France today. In the present context, another question is perhaps more to the point: how can the fact that these people make films (and not just any old films, assuredly) explain and even possibly legitimate the civic intervention of Pascale Ferran, Arnaud Desplechin, Claire Denis, Cedric Klapisch, Tonie Marshall (to name but those pushed forward by their peers into the position of spokespersons for the movement)? It is surely the nature of 'young French cinema', the evolution of cinema's political role, of ways of looking at 'reality', and more particularly of ways of looking at a reality that is close at hand (geographically, socially and in generational terms) that must now be examined. The only certainty is that, in just one season, French cinema showed us all unprecedented proof of its vitality.

Translated by Philippa Caine

2

'Qu'était-ce que le cinéma, Jean-Luc Godard?' An Analysis of the Cinema(s) at Work in and around Godard's *Histoire(s) du cinéma*

Michael Witt

'Il n'y a plus de cinéma.' ('There's no longer any cinema.')[1]

Godard's refrain since the early 1980s that the cinema is dying, replaced at the end of the decade by the flat assertion that the cinema is well and truly dead, is now widely familiar. Much of his work of the past two decades has played with this notion, and served to spin a Godardian 'death of cinema' discourse. Widely appropriated and repeated by others, the root of this now fairly common critique in a Godardian polemic has largely disappeared from view, and the idea that the cinema may be 'unwell', 'dying' or 'dead' has permeated through into all manner of critical discourses on film, from the popular to the highbrow. The idea of the death of cinema invokes multiple 'deaths' and 'cinemas' simultaneously. I have explored the 'deaths' elsewhere, principally in terms of Godard's view of the pervasive degradation in the quality of films, in the desire to make them, the desire to watch them, and of his critique of television's role in 'programming' subjectivity (Witt 1999). Within this schema, the decline and fall of cinema is ascribed to the seemingly endless prolifera-tion of 'enemy' images and sounds on television and in the burgeoning digital media, or, perhaps more precisely, to the resultant televisual redefinition of our contemporary world-space that it has effected. As Susan Sontag wrote in her polemic on the 'decay' of cinema, which serves as a succinct summary of many of the tenets of Godard's position, what has been lost is an art-form that was 'quintessentially modern; distinctively accessible; poetic and mysterious and moral – all at the same time' (Sontag 1996: 60).

Figure 2. *Histoire(s) du cinéma* (1988–1998), Jean-Luc Godard. Courtesy British Film Institute.

Across the 1980s, in conjunction with a recognition of the winding down of cinema as a popular art-form and its reduction to just one of many image-based cultural forms, Godard repositions himself as historian, looking back in analytical and evaluative mode to reapproach the question 'Qu'est-ce le cinéma?' ('What is cinema?') from a vantage point after the cinema's demise, or, rather, to reformulate the question itself as 'Qu'était-ce que le cinéma?' ('What was cinema?'). The culmination of this repositioning is, of course, in the project that has ensured Godard's return to a central position in debates around audiovisual art and culture at the beginning of the twenty-first century: his monumental four-and-a-half-hour *Histoire(s) du cinéma* (1988–1998). Long in gestation and much anticipated, the finished eight-part series received its TV première in France on Canal Plus throughout July and August 1999, and is now commercially available not only as a set of four Gaumont videotapes, but also as a four-volume collection of Gallimard/Gaumont art books, and as five CDs (released on the ECM label). Jonathan Rosenbaum has suggested that 'Godard's babbling magnum opus [. . .] projects itself into the future to ask 'What was cinema?'' (Rosenbaum 1997: 13). More than this, I suggest that the era provocatively identified by Godard as 'after' cinema is the *present*. Rather than rehearse the 'deaths' to which cinema is viewed as having succumbed, my aim here is to appropriate the question endlessly posed by Godard himself in his early critical writings (and repeated in on-screen text in *La Monnaie de l'absolu*), 'Qu'est-ce que le cinéma?', so as to examine what is at stake in the term 'cinema' in and around the eight chapters of the project – 1A *Toutes les histoires* ('All the [Hi]Stories'), 1B *Une Histoire seule* ('A Solitary [Hi]Story', or 'Only One [Hi]Story'), 2A *Seul le cinéma* ('The Cinema Alone', or 'Only the Cinema'), 2B *Fatale beauté* ('Fatal Beauty'), 3A *La Monnaie de l'absolu* ('The Twilight of the Absolute'), 3B *Une Vague nouvelle* ('A New Wave', or 'A Vague Piece of News'), 4A *Le Contrôle de l'univers* ('The Control of the Universe'), and 4B *Les Signes parmi nous* ('The Signs Amongst Us') – and especially in the idea of 'cinema' that permeates *Toutes les histoires, Une Vague nouvelle, La Monnaie de l'absolu,* and *Les Signes parmi nous*. Such an analysis will inevitably go against the grain of Godard's strategy of constructing a nebulous evocative discourse that seeks to demarcate a critical position whilst refusing linear argument, and whose culmination we see in the experimental essayistic use of video in *Histoire(s)*. Rather than receive the dense layers of meaning packed into each episode of *Histoire(s)* with an exasperated cry of 'incomprehensible', however, I will seek to separate out the multiple models of cinema invoked by Godard, and so consider the extent to which the logic they draw on is supported by a sustainable critical method that might be retrieved for film studies.

In the late 1970s, Godard took over from Henri Langlois the task of delivering a series of lectures on cinema history at the Conservatoire d'Art Cinématographique in Montreal. These lectures, partially transcribed as *Introduction à une véritable histoire du cinéma* (Godard 1980), contain the seeds of the core ideas about cinema and history that simmer across Godard's concerns of the 1980s, and coalesce in *Histoire(s)*. Key underlying premises on which Godard's conception of cinema rests, all constantly reinvoked in the Montreal lectures and thereafter, are that for cinema to flourish there must already be in existence (1) an industrial infrastructure, (2) a bedrock of creative desire amongst those involved in film production to ensure the provision of a sustained quota of average films amongst which the occasional one will aspire to and attain artistic excellence, and (3) collective desire on the part of the consumers of these products to moderate and sustain the cycle. In other words, embracing all three facets of this model, there must be an appropriate *climate* within which film production operates before 'cinema', as understood and used by Godard, can come into existence. It is not sufficient to produce great quantities of films in purely numerical terms, nor for audiences to crave and eagerly consume vast numbers of non-indigenously made films. For 'cinema' to exist, within the parameters established by Godard as cinema historian, there must be a wealth of more or less average films that engage with, rework and reflect contemporary concerns of direct relevance to the audience in question, concerns in turn desired and engaged with by that national audience.

One's immediate reaction to this defence of the popular by Godard is perhaps one of astonishment: 'Godard', so often invoked as arch-exemplar of the avant-garde *auteur*, pleading the cause of the mainstream. But it is worth recalling that a little-acknowledged aspect of Godard's early critical articles, besides a well-known emphasis on contemporaneous post-war American cinema (especially the low-budget B-movie), is the considerable attention devoted to the average artisanal French cinema (the films of Norbert Carbonneaux, for instance) that fell outside the damning terms of the 'cinéma de qualité'/'cinéma de papa' (the 'quality' or 'daddy's' cinema). The cinema as *popular* is central to Godard's position. But this term, as Richard Dyer and Ginette Vincendeau have observed, is fraught with multiple meanings, embracing a range of conflicting connotations in its dual 'market' and 'anthropological' modes (Dyer and Vincendeau 1992). The term within the context of Godard's criteria for cinema cuts across both these senses. Films should be designed for popular consumption (as opposed to marginal products with their own specialist constituent audiences) and both desired and valued by that popular audience, literally 'popular' amongst them:

> Painting never experienced this: Goya was seen by very few people; Beethoven was little heard. [. . .] But cinema was immediately seen by 100 people at the Grand Café. And then came phenomenal expansion. It took hold in a truly popular way, whether this was intentional or not, or for economic reasons or not. (Godard 1983: 6)

This is a crucial characteristic repeatedly emphasized by Godard. Unlike painting or music, the cinema was immediately widely distributed and 'popular': people liked it and wanted more. The cinema was a real art, 'High Art' even, and the only art ever to find a widespread popular audience and be popular with that audience: 'Everyone can love a Van Gogh, but here was someone who had invented a means of broadcasting Van Gogh's crows everywhere (albeit in a slightly less dreadful form) in a way that made everyone love it and feel close to it' (Godard 1988, 26).

Turning first to the notion of the existence of a cinema *industry* as prerequisite for 'cinema', those who lost sight of Godard in the 1960s, and continue to view him with some scepticism as champion of a quirky brand of *auteurism* (both as a critic, and then as embodying *auteurist* excesses in his art cinema of the 1960s), may greet such an assertion with incredulity. Likewise, those with one foot in the post-'Hollywood–Mosfilm' polemics around May 1968, in which all industrially-produced cinema was cast as an industry for reproducing conventional forms and corresponding 'identikit' viewers, may find such a suggestion difficult to accept. But Godard has long since played down and thoroughly revised any *auteurist* inclination, claiming repeatedly that the concept, always only a critical tool applicable to a specific moment in film history, has been sullied beyond recognition in a televisual era where film-makers are less interested in contributing to 'cinema' than in their self-promotion as *auteurs*. If Godard contributed to, and lived to regret, the invention of the *auteur*, then his critical position for the past twenty years is marked by an attempt to bury any such notion beneath what we might term a 'politique du producteur' (a kind of 'producer theory', as exemplified in the paean in *Toutes les histoires* to Irving Thalberg, head of MGM).

If the cinema for Godard is now less the product of a unique unifying *auteurist* vision, it has become the collaborative art-form *par excellence*. The Hollywood studio system, far from being denigrated as a source of manipulative reactionary products, is cast by Godard in his *Histoire(s)* as the socio-economic and industrial context – the dream factory – that allowed film-makers such as Murnau, Hitchcock, Ford, and Lang to flourish, even if only in opposition to institutional structures. Over and over again, Godard returns to the idea that it was the collaborative nature of the film-making process within an industrial context that constituted the strength of the American cinema and meant that even mediocre films were generally of a higher quality than films produced outside such an environment: 'an industrial context, where people saw one another and talked a bit about films' (Godard 1980: 32). Godard has often anecdotally claimed that for cinema to exist, a film studio must have a canteen, and specifically a canteen where all those implicated in the film-making process go, discussing the films they are working on whilst they are there. It is this desire to produce an artistic construct through collective work that characterizes this facet of 'cinema' for Godard, and that he sees as having evaporated in the televisual era. Directors and technicians may still share the same canteen, but they now talk about what was on television last night as opposed to the film they are working on:

I realised quite recently that the strength of the Nouvelle Vague, that which allowed it to break through in France at a given moment in time, was simply due to there being three or four of us who were discussing cinema amongst ourselves. The strength of the average pre-war American cinema came from those who were together all day, talking in the morning, in the canteen, and in a space other than a factory; it was a factory, but a very specific type of factory where they were able to talk. (Godard 1980: 101)

Godard proceeds to link this conception of discussion and debate to the notion of 'schools' or movements in both painting (he cites Impressionism and Cubism) and the cinema, remarking that such genuine collaboration underpins all moments in cinematic history where traces of innovation in film language can be seen at work. These moments, in brief, encompass the Nouvelle Vague, the German cinema industry after the First World War, Italian neo-realism, and the American cinema of the 1970s (Scorsese; Coppola; De Palma, etc.). Concluding his remarks here is the blunt but unequivocal statement that without the stimulus of the discussion and collaboration between the directors and technicians within national cinema industries, cinema is not only less good, but, according to the specific gloss given the term at this stage in Godard's research, simply absent. 'Otherwise, you don't make cinema' (Godard 1980: 101).

It is within such a context that we can begin to comprehend Godard assertions across the 1980s and 1990s that cinema, in the sense of a healthy national cinematic environment for the production and consumption of films, has more or less ceased to exist; claims that 'cinema' is dead no longer seem quite so arbitrarily provocative. It is more that it is conceived, constructed and played out within a framework that no longer requires or fosters cohesion, collaboration, or a sense of a cinematic community: 'I come back to the idea that our films have lost the need to be cinema, that they're primarily films. Because we have only an individual reason for doing things' (Godard 1989: 86). For Godard, whilst films are clearly still being made, often of a high quality, they are no longer 'cinema' in so far as the entire context, which in his critical view sanctions the use of the term, has been obliterated by the televisual mutation that has irreversibly altered the 'climate'. So a distinction emerges in Godardian discourse between 'cinema' and 'films'. Films may have constituted the individual units of 'cinema', but, if we follow Godard's line of argument, we can no longer speak of the existence of cinema in any meaningful sense other than as a pale imitation of the real 'cinema' outlined above, and we are inevitably left with a disjointed collection of *films*: 'We make films, but not cinema' (Godard 1989: 84). We are left with nothing but films, isolated, encircled and adrift within the realm of the audiovisual and the digital, a bleak scenario that provides the backdrop to Godard's frequent laconic self-representation since the early 1980s as a dinosaur on the verge of extinction, along with comparable survivors such as Jean-Pierre Mocky, Jacques Rivette, Jean-Marie Straub and Danièle Huillet, adrift, ill at ease, and having to barter and collaborate with the 'occupying power' of television for their survival.

It is also in this context that we may situate Godard's long-standing provocative refusal to entertain the notion of a British cinema. Whilst there is clearly an element within this polemic that states quite simply that British films are badly made or lacking in creative flair, Godard's accusation extends to the apparent lack of a British cinema industry and culture. Godard's recurrent critique of British cinema is traceable to his earliest critical articles: 'You really have to rack your brains to find something to say about an English film. Why, we ask ourselves? That's just the way it is. There's not even an exception to prove the rule. [. . .] No, it's a really hopeless situation. But to despair of English cinema would be to admit that it exists' (Godard 1958: 137). Similar statements, echoing Truffaut's contention that British cinema is a contradiction in terms, recur across interviews with Godard, particularly in the 1960s, after which – with the notable exception of Terence Davies's *Distant Voices, Still Lives* (1988) – he loses interest altogether and generally fails to acknowledge its existence, suggesting that it revolves less around *mise-en-scène* than an awkward 'mise-en-place': 'The British don't really create films – they just set them up' (Godard in Ardagh 1966). But beneath the evident provocation of such attacks resides Godard's promotion of a concept of cinema that insists on the fusion of an existing vibrant industry with a *popular* need and response to the products of that industry. In other words, Britain, possibly at least partially owing to the linguistic proximity of Hollywood, has lacked an indigenous 'cinema' in which the collective desires and anguishes of a nation have been worked through and played out in cinematic form.[2]

Cinema is seen in explicitly national terms in *Histoire(s)*, and in Godard's discourse on film and history as it has evolved since the 1970s. This is in many ways very surprising in the light of the international heritage of that most emphatically transnational of movements, the Nouvelle Vague, and of the huge importance of the role played by Henri Langlois's Cinémathèque. It is here that the Nouvelle Vague film-makers immersed themselves not only in post-war American cinema, but films from every era, every continent, every national cinema, and were propelled into film-making from this multicultural base. The intrinsically transnational intertextual generic puzzles of Godard's early Nouvelle

Figure 3. *Histoire(s) du cinéma* (1988–1998), Jean-Luc Godard. Courtesy British Film Institute.

Vague films apparently belie (or are at the very least somewhat startling in the light of) his subsequent sustained insistence on a reading of 'cinema' as containing a privileged link to indigenous production and the construction of nationhood. Jonathan Rosenbaum, in an otherwise enthusiastic response to Godard and Miéville's *Deux fois cinquante ans de cinéma français* (*2 x 50 Years of French Cinema*, 1995) points out that this acidic audiovisual missive calls into question every assumption underpinning both the centenary of cinema and the logic implicit in the series to which it belongs except one: the favouring of an approach to film history through national cinemas. Rosenbaum argues that the 'national cinema' bias underpinning the series intrinsically 'fosters insularity, mishandles many major figures who are transnational or multinational [. . .], and often honors sociology over aesthetics and the typical over the exceptional' (Rosenbaum 1996: 38). This omission, however, is far from inadvertent or incidental in Godard/Miéville's film. On the contrary, the acquiescence in the 'national' slant to the project's conception is emblematic of the critical position arrived at by Godard in his voyage to identify and pin down the specificity of what characterizes for him the essence of 'cinema' in its historical context.

Godard suggests in *Histoire(s)* that not only is the cinema dead in the sense of having been relegated to the status of *just another* distraction in the televisual/digital era, but that the precise moment of the start of its demise is its failure in the face of the unbearable reality of the Holocaust. For Godard, the cinema is a kind of unique seismograph through which a visionary ethnology of imminent social mutation and change is possible. He has talked of cinema as a mechanism through which an embryology of emergent social form can be conducted (Godard 1980: 215): the ostensibly innocent narratives of popular cinema are the site where traces of nascent socio-political shifts, as yet not fully articulated in discourses outside the cinema, are identifiable. Cinema is thus prophetic in its capacity to *foresee* emergent patterns of social crisis and conflict, a thesis that clearly echoes the work of Kracauer on the German cinema of the 1920s in relation to Fascism. Likewise, fiction films are treated as the true *actualités* (newsreels) of the twentieth century, not in the sense of the daily television news (so disdained by Godard), but rather of the work of metaphor in the instant slippage between reality and its representation: cinema is the place in which the ever-changing present is worked into narratives, and momentous moments of social instability and conflict crystallized and given a form that is then widely distributed and subjected to criticism. Thus the unique double role of cinema is to *announce* and to *testify*. And it is the failure of the cinema to confront and represent – 'to bring in evidence', as Godard would say – the Holocaust and the Nazi genocide of the Jewish people that for Godard marks the beginning of cinema's demise. Cinema failed in the face of this atrocious reality, proved insubstantial in the face of such an onslaught, and so lost its honour, confidence, and future ability to face its documentary duties *vis-à-vis* reality. This is not to suggest that no films attempted to represent the Holocaust. Godard's point is that they are very much the exception, far too few, and generally too late: 'cinema', in the sense of a buoyant film industry working to construct an immediate, relevant image of contemporary reality, simply fell to pieces, never to recover. If cinema dies across the 1970s, 1980s and 1990s, smothered by television and the media generally, then it has been doomed since the Second World War. To push this thesis to its logical endpoint, there has been no real cinema, not in the sense of conforming to the criteria I have outlined, since the 1940s. And so we arrive at a reading and explanation of the title of *Deux fois cinquante ans de cinéma français*: a survey of the evolution of the cinema from 1895 to the Second World War, followed by a tracing of its decline to the present.

The idea that for 'cinema' to exist there must be a climate in which a cinema industry can flourish, and that the films produced by such an industry must, in part, function as *actualités*, dealing with the everyday concerns and realities of the audience they address, may meet many of the expectations one might have of a vibrant relevant contemporary art-form in relation to the epoch it inhabits. But within this fairly general notion, a far more reductive reading of 'cinema' is at work, one we might identify as 'cinema' pared down to its essence. Although reluctant to apportion the label 'Cinema' (with a capital 'C') to any particular type of cinema, not least because various 'genuine' or 'true' ideas of cinema have been promoted in this way to different ends (to claim one particular mode of cinema as superior to or purer than another, for instance), it is to the following 'cinema', operating directly in relation to emergent, shifting, or dissolving national identities, that I apply it here. For 'Cinema' to exist, the various criteria for 'cinema' outlined above must not only have been met, but simultaneously perturbed and redistributed in a surge of exploratory creativity when a nation's self-image is absent, in question, or under threat. Implicit in Godard's thesis is that the cinema has functioned as the privileged site for the quest for a national image to reflect back on the nation and outwards to the rest of the world. Thus in addition to the quest for identity through the cinema – and this is the major stumbling-block that excludes virtually all nations and all cinemas from entering Godard's select pantheon – this surge of collective national desire to construct or resurrect a national self-image must be through *a simultaneous revolution in the language of cinema itself.* It is not sufficient to appropriate wholesale the forms, technology and genres of previous generations. For 'Cinema' to exist, the quest for a national image must itself throw into question and reinvent the means through which it is sought and articulated. Such a premise clearly puts a very different gloss on the whole concept of a 'national cinema': for Godard, this combination of terms assumes the mutual interaction and realignment of each in relation to the other. While he might welcome the general reorientation of film studies away from a limited canon of 'great' directors to a representative cross-section of cinematic production, Godard refuses, or at least accepts only on his own intransigent terms, the notion of what constitutes cinema: 'Cinema' denotes not merely a representative cross-section of film production, but a means of communication undergoing a process of internal revolution.

Before exploring the specificities of *which* cinemas make up a role-call of 'Cinema', a brief detour is required through the evolution of

Godard's engagement with questions of national identity that prepares the ground for the conclusions he presents in the 1990s. Questions of individual, collective and national identity have long been central to Godard's practice, and it is in this context that he was invited as guest interviewee at the 1991 conference at the National Film Theatre on 'Image and Identity in Contemporary European Cinema' (Godard 1992a). The work of the Sonimage period, that of Godard's collaborative venture with Anne-Marie Miéville from 1973 to 1978, takes questions of individual identity as its key point of departure. As such, it draws heavily on the psychoanalytic paradigm so influential within the post-structuralist context of the time, as evidenced in the title of the first, and eventually abandoned, Sonimage video project, *Moi je* ('Me, I'). In a recent essay suggesting the theory of globalization as a framework within which to analyse films in relation to questions of national and cultural identity, Ian Aitkin suggests a direct analogy between the static conception of the unitary subject in its classical (Enlightenment) embodiment and traditional conceptions of nationhood as a collective extension of this unified subject (Aitkin 1996, 77). Precisely this slippage is at work within Godard and Miéville's Sonimage project. If *Moi je* announces an insistence on the subject in Godard's work as fractured, decentred and essentially volatile, then the ambitious and again ultimately unrealised *Naissance (de l'image) d'une nation* ('Birth [of the image] of a nation', 1977–9) transposes the problematic onto the emergence of the Popular Republic of Mozambique. At the invitation of the Mozambican government, Miéville and Godard were asked to collaborate on that nation's desire to construct a national television infrastructure whilst taking into account the need simultaneously to construct a sense of national identity through the medium of images and sounds unfamiliar to the majority of the Mozambican population at the time: 'To recognize a projection of oneself, to need to project oneself so as to see oneself . . .' (Godard 1984–5: 14).[3]

Cinema, along with all forms of cultural representation, plays a role in mediating and holding in place a certain national image. But for Godard, the use of cinema as a phatic information circuit, a conduit for the passage of any and all representations, has little in common with 'Cinema'. This misunderstanding over the notion of cinema was clearly at the heart of disagreements between Godard and Colin MacCabe in their dialogue at the 1991 NFT conference. It should be pointed out that the extent of the disagreement was more pronounced than the impression given by the published transcript of this dialogue, and, notably, omits MacCabe's comment the following day (when Godard was no longer present) that although it was always a pleasure to talk to Godard, he disagreed with virtually everything he had said. MacCabe argued that the cinema is surely one of the forms through which emerging new European identities will evolve in the face of the growing disparities between dominant cultural stereotypes and rapidly shifting socio-economic realities in Europe. Godard may well in fact agree with this in principle, but steadfastly refused to entertain the idea that it is through cinema, *his* concept of cinema, that such emerging identities will be formed: '. . . maybe it doesn't go through movies any more because it's so corrupted' (Godard 1992a: 102). Cinema, according to Godard, has certainly performed this function at isolated moments when nations have sought to (re)construct a national image; but, he argues, the context, climate and desire for such a cinema through which the struggle can take place have long since evaporated.

The conclusion of Godard's research, one that constitutes a key thesis running through *Histoire(s)*, is that 'Cinema' has only existed at the following points in (cinema) history: Russian cinema of the 1920s, German cinema between the wars, Italian neo-realism, and classical Hollywood cinema of the 1940s and 1950s. All other nations, all other cinemas have done something else, but it is not 'Cinema' in this highly reductive sense arrived at by Godard, where the cinematic apparatus has mutated under the collective desire to dissolve and trace the outline of a new national image in response to a loss or absence of national identity. Godard has articulated this thesis in many different guises since the beginning of the 1980s. The following, taken from his dialogue with MacCabe, is one of its fullest formulations:

> There have only been a handful of cinemas: Italian, German, American, Russian. This is because when countries were inventing and using motion pictures, they needed an image of themselves. The Russian cinema arrived at a time when they needed a new image. And in the case of Germany, they had lost a war and were completely corrupted and needed a new idea of Germany. At the time the new Italian cinema emerged, Italy was completely lost – it was the only country which fought with the Germans, then against the Germans. They strongly needed to see a new reality, and this was provided by neo-realism. (Godard 1992a: 98)

It works its way into *Histoire(s)* through Godard's melancholic reflections on the Second World War, cinema, and the lack of a cinema of resistance in *La Monnaie de l'absolu*:

> How is it that in 40–45, there was no cinema of resistance? Not that there wasn't the odd *film* of resistance dotted around here and there. But the only film in the sense of 'cinema' that resisted the American occupation of the

cinema, and a certain uniform mode of film-making, was an Italian film. This is no coincidence. Italy was the country that fought the least, suffered greatly, is guilty of a double betrayal, and so suffered from a loss of identity. And if it rediscovered this identity with *Rome, Open City*, it's because the film was made by people not wearing uniforms. It's the only time. The Russians made films of martyrdom. The Americans made advertising films. The English did what they always do in the cinema: nothing. Germany had no cinema, or no more cinema. [. . .] Whereas with *Rome, Open City*, Italy simply won back a nation's right to look itself in the face.

Two aspects of the model of cinema invoked here are particularly striking: the centrality of nations and questions of identity, and the inclusion only of moments in cinema history where not only national identity is at stake, but where a new relationship to reality is being forged and articulated through an exploration of cinema itself as a form of expression. In other words, an insistence on form at the core of a model that excludes the overwhelming majority of national cinemas, and embraces only those privileged moments in which the cinema as cultural form is itself interrogated and undergoing internal mutation.

To arrive at this select few, Godard has to overcome several problems, and indeed his position shifts across the 1980s as he seeks to map his rationale. The basis to his thesis is already in place by 1982: '. . . it's when nations lose their identity that they need something that's ineffable and ephemeral through which to provide an account of themselves: an image' (Godard 1982: 58). At this stage, he has narrowed his selection down to those few cinemas in which, in his view, a new relation to reality is being explored through a quest for a national image: post-Revolution Russian cinema, German expressionism, and Italian neo-realism. His two problems are American cinema and French cinema (and specifically the Nouvelle Vague): 'Two questions remain to be explored: that of American cinema, and that of the Nouvelle Vague, which changed quite a few things' (Godard 1982: 59). American cinema is ushered in relatively unproblematically on the grounds that the United States, as a nation in its infancy, badly needed a self-image. In fact it is to the very lack of a national history that Godard ascribes the thirst to construct and project an image to the outside world, a desire so powerful that it ended by enveloping the globe, first through cinema, and then through television. It was the inscription of this desire into the narratives of American cinema that seduced the world; other nations may not have seen themselves in Hollywood cinema, but recognized, identified with, and themselves desired the very intensity of that desire.

French cinema poses a greater problem for Godard and leads to considerable intellectual gymnastics. On the one hand, he views the Nouvelle Vague as having had, at least in a minor way, an impact on cinematic language and as having renegotiated the contract between reality and its representation. On the other hand, it is intensely problematic to his thesis, taking place long after the 'death' of cinema (during and after the Second World War). If Italian neo-realism can be read as dealing with the aftermath of war, a sort of 'dernier sursaut' ('final burst') (Godard 1988: 26) in 'Cinema', then in relation to what major socio-political upheavals or internal shifts is a new national image being projected through the Nouvelle Vague? Godard toys with the idea of its responding to the aftermath of Vichy, the Occupation, and the dissolution of France's self-image as a colonial power (as figured, particularly, in Vietnam and Algeria); but, with an eye on the films that constitute this body of work, such an idea is hardly sustainable (Godard 1989, 84). So, for Godard, the Nouvelle Vague does not qualify for 'Cinema' status, a point made clearly through Anne-Marie Miéville's voice-off (borrowed from Cocteau) in *Une Vague nouvelle*: 'oui, c'est beau, mais c'est pas du cinéma' ('yes, it's beautiful, but it's not cinema'). Nor, for that matter does French cinema as a whole. Drawing on the distinction between 'cinema' and 'films' discussed earlier, Godard concludes that the French had lots of films, even a 'cinema' in the broad sense of the climate outlined above, but no 'Cinema' in the ultimate sense of a nation and a medium of expression in a process of interaction and mutual realignment: 'And then, too, the French had so many film-makers that people ended up believing that they had a cinema' (Godard 1992b: 20).

In an ingenious way, albeit a methodologically highly unconventional one, Godard invents a way of half-including the Nouvelle Vague via the back door through the contention that, while the Nouvelle Vague falls outside the criterion of having responded to popular desire for a new national image, it nevertheless invented a new concept of cinema through cinephilia. From a background in film history, and a passion brought to the cinema by the film-maker/critics of the Nouvelle Vague, a new 'country' was born, that of *cinema*: 'Cinema was a place, a territory' (Godard 1988: 24),[4] or, as Serge Daney (who developed this same idea) put it, 'Cinema is the country that was missing from my geography map'.[5] So French cinema, in the guise of the Nouvelle Vague, is accorded a sort of secondary ranking within the terms of Godard's 'Cinema' through the bizarre yet seductive invention of the cinema as nation, giving us, finally, Russia, Germany, America, Italy, and cinema itself (within which France, via the Nouvelle Vague, is implicated) as a definitive role-call. As I have suggested, the paradox here in the use of an inherently transnational movement, the Nouvelle Vague, as point of departure for the construction of a model that ties 'Cinema' tightly to individual nations should not go unnoticed. And what of any subsequent movements? Nothing, according to Godard. Perhaps, at a stretch, elements of the New German Cinema through which is figured the desire to re-construct yet another national self-image following the Second World War. But this cinema falls at the formal hurdle: it is clearly a site of national self-examination, but one in which the cinema itself is not called into question. Fassbinder alone is accorded a privileged position within the Godardian hierarchy, a sort of wayward unique shooting star who attempted single-handedly to re-invent a German cinema for the German nation, and, according to Godard, died of 'une espèce d'overdoses d'obligations créatives' ('a kind of overdose of creative duties') (Godard 1988: 26) in the process:

> Fassbinder, who made almost exclusively very bad films, or at least not very good ones, was one of the last film-makers to still make cinema. I didn't like his films much, but I so loved the fact that he was driven to make them, which was more important. He said: 'I'm German, and I make films for German people.' As soon as he made a Hollywood film like *Despair*, it really wasn't any good, it wasn't his thing. But whilst he was making *Maria Braun* and so on, five identical films with the same actors etc., *that* was cinema, and had no need to be films. (Godard 1989: 84)

If Italian neo-realism constitutes the last reciprocal mutation of cinema and nation within Godard's schema, and the Nouvelle Vague functions as an awkward appendage, then Fassbinder represents the final death throes of an irretrievable form.

The principal point to be retained from this unravelling of the over-lapping notions of 'cinema' and 'Cinema' at work in *Histoire(s)* and the discourse that Godard has spun around cinema and history for the last twenty years is that when Godard speaks of the death or absence of cinema in any particular context, it is not only in purely provocative terms (although it clearly carries within it a provocative charge), but in relation to this extremely specific model of 'Cinema', wherein a cultural form is revolutionized through the collective desire of a nation for a new image. We may well refute such a model as idiosyncratic in the extreme, absurdly reductive in its exclusively occidental focus, ignoring virtually all the most prolific international film industries, and, as I have suggested, turning on a core formalist premise that many might find unacceptable. But the insistence on the interrogation of form in Godard's voyage through cinema history should hardly take us unawares: cinema is a communications circuit like any other, and Godard has long insisted on a radical communications model. The Sonimage project, 'on and under communication', represents above all a quest to identify and interpret 'communication' in the televisual era. Its conclusion: what we habitually term communication has nothing to do with *real* 'Communication', for which a mutual realignment of subject, object and representation is required, form and content mutating, taking the subject with them.

To return to my point of departure, my aim was to distinguish the 'cinema(s)' contained in Godard's pronouncement of the death of cinema, and to evaluate the uses of the term 'cinema' in and around *Histoire(s) du cinéma*. The presence of so many cinemas, all coiled within Godard's use of the term, erupting each time it is used in a clash of multiple meanings, make the term hugely suggestive, provocatively imprecise, always allowing Godard to shift ground in mid-argument from one meaning to another, ever illusive, impossible to pin down. As already suggested, this also exemplifies the very conception and functioning of the Godard text, always discoursing around and between the subject(s), never sustaining a linear argument. Both principal notions of cinema I have outlined are at work in Godard's appropriation and (ab)use of the term: cinema in the rather loose sense of a healthy climate for contemporary film production and consumption, and 'Cinema', which functions exclusively within a national perspective and, as we have seen, is one of the key platforms around which the heterogeneous audiovisual fragments of *Histoire(s)* revolve. As the tracing of the evolution of Godard's use of the term 'cinema' across the 1980s and 1990s has shown, the models it draws on are based less on any systematically developed thesis than on mercurial waves of *rapprochements* and intuitions, and, as such, are unlikely to be appropriated by the world of academic film studies. What is already happening, however, is that the poetic provocations that demarcate the series's parameters, both in the guise of intertitles and Godard's doom-laden voice-over, are entering the ranks of the oft-quoted Godardian aphorisms that so often punctuate writing on film. If such formulae cannot be said to be generated by a sustained methodology, they derive nevertheless from a logic of sorts, albeit one as personal as it is aleatory. Rather than dismiss Godard's research as impenetrable or meaningless, I have sought here to demonstrate the development of this logic. Before either glibly dismissing or appropriating Godard's aphorisms, we should be alert to the fact that, far from an unconnected kaleidoscopic collage of miscellany, these formulae have a context and come with their own history. Likewise, before we can engage with, discuss or refute Godard's wider discourse on cinema and history, particularly as played out in *Histoire(s) du cinéma*, the divergent connotations of the terms through which it operates must first be separated out, analysed and elucidated, foremost amongst them the concept of *cinema* itself.

Notes

1. Godard to Bernard Pivot, live on *Bouillon de Culture*, France 2, 10 September 1993, 22.25.

2. For an interesting exploration of the potential reasons for the absence of a British film culture, see Christopher Williams (1996), 'The Social Art Cinema: A Moment in the History of British Film and Television Culture', in Christopher Williams (ed.) (1996), *Cinema: The Beginnings and the Future*, London, University of Westminster Press, pp. 190–200. Williams addresses and partially concedes this apparent lack of a cinematic heritage and tradition, along with its function as both filter and reflection of the national psyche, arguing that it is not just through popular cinematic forms, but also through experimental and avant-garde traditions, that pressing issues pertaining to national cultural identity are played out. He suggests (p. 194) that the absence of a British film culture is at least partially due to the absence of an art cinema tradition in Britain in which, as he says, 'the leading issues of subjectivity (individual identity, sexuality, personal relations) or of socio-cultural developments and consciousness (history, community and national relationships) could be directly addressed in image-related forms'.

3. Godard interpreted the title, before the project foundered, in the following terms: 'birth of a nation through the image it constructs of itself, would like to construct, or succeeds in constructing, and then wants to pass on to others' (Godard 1980: 70). Negotiations began in 1977, followed by working visits by Godard and Miéville to the Popular Republic of Mozambique in 1978. The series aimed to employ a multiplicity of formats (Polaroid, still photography, video and Super 8) to explore the opposition between a culture devoid of media imagery (Mozambique) and a society awash in images and sounds (France), with the aim of drawing lessons for the nascent Mozambican audio-visual infrastructure. While none of the five 'émissions TV-cinéma' ('TV/cinema programmes') envisaged by Sonimage were completed,

documentation on the failed collaborative venture is available as Jean-Luc Godard (1979), 'Le Dernier rêve d'un producteur: Nord contre sud, ou Naissance (de l'image) d'une nation', in Godard (ed.), *Les Cahiers du Cinéma*, 300, pp. 70–129. The theoretical portion of a document produced by Sonimage regarding television in relation to the Mozambique project is reproduced in Colin MacCabe, with Laura Mulvey and Mick Eaton (1980), *Godard: Images, Sounds, Politics,* London, Macmillan/British Film Institute, pp. 138–40. A useful discussion and critique of Godard and Miéville's project in Mozambique can be found in Manthia Diawara (1992), *African Cinema: Politics and Culture,* Bloomington, Indiana University Press, pp. 93–103.

4. See too the exchange between Godard and *Les Cahiers du cinéma* around this notion of the love of cinema giving birth to the cinema as country in Godard (1982: 59).
5. Serge Daney (1994), *Persévérance: entretien avec Serge Toubiana,* Paris, Denoël, pp. 94–5. Daney talks here extensively of the notion of cinema as a country, specifically ascribing its origin to Godard, and proceeding to give the notion his own particular gloss. He also engages (p. 104) with Godard's notion of the crucial link between cinema and national identity: 'se refaire un pays, un visage' ('to reconstruct a country, a face').

References

Aitkin, Ian (1996), 'Current Problems in the Study of European Cinema and the Role of Questions on Cultural Identity', in Wendy Everett (ed.) (1996), *European Identity in Cinema*, pp. 75–82, Exeter, Intellect.

Ardagh, John (1966), 'An Alpha for Godard?', *The Guardian* (12 December): 7.

Dyer, Richard and Vincendeau, Ginette (1992), 'Introduction', in Richard Dyer and Ginette Vincendeau (eds) (1992), pp. 1–14, *Popular European Cinema*, London & New York, Routledge.

Godard, Jean-Luc (1958), 'Désespérant', *Arts*, 680. Reprinted in Jean-Luc Godard (1985), *Jean-Luc Godard par Jean-Luc Godard*, ed. Alain Bergala, pp. 137–8, Paris, Cahiers du Cinéma/Editions de l'Etoile.

—— (1980), *Introduction à une véritable histoire du cinéma*, Paris, Albatros.

—— (1982), 'Le chemin vers la parole' (Interview with Alain Bergala, Serge Daney and Serge Toubiana), *Les Cahiers du cinéma*, 336: 8–14, 57–66.

—— (1983), 'Godard à Venise', *Cinématographe*, 95: 3–7 (transcription of Godard's press conference at the 1983 Venice Film Festival).

—— (1984–5), 'Jean-Luc Godard: la curiosité du sujet' (Interview with Dominique Païni and Guy Scarpetta), *art press* (sic), («Spécial Godard»), hors série 4 (December 1984 – January/February 1985): 4–18.

—— (1988), 'Godard fait des histoires' (Interview with Serge Daney), *Libération* (26 December): 24–7. In English as 'Godard Makes (Hi)stories', in Raymond Bellour and Mary Lea Bandy (eds) (1992), *Jean-Luc Godard: Son + Image, 1974–1991*, pp. 159–67, New York, The Museum of Modern Art.

—— (1989), '«Cultivons notre jardin»: Une interview de Jean-Luc Godard' (Interview with François Albéra), *CinémAction* 52, («*Le cinéma selon Godard*»), ed. René Prédal, pp. 81–9.

—— (1992a), 'Jean-Luc Godard in Conversation with Colin MacCabe', in Duncan Petrie (ed.) (1992), *Screening Europe: Image and Identity in Contemporary European Cinema*, pp. 97–105, London, BFI.

—— (1992b), 'Entretien avec Jean-Luc Godard: Le Briquet de Capitaine Cook' (Interview with François Albéra and Mikhaïl Iampolski), *Les Lettres Françaises* (19 April): 17–21.

Rosenbaum, Jonathan (1996), 'International Harvest', *Chicago Reader* (22 November): 38–41.

—— (1997), 'Trailer for Godard's *Histoire(s) du cinéma*', *Vertigo*, 7: 13–20. First published as Rosenbaum, Jonathan (1997) 'Bande-annonce pour les *Histoire(s) du cinéma* de Godard', *Trafic*, 21: 5–18.

Sontag, Susan (1996), 'The decay of cinema', *New York Times Magazine* (25 February): 60–1.

Witt, Michael (1999), 'The death(s) of cinema according to Godard', *Screen*, 40 (3): 331–46.

3

Le Chêne et le Roseau: The French Communist Critics and the New Wave
Laurent Marie

Resnais's burning acuteness, Chabrol's penetrating good nature, Truffaut's fierce generosity, Bernard-Aubert's wild sense of the polemical, Camus's colourful vibrancy, Baratier's refined poetry, Franju's tender cruelty, Chris Marker's inspired comical nature, Rouch's passionate humanity, Malle's acute vision, Varda's peculiar sense of comedy, Astruc's haughty anxiety . . . (Sadoul 1959e: 117)

. . . Belmondo's blasé romanticism, Brialy's twirling brilliance, Blain's persistent physical presence, Bardot's pouting lips, Léaud's anxious youthfulness, Moreau's sovereign freedom, Anna Karina's nervy boredom, Alexandra Stewart's sophisticated charm, and the ephemeral and dazzling appearances of Juliette Mayniel, Corinne Marchand or Clothilde Joano . . . (Baecque 1998: 112)

In *L'Âge moderne du cinéma français*, published in 1995, Jean-Michel Frodon gives a brief outline of the way Communist critics responded to the New Wave. His argument may be summed up as follows: the Communist critics' position was predictably negative, or when it was not, their praise was short-lived. More recently, the New Wave has received the attention of film specialists such as Antoine de Baecque (1998), Jean Douchet (1998) and Michel Marie (1998), but none of them focus on the French Communist response. I would like to show here that Frodon's view is somehow misleading, since the reception given by the Communists to the New Wave was rather more complex. This reception warrants a comprehensive analysis, as it marked an important change in the French Communist Party's (PCF's) critical discourse. After a brief summary of the essential features of this discourse during the years preceding the New Wave, the reaction of the French Communist critics to the new generation of film-makers will be addressed here by examining both the main changes that took place from the year 1958 onwards in the critics' reviews as well as the signs of continuity apparent in their analyses.

Finally, the subsequent reactions this reception gave rise to will be considered, as these illustrate both a critical debate among leftist critics and a wider debate within French society at large.

In 1958, the Party's intellectuals were still feeling the shock wave of the Twentieth Congress of the Communist Party of the USSR, which in 1956 denounced Stalin's errors and faults. New Realism, a French version of Zhdanovism (in other words a Socialist Realism '*aux couleurs de la France*', which had been defended for most of the decade), seemed in 1958 rather inadequate. New Realism was the brand of aesthetics advocated by the Party, which, at the time, was asking its artists and intellectuals 'to take up all the ideological and political positions of the working class, to defend with the strongest resolution all the Party's positions, whatever the circumstances, and to cultivate in themselves the love of the Party (*l'esprit de parti*), in its most conscious form'. The Cold War was a period when Laurent Casanova, who was in charge of the intellectuals in the party, could say without blushing: 'There are still some Communists who are incredibly wooden when they come to deal with this living, breathing entity that is the struggling working class' (Casanova 1949: 30–1). What did this doctrine mean in terms of film as an art form? Irwin Wall explains that in Socialist Realism 'plots must be objectively set in an historical context and demonstrate plausible characters acting in authentic situations' (Wall 1983: 128) and that 'Socialist Realism promised to bring together elite and popular culture, so as to simplify high culture, to render it comprehensible to the masses' (1983: 129). In real terms this meant a condemnation of formalism, implying the pre-eminence of subject-matter over style, as well as a total rejection of intellectualism. To this the PCF added its own nationalist rhetoric. As most French directors remained impervious to New Realism, Communist critics marked their difference on the issue of style and content in the party's press. The defence of the subject-matter, combined with a fair amount of patriotism, led Communist critics to defend *la tradition de qualité*. Essentially, their support for directors such as Becker, Le Chanois, Daquin, Cayatte, Clouzot, Grémillon or Christian-Jaque proved constant.

How then did Communist critics react in 1958–9 when a number of directors released their first feature films and showed a new approach in terms of style, subject-matter and production methods? During the 1958–62 period, the main Communist critics (Albert Cervoni who, in 1959, was 31, Samuel Lachize, 34, Michel Capdenac, 30, and Marcel Martin, 33), were headed by a father figure, Georges Sadoul who, at 55, predictably set the tone of the Communist response, as he had invariably done since the Liberation.

Figure 4. Georges Sadoul and Henri Langlois. Courtesy Cinémathèque Française Bibliothèque du Film.

In January 1958, Sadoul wondered whether French cinema had not
lost its courage. And when he spoke of a crisis, what he had in mind was
a crisis in *quality* rather than the crisis in *quantity* that had preoccupied
him over the previous twelve years: 'Notwithstanding René Clair's *Porte
des Lilas*, French directors – whether excellent, good, or simply worthy
– have shown in their latest production a decline in content as well as in
form' (Sadoul 1958a: 2). Sadoul did not explain precisely why he thought
there was a decline, but considered for instance that Cayatte's and
Clouzot's latest films were going nowhere and were ideologically flawed.
The newcomers enjoyed better treatment, and several of them aroused
Sadoul's hopes: he liked Vadim and Bernard-Aubert's début, thought
Louis Malle's *Ascenseur pour l'échafaud* augured well for 1958, put his
trust in the documentary school and announced that a number of new
talents who were under thirty were preparing their first films. He
concluded this article of January 1958 thus: 'We should therefore hope
that the current weakness of French cinema will be short-lived and that
our production will soon prove that it has lost nothing of its strength and
courage.'

– 45 –

Twelve months later, Sadoul's assessment of the past year was extremely positive. 'The last semester of 1958 has been beneficial to French cinema', Sadoul wrote in December of the same year (1958d: 1). He ranked Louis Malle as one of the best film directors, and appreciated Chris Marker, whose 'sincere honesty and original talent cannot be denied' (1958d: 9–10). In the aftermath of the 1959 Cannes Film Festival, Sadoul let out a sigh of relief: 'The disturbing artistic stagnation which ruled the years 1955–1957 is over. The new movement is transforming and renewing French cinema, despite the economic and other problems which still have inevitably to be faced' (Sadoul 1959e: 117). The same year, Cervoni declared that 'if one had to make a choice, there would be no hesitation. Between Duvivier and Chabrol, between Jeanson and Truffaut, one would choose Chabrol and Truffaut' (Cervoni 1959b: 28). Four years later, in January 1963, Sadoul found Varda's *Cléo de 5 à 7* 'a heart-rending picture' and *Vivre sa vie* 'the best Godard film', while suggesting that *Jules et Jim* illustrated 'the evolution and confirmation of Truffaut's talent' (Sadoul 1963: 1). Apart from the dissenting and undiscerning voice of an ageing Moussinac, who castigated the New Wave for showing 'an evident liking for perversion' (Moussinac, n.d.: 9–12), the Communist assessment of the New Wave was therefore '*globalement positif*', to use a notorious French Communist expression.

Let us now look at what changed and what remained from the prevailing Communist critical discourse of the 1950s. There were two main changes: on the one hand, an evolution in the critics' discourse on film aesthetics and formalism; and on the other, a shift from the earlier New Realist stance regarding the pre-eminence of subject-matter. In order to illustrate the Communist critics' recognition of the role and importance of style, I have chosen a film, *Hiroshima mon amour*, and a director who was not part of the New Wave: Orson Welles.

As was to be expected, Resnais's first long feature film elicited a certain amount of controversy.[1] A number of objections were raised about the Nevers episode. Armand Monjo thought the film could only appeal to collaborationists and Pétain's followers (Monjo 1959: 2). While Sadoul also had some reservations about the validity of the Nevers episode, these were not strong enough to deny Resnais's talent: 'This film is spellbinding. The *mise-en-scène* of *Hiroshima mon amour* is a marvel. Alain Resnais is a great director, one of the best directors of our time. *Hiroshima* has given me no end of enjoyment. But the more I remember this unforgettable film, the more uneasy I feel about Marguerite Duras's scenario' (Sadoul 1959d: 6). On this count, Cervoni shows more alertness and instinct than Sadoul. 'Resnais', he writes, 'is the only one among the young authors who looks at the world with a sharp critical eye, who is not at peace with himself, who never forgets his own responsibility and that of his viewers. This is why he is the only one of the young authors of whom one can say he is a genius, as Truffaut declared. [Resnais] is the only one who uses cinema not merely as a clever illustration of an event but as a truly new form of thought' (Cervoni 1959b: 29). For Cervoni, the harmony between Duras's text and Resnais's cinematography is complete, the film is a unified whole. To separate Duras and Resnais, as Sadoul did, goes against the film itself, where words, shots and montage are intricately and intimately connected (Cervoni 1959a: 29).

Another emblematic example of the evolution of Communist discourse on style and content can be found in Albert Cervoni's reappraisal of Orson Welles's output and of his place in world cinema in November 1959. According to Cervoni, Orson Welles – 'Broadway's Hugo', he called him when referring to his theatrical début (Cervoni 1959c: 24) – brought to American culture, with which he was very much in tune, an 'extra-American dimension' (*ibid.*), which could be witnessed in the director's 'refinement and openness to social issues'. *Citizen Kane* would remain 'a monument of the Seventh Art', *The Magnificent Ambersons* reached 'a Balzacian density' (*ibid.*), and *A Touch of Evil* was a 'moralist's film' (*ibid.*), exposing the dark reality of America to which Welles opposed his 'passionate liberalism, albeit with a shade of idealism'. Cervoni also applauds the American film-director's contribution in terms of *mise-en-scène*, pointing to his use of depth of field, his sense of framing, lighting and his expressionism: 'In terms of form, Welles has enriched contemporary cinema' (1959c: 25). Fifteen years earlier, *L'Humanité* had argued that the film would only appeal to 'technicians and snobs', while in the *Lettres françaises*, Georges Sadoul followed suit: entitling his article 'Hypertrophy of the brain', Sadoul considered the film to be 'an encyclopedia of outmoded techniques directed by an artless, impetuous and clumsy beginner' and saw no future for it: 'An avant-garde film', he continued, 'often ages very quickly, and *Citizen Kane*, which was made five years ago, is already beginning to date' (Sadoul 1946: 9).

Both the recognition of the formal qualities of Resnais's direction and the reappraisal of Orson Welles's pioneering talent are clear signs of the change that was taking place in Communist film criticism. Added to these two examples, one only needs to mention Cervoni's review of *Les 400 coups* to underline the *rapprochement* of the Communist critics' position with that of André Bazin, one of the foremost champions of the New Wave. Cervoni claimed that Truffaut did not go far enough in his use of ambiguity, which Bazin considered quintessential to film: 'When I spoke

Figure 5. André Bazin. Photo: Carlos Cisventi. Courtesy Cinémathèque Française Bibliothèque du Film.

of ambiguity, I did not mean it as a reproach. On the contrary, I meant it as a celebration of the main merit of a film which does not resort to the dishonest clear-cut structure of a spectacular demonstration' (Cervoni 1959a).

André Bazin died in November 1958. The same month, in a moving tribute to the film critic, Sadoul wrote ecstatic lines about André Bazin's latest opus, the first of four volumes of his collected essays entitled *Qu'est-ce que le cinéma?* As he declared his admiration for Bazin, Sadoul also seemed to engage in some kind of self-criticism. According to Sadoul, Bazin's approach to film criticism was generous, open to contradiction, inspiring:

> One is dead, really dead, when one's voice cannot find an echo or when one's voice is transformed into empty and meaningless incantations or is frozen into sterile and fossilised, not to say distorting and absurd, formulas. [. . .] Bazin's mind refused patterns that were as heavy and ponderous as an oak stake. His nomadic reflections were rather like reeds [*L'esprit de Bazin refusait les schémas pesants et massifs comme des pieux de chêne. Elles étaient plutôt roseaux ses pensées mouvantes*]. Whoever engaged in a discussion with Bazin could see him bow under tempestuous arguments. Bazin stood his ground firmly, bowed yet never broke. [. . .] A series of principles may be drawn from Bazin's just vehemence and any film critic and any film historian would be well inspired to take them up, inspired as they are by life itself and not by fossilised dogmatic considerations (Sadoul 1958b: 5).[2]

There is little doubt that Sadoul was acknowledging Bazin's superiority as a film theorist, while at the same time reflecting on his own mistakes. In other words, the Communist film historian was admitting that he and his colleagues had gone astray, betraying the ethics of film criticism. Thus, a first major change: the issues of style and form ceased to be dismissed as bourgeois preoccupations.

This raises the question of the pre-eminence of social content over form. Was this, a central part of the Communist discourse since the end of the war, affected in any way? It is well established today that the New Wave directors did not go out of their way to tackle real social and political issues. There was little trace of any serious political commitment in their films, let alone left-wing activism. Yet the overall apolitical nature of the New Wave production doesn't seem to have proved a major obstacle to the Party's critics. Here and there they question the social dimension of the new films. Sadoul, reviewing Louis Malle's *Les Amants*, agrees that 'social critique is not the main objective of this great poem' (Sadoul 1958c: 6), while Samuel Lachize, who finds *A Bout de souffle* attractive, regrets that its subject-matter leaves him more or less indifferent, although the film's direction is full of qualities' (Lachize 1960: 2). Sadoul tries hard to play down their non-involvement : 'One should not limit the [young directors'] contribution simply to their search for new art-forms in film. Their "aestheticism" or "formalism" is less significant than one might have thought. Social concern is not at all absent from their films' (Sadoul 1959e: 117). Sadoul must have felt that he was somehow stretching the truth, otherwise why would he have concluded by asking whether the work of these film-makers would remain socially conscious in the future? (*ibid.*). Whatever Sadoul's self-contradictions, the answer to his question is well known: the young generation did not make social issues central to their work until the mid-1960s. Yet, generally speaking, Communist critics were careful not to push their questioning to its logical conclusion and, apart from some individual hostile reactions, gave their approval to the new films despite their political blandness.[3] The emotional troubles and adventures of the privileged youth portrayed by many New Wave films did not unleash any class conflict. The militant demands of New Realism, with its pro-working-class stance, seemed consigned to oblivion. This marks the second major development in the Communist critical discourse.

One facet of the earlier discourse of New Realism was nevertheless retained, a facet more readily compatible with the New Wave. This I will examine through Sadoul's reception of *Les Amants*, as it exemplifies both the continuity – in terms of contextualizing new art within the national heritage – and the change of tone that was coming about:

> Some have spoken of eroticism or even pornography with regard to certain scenes of *Les Amants*, which are no more obscene or naughty than Rodin's *Kiss* or Tintoretto's *Mars and Venus*. French artists, whether it be in literature, in painting or in sculpture have been dealing with physical love for a very long time. In other countries with other customs, the film might cause a scandal. Whatever one's opinion about the film, it does bear the hallmarks of its director's strong personality: Louis Malle is now among the best French film-makers (Sadoul 1958c: 6).[4]

Although the reaction to *Les Amants* might seem to provide a trivial illustration of the changes taking place within Communist criticism, it is nevertheless a revealing example. It is new if one remembers that only five years before a brief shot of a breast could be cited as proof of the decadence of the American regime. But above all it is characteristic of the way Communist critics of art, literature, and film always tend to anchor novelty within tradition. It was important for Sadoul that the New Wave should not be regarded as anomalous but as part and parcel of France's cultural heritage. No sooner had the new directors taken their first steps than Sadoul coined a few labels for them: 'The New School of Paris', 'Generation 1960', 'Neo-romanticism''. These were carefully chosen, as they echoed earlier French artistic movements in literature, painting, and film. The new directors became the descendants of Victor Hugo as well as of Carné. In March 1960, Sadoul explains: 'the New Wave's portrayal of France, its inhabitants and its trends is no further from our best national traditions (Rousseau, Diderot, Voltaire, Stendhal or Balzac) than Zola's and Maupassant's novels were' (Sadoul 1960a: 2).

In view of the fact that many of the newcomers – Kast, Kyrou, Astruc, Malle, Bernard-Aubert – refused to be drawn into a group or a movement, Sadoul agreed to drop the term 'Generation 1960', but argued that they had misunderstood him when he proposed the label 'The New School of Paris'. He had not meant it as a sect or a doctrine. 'It referred', he writes, 'to the definition given by Littré: 'a group of famous painters who worked in the "taste of this country" – most of whom were French' (Sadoul 1959c: 11).[5] This definition suited Roger Vadim and Georges Franju. As to his defining the newcomers as neo-romantics, Sadoul argued that realism and romanticism have never been incompatible, contrary to what Alexandre Astruc subsequently argued (*ibid.*).[6] Sadoul refers to Aragon, who in 1935 declared: 'Socialist Realism or Revolutionary romanticism, two names for the same thing, and this is where the Zola of *Germinal* and the Hugo of *Les Châtiments* come together' (*ibid.*). He also quotes Victor Hugo: 'Romanticism is the French Revolution incarnated in literature' (*ibid.*). Sadoul thus compares the new generation of film-makers to the literary group of the 1830s, reminding his readers that many of these writers, at their prime, were under thirty (Gautier, Musset, Hugo) and that the others reached fame in the same years (Balzac, Lamartine, Stendhal). What links the cinema of the New Wave with the poetry of the 1830s is 'a certain kind of lust for life, a liking for scandal, a certain wryness and a certain dandyism' (Sadoul 1960c: 10–11). This is an amazing change from the early 1950s, when such terms would inevitably have been used to vilify what the Communists regarded as immoral, unhealthy, Hollywood-influenced, and, therefore, anti-national cinema. What had once been considered bourgeois libertinage had now become part of French culture. A quarter of a century earlier, a younger Sadoul had branded poetic realism 'the French school of realism'. In 1950 it was New Realism that was portrayed as the only true heir of French culture. Now, in 1960, it was the New Wave.

The largely positive reception the Communist critics gave to the New Wave did not go unnoticed, and sparked reactions within both the PCF and French Marxist criticism at large. Among Communists, there seems to have been a rift between the critics and the film industry personnel, be they directors or technicians. This does not come as a surprise. Apparent in the stylistic novelty of many New Wave films, the freedom with which some of their directors tackled issues of production was bound to send shock waves across the well-established routine of France's film-making practice. The way they refused to conform to the governing set of rules – put in place and enforced since the Liberation through the relentless activism of the film unions – triggered a hostile response from the unions, which in 1960 were still extremely powerful.[7] Any move outside the system was therefore seen as going against the interests of French film workers.

When *Le Beau Serge* came out in February 1959, Georges Sadoul and Samuel Lachize were careful not to condone Chabrol's independence of mind while showing their appreciation of his free spirit. Lachize underlines Chabrol's 'courage', but explains that Chabrol's first long feature film 'is by no means to be set up as an example of the kind of film which could be made outside established customs' (Lachize 1959: 2). For Sadoul, the film could be produced because 'film authorities and unions turned a blind eye so as to allow it to be made outside legitimate and indispensable but onerous professional norms' (Sadoul 1959b: 6). Yet he also lends his support to the young directors, who 'prefer the rags of independence to the gilded livery of superproductions' (*ibid.*). In January 1963, at a time when the New Wave was facing public and critical disaffection, Georges Sadoul was one of the few critics who remained supportive of the young generation. He seemed even fully to endorse their production methods: 'those who blame the New Wave for losing twenty to thirty million francs forget to mention the hundreds of millions wasted in "commercial" productions' (Sadoul, 1963: 7). Louis Daquin and Jean-Paul Le Chanois exhibited a much less tolerant attitude towards their younger peers' methods of production. Both directors, who held positions of high responsibility in the *Fédération du Spectacle* CGT, condemned the way young directors approached film-making: 'Some take advantage of the situation to jump the queue and stir up trouble in order for their film to come out quicker. Other than a few interesting artistic temperaments, watch out for the smart cookies whose individualism has led to the forsaking of union gains which could prove harmful to the industry, as well as leading to an insane selfishness and to an *après moi le déluge* drift' (*Cellule des cinéastes*, n.d.: 2). Whereas Sadoul stressed

Chabrol's risk-taking, while acknowledging the chance factor that helped him start his film-making career, the Communist directors' cell (i.e., the smallest unit in the PCF's organization), in which Daquin and Le Chanois were the leading voices, contemptuously portrayed the young directors as spoiled rich kids, while conceding that their fortune was better spent making films than living it up.

The dispute that took place within French Marxist criticism at large proved far more serious. Its origins and outcome went far beyond the boundaries of film criticism. In 1959, Raymond Borde, speaking in the name of a number of critics – Edgar Morin, Ado Kyrou, Roger Tailleur, Marcel Oms – defended the existence of a non-Stalinist Marxist criticism: 'the notion of Marxist criticism has been too narrow until now, since it only takes into account *Les Lettres françaises* and *L'Humanité*, which simplify every issue according to the current dogma' (Borde 1959: 105). Defining the credo to which a number of critics adhered, Raymond Borde wrote: 'We are of the left. The concept was still rather vague a few months ago. Today it has got a precise meaning. We abhor man's exploitation of man, colonialism, ideological enslavement, and the so-called "sacred" values' (*Ibid.*).

Three years later, in 1962, the June issue of *Positif* epitomized the divisions within French Marxist film criticism. While on the surface it vehemently denounces the reception given by the Communists to the New Wave, the very ferocity of the criticism betrays a much wider ideological split among French Marxists. At the end of a devastating portrayal of Sadoul, Raymond Borde concludes that the communist critic 'no longer has his place among leftist critics', because 'he has already done enough damage' (Borde 1962b: 76).[8]

There are two possible explanations for such a violent tone even for the editorial team of *Positif*, who were well known for their bad manners. The first one belongs to the sphere of film criticism, while the other concerns French society at large. First, the hostility reflects the well-documented controversy between *Positif* and *Cahiers du Cinéma*. For *Positif*, the New Wave was a conformist and fundamentally right-wing phenomenon, while André Bazin was accused of conservatism and bourgeois idealism of the most insipid kind (Gozlan 1962a: 42). Alongside Borde's character assassination of Sadoul, *Positif* published a long study of André Bazin's legacy by Gérard Gozlan. Bazin is designated the forefather of Georges Sadoul: 'Bazin was one of those who unite what should be kept apart. And his successor today is Georges Sadoul. Instead of looking for contradictions, of setting up oppositions, Sadoul contributes to the levelling of everything' (Gozlan 1962b: 60). In short, for *Positif*, 'left-wing criticism, Communist included, has become – through its decomposition, its degradation, its lack of culture and rigour – humanist, liberal, moralising and, above all else, its critics have become scroungers since they are reduced to asking bourgeois films to provide less individualistic solutions and happier perspectives' (Gozlan 1962b: 56–7 note).

Yet what the attitude of *Positif* also betrays is the frustration felt by leftist critics faced with the notable absence of the Algerian War from French screens (though for a different view of the role of the war in French cinema see Breton 1992: 21–22). There is little doubt that this absence is partly responsible for the fierce enterprise of demolition orchestrated by *Positif*. Indeed, the PCF is also blamed for not having become more involved in the production or the backing of marginal and militant films made at the time. René Vautier, a Communist director who directed several such films, points out that the Communist critics and the Communist press ignored his films, but also goes on to blame the French directors' failure of nerve. As he ironically puts it, 'Alain Resnais himself dropped his project for a film on Algeria and went to film *L'Année dernière à Marienbad* in Germany' (Vautier 1998: 96). In her comprehensive study of the PCF and the Algerian War, Danièle Joly emphasizes that the party's Algerian policy was criticized by some of its members as well as by a large part of the French left (Joly 1991: 130–44). *Positif*'s attacks on the Communist critics metonymically echoed the French left's criticism of the PCF's stance over Algeria, particularly its alleged lack of a clear involvement with the Algerian people's struggle for independence.

This controversy raised the whole question of the possibility of a political cinema in France. In a violently anti-Communist article, Marcel Oms expresses his hopes that a marginal/militant cinema would take up the cause of French radical cinema (Oms 1962: 5). The seeds of May 1968 were sown. The rift between Marxist critics over the New Wave contained in an embryonic form the future debates of May 1968. In this respect, Sadoul seems to have had more instinct than the critics from *Positif*. Borde defines Godard as 'unrepentantly wasting film and uttering the most idiotic statements' resulting in his being '*the* most painful regression of French cinema towards intellectual illiteracy and plastic pretence' (Borde 1962a: 27). During the summer of 1960, after the release of *A bout de souffle*, Sadoul wrote of Godard: 'It is not because a young director manifests some bitterness in his first picture that he will necessarily become a "Fascist". This bitterness may, on the contrary, be the first sign of a critical consciousness that will eventually bring him towards a real optimism. Let's take him in his dialectical progress where a negation of bourgeois optimism might in some cases lead to a true optimism, which is not metaphysical, but revolutionary' (Sadoul 1960d: 6). Knowing the future of Godard's career as we do now, it is interesting to see which of the two critics, Sadoul or Borde, had the most insight.

More open, less dogmatic, Communist film criticism during the New Wave was a welcome departure from the tiresome *langue de bois* to which readers had become accustomed. Yet one wonders whether the baby was not thrown out with the bath water. Philippe Esnault in *Les Lettres françaises* underlined the discrepancy between the privileged lives portrayed in many New Wave films and that of the great majority of French youth: 'rural youth, working-class youth, students who work to study seem not to exist' (Esnault 1960: 10). Georges Sadoul and his followers demonstrated unusual leniency towards many of the New Wave directors. This trend was picked up very early in Communist circles. On the agenda of the directors' cell meeting of 3 February 1959, the third item reads: 'need for a Marxist analysis of the situation of cinema in France, as well as of the means we as Communists must put forward to fight against the confusion which holds sway in the film industry . . . and also in our ranks' (*Cellule des cinéastes* 1959: 1). It was only after the demise of the New Wave that Albert Cervoni would reflect on the questions raised by the Communist response to the young generation. Cervoni's analysis plays down earlier enthusiasm: 'While it would have been a mistake to turn a blind eye to the relative improvement brought about by the New Wave, we didn't need to give in – as we all did to some extent – to the temptation of unity at all costs, which in turn led to excessive herd instinct' (Cervoni 1965: 6).[9] When Cervoni criticizes the New Wave as a whole for depicting situations that are too remote from the life of most of the working population, he nevertheless acknowledges the right of the artist to do so, the right of the film directors to choose and shoot whatever they want. According to the Communist critic, the film-makers' work may be criticized on ideological grounds, but their talent or individual expression should also be recognized and praised when they deserve this praise. Such a viewpoint anticipates the 1966 Central Committee of Argenteuil, which would officialise the recognition of artists' and intellectuals' creative independence. It is also worth noticing Georges Sadoul's faithfulness to the New Wave. Significantly, the film historian kept defending small budgets over expensive productions[10] and the work of young independent-minded authors, such as Luc Moullet's *Brigitte et Brigitte*.[11] His fidelity and ongoing support were movingly acknowledged by Agnès Varda and Louis Malle upon Sadoul's untimely death in October 1967.[12]

The discussion within the Party as to the validity of the critics' views on the new generation demonstrates that the reception given by the

Communists to the New Wave was much more problematic than Jean-Michel Frodon's simplistic portrayal suggests. The French Communist film critics seem to have preferred the flexibility of the reed to the rigidity of the oak. In a way, they had more in common with Maïté, the young Communist heroine of Téchiné's *Les Roseaux sauvages*, than with her mother, Madame Alvarez, a schoolteacher whose positions are so rigid that she ends up having a nervous breakdown. Indeed, André Téchiné's shorter TV version of his feature film is entitled *Le Chêne et le roseau*.

Notes

1. *La Croix*, the Catholic daily, approved the decision of the Centrale catholique du cinéma (Catholic Film Office) to classify *Hiroshima mon amour* as 4B, or not recommended: Jean Rochereau (1959), '*Hiroshima mon amour*', *La Croix*, n° 23257, 24 June, p. 6.
2. A different, shorter version of this text, which does not contain the references to the oak and the reed, was published two months later: see Georges Sadoul, 'Livres de cinéma', *Les Lettres françaises*, n° 757, January 1959, p. 7.
3. Such as Michel Capdenac's rejection of *Les Bonnes Femmes*, 'Non, Monsieur Chabrol!', *Les Lettres françaises*, n° 822, 28 April 1960, pp. 1, 7; but the film was defended by Liliane Lurçat (1960) seven months later in 'Du cinéma, école de psychologie et des *Bonnes femmes*', *L'Humanité*, n° 5031, 2 November, p. 2.
4. While Sadoul was now more tolerant, it is worth noting that Force Ouvrière's Raymond le Bourre strongly objected to *Les Amants*, *En Cas de malheur* and *Les Tricheurs*, which he found 'all the more pernicious as they are destined for a popular and familial public' and 'very damaging to our youth and France's prestige abroad': Raymond le Bourre, 'Une autre forme d'abandon', *Carrefour*, n° 748, 14 January 1959, p. 10, in Jean Pivasset (1970), *Essai sur la signification politique du cinéma ; l'exemple français, de la libération aux événements de Mai 1968* (Paris, Cujas), p. 210.
5. In *Esprit*, once again Sadoul goes down the path of French history in order to find the sources of the new French cinema, refering to Molière, Jacques Callot, Le Tintoret, Le Nain, Le Cavalier Bernin and Georges

de La Tour: Georges Sadoul (1960b), 'Quelques sources du nouveau cinéma français', *Esprit*, n° 6, 1 June 1960, pp. 968–78.

6. 'Sadoul speaks of romanticism. How wrong he is! Cinema is and can only be realist', Alexandre Astruc, *Les Lettres françaises*, 8 April 1958.

7. See Jean Pivasset (1970), *Essai sur la signification politique du cinéma; l'exemple français, de la libération aux événements de Mai 1968* (Paris, Cujas), pp. 58–9.

8. While Borde considers Sadoul to have been harmful in terms of French film criticism, he also refers to the aura of respect Sadoul enjoys abroad. As the most translated French critic, Sadoul is blamed for giving a false image of the New Wave, i.e. for making his foreign readers think that it was a cinema of the left. Here is how Borde describes their reactions when told otherwise: 'They look at you with an expression of disbelief and say: "But Sadoul is a Communist, isn't he?"' The title of an article published in a Mexican newspaper illustrates that, in many foreign countries – especially in Eastern Europe and in the Third World, Sadoul's words are gospel: 'Interview with Georges Sadoul, the Pope of film criticism' ('*Entrevista con Georges Sadoul, el Papa de la Critica Cinematographica*') in *Novedades*, Mexico, 29 June 1962, Paris, BIFI, Archives Sadoul, GS-E 26 (Sadoul 1962a).

9. Albert Cervoni, untitled, in a letter dated June 1965 addressed to Georges Sadoul by Gaston Plissonier, a member of the Party's political bureau, which contains Cervoni's unpublished internal document, Paris, BIFI, Archives Sadoul, GS-D 10.

10. See for instance Georges Sadoul (1965a), 'Le cinéma français est-il un luxe?', *Les Lettres françaises*, n° 1062, 7–13 January 1965, pp 1, 10 or (1965b) 'Les films à gros budgets tuent-ils le cinéma ?', *Les Lettres françaises*, n° 1065, 28 January–3 February 1965, p. 8.

11. See Georges Sadoul (1966), 'Comme l'as de pique', *Les Lettres françaises*, n° 1161, 15 December 1966, p. 36.

12. See photos. Louis Malle in *L'Humanité*, n° 7202, 18 October 1967, p. 10; Agnès Varda in *Lettres françaises*, n° 1204, 18 October–24 October 1967, p. 15.

References

Baecque, Antoine de (1998), *La Nouvelle Vague*, Paris: Flammarion.

Borde, Raymond (1959), 'Critique et marxisme vivant', *Cinéma 59*, n° 33, pp. 104–6.

—— (1962a), 'Dictionnaire partiel et partial d'un nouveau cinéma français', *Positif*, n° 46, June, pp. 19–38.

—— (1962b), 'L'hypothèque Sadoul', *Positif*, n° 46, June, pp. 70–7.

Breton, Emile (1992), 'Quand les plantes exotiques parlaient', *Les Lettres Françaises*, n° hors-série Spécial Algérie, April, pp. 21–22.

Capdenac, Michel (1960), 'Non, Monsieur Chabrol!', *Les Lettres françaises*, n° 822, 28 April, pp. 1, 7.

Casanova, Laurent (1949), *Responsabilité de l'intellectuel communiste*, Paris: Éditions de la Nouvelle Critique.

Cellule des Cinéastes (1959), 'Ordre du jour du 3 février 1959', Paris, BIFI, Fonds Jean-Paul Le Chanois, 163-B. 35.

—— (No date), 'Rapport de la commission chargée d'étudier les problèmes nouveaux et les méthodes de travail ou la structure de l'industrie cinématographique', Paris, BIFI, Fonds Jean-Paul Le Chanois, 163-B. 35.

Cervoni, Albert (1959a), 'Les points sur les « i » de *Hiroshima mon amour*', *France nouvelle*, n° 714, 2 July, pp. 28–9.

—— (1959b), '*Les 400 coups* . . . une vérité qui n'est pas sans limite', *France nouvelle*, n° 716, 16 July, pp. 28–9.

—— (1959c), 'Citizen Welles', *France nouvelle*, n° 735, 26 November 1959, pp. 24–5.

—— (1965), Paris, BIFI, archives Sadoul, GS-D 10.

Douchet, Jean (1998), *La Nouvelle Vague*, Paris: Hazan.

Esnault, Philippe (1960), 'Une industrie qui pourrait être un art – I. De la nécessité d'une relève', *Les Lettres francaises*, n° 817, 17 March, p. 10.

Gozlan, Gérard (1962a), 'Les délices de l'ambiguïté (éloge d'André Bazin)', *Positif*, n° 46, June, pp. 36–69.

—— (1962b), 'Éloge d'André Bazin (suite et fin)', *Positif*, n° 47, July, pp. 16–61.

Joly, Danièle (1991), *The French Communist Party and the Algerian War*, Paris: Macmillan.

Lachize, Samuel (1959), 'Une réussite (où personne n'a triché)', *L'Humanité*, n° 4495, 14 February, p. 2.

—— (1960), '*A bout de souffle* . . . (mais avec espérances!)', *L'Humanité*, n° 4836, 19 March, p. 2.

Lurçat, Liliane (1960), 'Du cinéma, école de psychologie et des *Bonnes femmes*', *L'Humanité*, n° 5031, 2 November, p. 2.

Marie, Michel (1998), *La Nouvelle Vague*, Paris: Nathan.

Monjo, Armand (1959), 'J'attendais beaucoup plus', in 'Le film le plus discuté de l'année divise aussi nos critiques', *L'Humanité*, n° 4596, 13 June, p. 2.

Moussinac, Léon (no date), 'Une Nouvelle Vague ?', original manuscript, Paris, Bibliothèque de l'Arsenal, fonds Léon Moussinac, 114 (13) 4340.

Oms, Marcel (1962), 'Le grand mensonge', *Positif*, n° 47, July, pp. 5–11.

Pivasset, Jean (1970), *Essai sur la signification politique du cinéma ; l'exemple français, de la libération aux événements de Mai 1968*, Paris, Cujas.

Rochereau, Jean (1959), '*Hiroshima mon amour*', *La Croix*, n° 23257, 24 June, p. 6.

Sadoul, Georges (1946), 'Hypertrophie du cerveau', *Les Lettres françaises*, n° 115, 5 July, p. 9.

—— (1958a), 'Depuis Octobre, le cinéma français connait une crise . . .', January, Paris, BIFI, archives Sadoul, GS-A 137.

—— (1958b), 'André Bazin', November, Paris, BIFI, archives Sadoul, GS-A 143.

—— (1958c), 'Enfin un film d'amour', *Les Lettres françaises*, n° 747, 13 November, p. 6.

—— (1958d), 'Sur le plan de l'art, le dernier semestre 1958 a été bénéfique pour le cinéma français', December, Paris, BIFI, archives Sadoul, GS-A 147.

—— (1959a), 'Livres de cinéma', *Les Lettres françaises*, n° 757, 22 January, p. 7.

—— (1959b), 'Un jeune auteur complet', *Les Lettres françaises*, n° 761, 19 February, p. 6.

—— (1959c), 'Naissance d'un néo-romantisme', *Les Lettres françaises*, n° 768, 9 April, p. 11.

—— (1959d), 'L'univers et la rosée', *Les Lettres françaises*, n° 778, n° 18 June, p. 6.

—— (1959e), 'Notes on a new generation', *Sight and Sound*, vol. 28, n° 3/4, Summer/Autumn, pp. 111–17, originally in 'Nouveaux réalisateurs et nouveaux films français', June, Paris, BIFI, archives Sadoul, GS-A 149.

—— (1960a), 'Le cinéma français au début de 1960', March, Paris, BIFI, archives Sadoul, GS-A 159.

—— (1960b), 'Quelques sources du nouveau cinéma français', *Esprit*, n° 6, 1 June, pp. 968–78.

—— (1960c), 'Le néoréalisme est mort, vive le néoromantisme . . .', Paris, BIFI, archives Sadoul, GS-A 165.

—— (1960d), 'Le cinéma et l'homme de 1960', *Les Lettres françaises*, n° 837, 18 August, p. 6.

—— (1962), '*Entrevista con Georges Sadoul, el Papa de la Critica Cinematographica*' in *Novedades*, Mexico, 29 June, Paris, BIFI, archives Sadoul, GS-E 26.

—— (1963), 'Euthanasie du cinéma français', *Les Lettres françaises*, n° 961, 17 January, pp. 1, 7.

—— (1965a), 'Le cinéma français est-il un luxe?', *Les Lettres françaises*, n° 1062, 7 January, pp. 1,10.

—— (1965b), 'Les films à gros budgets tuent-ils le cinéma?', *Les Lettres françaises*, n° 1065, 28 January, p 8.

—— (1966), 'Comme l'as de pique', *Les Lettres françaises*, n° 1161, 15 December, p. 36 .

Vautier, René (1998), *Caméra citoyenne*, Paris: Éditions Apogée.

Wall, Irwin M. (1983), *French Communism in the Era of Stalin*, Westport, CT: Greenwood Press.

—4—

France and EU Policy-Making on Visual Culture: New Opportunities for National Identity?
Louise Strode

The 'Culture' of any given nation may be taken to mean those aspects of cultural life that can be understood as symbols of national identity, that is, those that are visible on an international level, such as films, music and language. Consequently, these symbols may be subject to the application of policy for varying motives from 'official' or 'elite' sources of power. This, of course, is one possible definition, and is used for this particular analysis, which examines how nations compare their identities with those of others. 'Visual culture' may take various forms, from film to advertising to theatre, but will be taken in this case as referring specifically to television and cinematic production. Recent debates in France have focused on certain areas of policy towards visual culture such as the protection and promotion of the French film or television product in what is becoming an increasingly global market-place.

From examination of such debates, and given the French State's historically strong role in the organization of culture in general, it would appear that visual culture represents a stage on which issues concerning French national identity are played out. Furthermore, visual culture is an example of a case where these issues have recently been discussed in a European context, given France's alignment with other European countries, yet in opposition to various cultural 'others', such as the USA and other non-European countries, especially Japan (see, for example, Forbes 1995a: 235, 260). French political leaders involved in the building of Europe since 1945, that is, Europe in terms of the construction of the European Community/Union, have often spoken of the desire to strengthen cultural links between countries and to develop cultural policies. These aims were reflected in France's request for the 1992 *Treaty on European Union* (the 'Maastricht' treaty) to include a 'Cultural Dimension' to encourage mutual respect and co-operation in areas of cultural policy through a legal competence, thus laying the basis for future European cultural legislation (*La Lettre de Matignon* 1992; Shore 1993: 784). This was achieved in the form of Article 128 of the *Treaty* (Commission of the EC 1992).

In the late 1980s, President Mitterrand pioneered the development of a programme known as *Euréka Audiovisuel*, which was designed to promote the distribution of European technology in the visual culture industries, for example high-definition television. In 1989, France was instrumental in the introduction of the 'Television without Frontiers' initiative, a project that envisaged the establishment of quotas stipulating the prioritizing of the broadcast of 'a majority' of European programmes (Looseley 1994: 126; *Conseil supérieur de la Langue française* 1994: 10; *Le Monde*: 26 July 1991; *The Independent*: 2 February 1995). This legislation was arguably aimed at limiting American broadcasts in particular. French policy-makers have more recently tried to reinforce such a strategy through European Union legislation, the development of funds for film production within the EU, and the insistence on the establishment of quotas for European-generated material (*The Guardian*: 23 March 1995; Forbes 1995a: 260). However, the re-negotiation of the General Agreement on Tariffs and Trade (GATT) in 1993 threatened such policies and generated considerable debate in France and throughout Europe. Since the GATT debate, notable policies in the area of visual culture policy include continually developing revisions of Television without Frontiers, and the programmes MEDIA I and II. France has also used its EU presidency opportunities, such as those of 1989 and 1995, to push its cultural policy objectives on to the European agenda (Drake 1994: 48; *La Lettre de Matignon* 1995).

This essay, however, will consider one case study example of a visual culture policy area reflecting French elite concerns with identity in a European context. The discussion will focus on French policy-making debates concerning the 'Uruguay cycle' of negotiations of 1993 on the General Agreement on Tariffs and Trade (GATT). These debates synthesized perhaps the strongest anti-American reaction on the part of French elites regarding European televisual and cinematic industries (including, of course – and perhaps sometimes exclusively – French productions). This reaction served to encourage further debate surrounding France's ongoing battle for the protection of such industries, a battle that has become increasingly interlinked with that of the European partner industries. Such a relationship has arguably led to French policy-making elites utilizing their European links to their own advantage. This will be suggested in the following analysis of contributions to the political debate on GATT made by the then French President, François Mitterrand, and the Minister for Culture and Francophone Affairs, Jacques Toubon (Mitterrand 1993; Toubon 1993b).

« L'Exception culturelle » and the GATT Debate

The political debate on GATT in France stemmed essentially from the fact that in Europe, cinematic and televisual creations have often been perceived and portrayed more as a form of expressive art, rather than as a 'product' to be marketed like any other (although there are arguments to suggest that this 'tradition' is in fact an 'invented' one).[1] This opinion fuelled much of the conflict between French and American political elites and film and television professionals, with the French side advocating a policy of *une exception culturelle* or a 'cultural exception' from the GATT agreements for any 'cultural product'. Without such a clause, existing protective policies such as Television without Frontiers would be jeopardized. Meanwhile, the United States negotiators argued against the continuation of quota restrictions, which they regarded as contrary to the notion of free trade.

French policy-makers' desire to support the French cinematic industry, which has a rather unbalanced import–export relationship with that of the USA, was clearly evident, but French anxieties concerning the cultural aspects of the GATT propositions seemed to be more firmly rooted in the long-standing ambivalence of the Franco-American cultural relationship. Americanization has often been held in suspicion by French political elites, who regard it as synonymous with an encroaching modernization (*Le Monde*, 12 December 1996; Morley 1996: 328).[2] Behind the more obvious commercial battle lay the long-standing struggle between France and the United States for economic, political and cultural power (Gaillard 1994: 9). The producer of the successful French film *Les Visiteurs*, Alain Terzian, summarized the situation arising from the United States' stance on GATT and culture as one where 'the essential interests of France are at stake', clearly linking economic factors with wider issues related to national identity (Terzian 1993: 7).

Political controversy arising from the GATT debate offers an interesting and suitable focus for an investigation of French national identity, since visual culture policy is an example of a site where this identity can be expressed, through symbols that are internationally visible, such as film and television 'products'.[3] What is interesting is that many examples of political debate or discourse on this subject reveal a kind of consensus of opinion amongst French cultural policy-makers on France and Europe that may not at first be apparent.

The discussion below concentrates on two examples of contributions to the French political debate surrounding GATT and cultural policy. Whilst these two texts are obviously a small-scale example, they can be used to illustrate the political consensus that the European Union may represent an opportunity for French cultural policy-making objectives concerning national identity. The two texts selected are worthy of in-depth analysis, since they contain key speeches made by important members of two opposing political groupings on the GATT issue.

The text by Jacques Toubon was produced in his role as RPR (*Rassemblement pour la République*, or 'Rally for the Republic') Minister of Culture, in an address to the 'Rencontres cinématographiques' in Beaune on 30 October 1993.[4] Although such events are immediately aimed at a specialist audience composed primarily of those involved in the cinema/television industries, the participation of Jacques Toubon, as France's Minister for Culture, was naturally open to close scrutiny and reporting by the international media, given the context of the impending Uruguay Round of the GATT talks and French political elites' concerns surrounding cultural issues in the agreements. Such events represented a good opportunity for Toubon to offer his opinions on the talks and to secure the support of creative industries in other countries.

The François Mitterrand text represents one of the few major presidential pronouncements on the GATT/cultural exception issue. The lack of contributions by Mitterrand may have been due to the President's wish to appear above the general political wrangling of the negotiations, choosing to confine his key contributions to issues that directly concern French national identity such as culture, rather than the more general economic arguments surrounding GATT. The speech was destined to attract media coverage, and hence wide attention in France and abroad, for several reasons. These included Mitterrand's status as President of the Republic, his position at the head of the Francophone movement in the midst of the political debate surrounding the 'cultural exception', and his well-documented personal interest in both European integration and culture. Furthermore, Mitterrand's speech, given during his acceptance of an honorary doctorate at Gdansk University on 21 September 1993, was the first time the President was to launch himself explicitly into the French professional and governmental crusade for a clearly demanded *exception culturelle,* having previously only hinted at an intention to comment on the issue (*Libération*, 22 September 1993). Interestingly, the city in which the speech was delivered symbolizes a history of conflict and struggle against totalitarianism, a background that Mitterrand perhaps thought would support his arguments, although press reports at the time suggested that the Poles themselves were not expecting such a forceful statement on a particularly French concern (*ibid.*).

By comparing these examples of contributions to the GATT debate, we can consider how Europe may be presented by different political groups as an opportunity for French visual culture policy. Examination of these texts by Toubon and Mitterand suggests that Europe is invoked for a variety of reasons, and there are some clear points of convergence in the discourse of the two actors.

A Threatened 'Europe'

Both speakers start from the idea that 'Europe' is under threat in some way. France is situated definitely 'in' Europe, whichever definition is used (and what exactly constitutes 'Europe' is not always clear). Both Europe and France are suggested to be under threat from certain cultural 'others', particularly America, although threats such as Japanese technology are mentioned too. The need for the defence of European cultural identity is emphasized, together with the implication that it is France that is leading the European fight.

For example, in justifying the French government's position regarding *l'exception culturelle* in the GATT agreements, Toubon argues that the issue concerning the French 'ne se limite pas à l'identité, il est pour l'universalité' (is not limited to identity, it concerns universality). 'L'universalité' is obviously a loaded word in the mouth of a French politician, suggesting as it does links with the French Revolution and Jacobin, universalist conceptions of civilization. Toubon also suggests that other countries' cultural identities may be equally at stake. To critics of the government's stance, Toubon argues that France's policy is based on openness to other cultures and ideas rather than a closed, defensive attitude, of which it may be accused. He argues that the success of various European film-makers, previously due to European support systems, is now jeopardized owing to American-led demands for renegotiation of the GATT agreements. But he claims that the French 'battle' – as it is presented here – is not an identity issue, but rather concerns the promotion of the right for different types of cinematic products – French and European – to flourish in the world market-place: 'Our struggle is not based on an identity battle at all. It defends the cause of French, European and World cinema.' Yet this statement is somewhat contradictory, since the French film industry is doubtless a cultural symbol, and furthermore, given the existence of various government agencies designed to support French film production and exports, is frequently held as a measure of the independence or otherwise of French cultural and national identity (Looseley 1995: 27).

A military metaphor is present throughout this speech, with frequent references to the notion of a battle or struggle. This is arguably inherent in the construction of French identity, given the Republican 'story' of the defence of identity against a threat, which is a military 'other' first and foremost. Examples such as the words of the *Marseillaise*, the military format of the 14 July celebrations, the Tomb of the Unknown Soldier, and Charles de Gaulle as a Resistance hero may be considered here.

Mitterrand, too, speaks in terms of threats and the need for protection. He praises the European film industry, and argues that Europe is both rich in cultural heritage, and successful in the nurturing of creation, of arts and ideas, and of national identities, alongside competitiveness, but that now this is under threat. He argues against the resultant 'assimilation' by Europe of American culture, presenting older 'valeurs fondatrices' (founding values) of Europe in opposition to 'le mercantilisme, le pouvoir de l'argent' (mercantilism, the power of money), as he appeals to the notion of Europe as a 'vieux continent' (old continent), in opposition to the 'Nouveau Monde' (New World).[5] Whilst Europe's 'spirit' may have survived 'wars' and 'the great totalitarian machines' before the end of the Cold War, Mitterrand claims this is now threatened by the domination of economic power and the advance of technology, led by America's drive towards increased liberalization of the world visual culture market-place. Here, the emphasis is on the whole of Europe's being affected, rather than just France. These statements develop the portrayal of France as a victim, by invoking Europe's cultural past: France is within a Europe dominated by American influence, but will rise again, and find new glory. However, much of the past European identity, which is appealed to, is arguably mythical, since no account is taken of the harsh reality of the Europe of the Second World War, for example. The creation of present-day 'Europe' was, after all, inspired by the necessity to form alliances in response to military threats. Given France's comparatively recent experiences of war, and the centrality of the military metaphor in the republican construction of French identity, the conception of 'Europe' assumes a great significance. Yet the vision of Europe that is discussed in French political discourse can really only look to the pre-wars era, or to developments since 1945, in order to avoid re-invoking painful and divisive personal experiences. Thus a Europe *beyond* war must be referred to, which Mitterrand does when he speaks of 'the tradition of the Middle Ages', 'the Enlightenment philosophers', and the Maastricht Treaty.

Toubon, meanwhile, develops his claim that the French government does not seek to close off the European cinema market-place to outside influence, but rather to prevent it becoming the victim of an over-powerful monopoly, characterized, with racial overtones, as 'le monopole nippo-américain' (Japanese–American monopoly).[6] So the implied major threats to the European market of Japan and the USA are accused of monopolistic practices and the formation of an opposition to France, itself presented again as open to new ideas and new influences. Here, imagery concerning struggling and fighting is present once more – 'nous battons . . .' (we struggle), 'la bataille que nous menons . . .' (the battle that we are waging) – suggesting feelings of urgency, and reaction to an external threat. A Gaullist vision of French identity is invoked, depicting France as a 'guardian of civilization', standing proud and independent in the face of various aggressors.[7]

Europe and A New World Order?

Besides these rallying cries for the protection of European cultural identity, both speeches refer to the position of Europe in a post-Cold War world. Toubon, for example, interprets 'uniformization' as signifying the power of American cultural influence, which may be brought about by globaliza-tion, when he asks 'Are we moving towards one world? A unified world?', wondering if 'a single cultural model' could be imposed by the power of the market. He suggests a situation of passing 'from Soviet tyranny to American monopoly', revealing a Gaullist vision of France constantly caught between two opposing 'blocks'.[8] Mitterrand, too, argues that the GATT dispute is not essentially about setting up 'the cultures of Europe' against 'that of the New World' (i.e., America), but the wish to preserve 'l'idée universelle de la culture' (the universal idea of culture) against market forces. This phrase is also significant, as it again implies a 'monoculture' emanating from the USA. He too makes reference to a new form of totalitarianism threatening Europe in the form of American economic power, rather than Soviet military might.

Thus both actors employ arguments related to the effects of what could be termed 'globalization' on cultural identity, and indicate feelings of uncertainty and suspicion regarding world structures following the end of the Cold War in what may be described as a 'postmodern' condition, where old sources of conflict and co-operation may have changed or even disappeared, with inevitable consequences for national identity. This fear of *mondialisation* (globalization) may at first appear to be the same as older thinking on Americanization. Doubtless there are strong links, particularly given the role of visual culture in the process of Americanization, and now in the process of globalization as communication technologies continue to develop at a rapid pace. However, given the references to threats from other countries besides the United States, to Europe in a post-Cold War age, and to the growth of new technologies, together with the actual use of the term 'mondialization', it would seem that 'globalization' encapsulates more effectively the fears of French politicians displayed in these texts. Furthermore, the seductive nature of Americanization for France has been well documented (for example Kuisel 1993), while, as Taylor argues, globalization suggests not so much a better world, as a threatening world of 'shifting jobs and downsizing' (1997: 20).

'Europe' as France's Opportunity

Besides the considerable attention given to the notion of a threat to European cultural and national identity, both Mitterrand and Toubon present Europe as a site or source of opportunity for France's future policy-making, as a chance to gain influence for its own visual culture policy agenda, through the GATT issue.

Europe is first described as an opportunity for protection. Although both Mitterrand and Toubon may criticize some aspects of European policy as being too weak, they demonstrate their support for the French agenda of protection when they argue that the laws such as those represented by the EU quota system are necessary to allow the weaker players in the market some degree of freedom. Furthermore, we have seen that they stress Europe and France as places favouring diversity represented in visual culture products (even though they themselves may wish to limit the influence of some cultures).

Both speakers try to rally the support of their audiences, which include France and other EU countries, and those belonging to a wider Europe. They advocate co-operation in production and marketing, and the establishment of distribution networks, thus creating an economic alliance against US domination. So a European market-place may offer an opportunity for defence – both immediately and in the future – against America's 'invasion'. Moreover, refusal to fight together may spell disaster for Europe. To support this argument, the need for a 'Europe des cultures' is highlighted, as both Mitterrand and Toubon urge a kind of cohesion in terms of cultural identity, highlighting the validity of the aims of the

Maastricht Treaty, especially in an increasingly globalized market-place for visual culture and cultural 'products' in general.

Toubon, for example, emphasizes the future of European policy, following GATT and the agreement of an *exception culturelle* clause, describing his ideas for production and distribution of visual culture in the world market-place. Highlighting the theme of *liberté*, Toubon urges Europeans to act to safeguard the future, since only the inclusion of a 'cultural exception' clause can make a difference, together with stronger policies for European visual culture products. Both Mitterrand and Toubon use a kind of 'slippage' between the 'discursive characters' of France and Europe in their discourse, made possible since 'Europe' is not clearly defined. When first introducing his discussion of the GATT debate, Toubon indicates his personal contribution to policy-making with phrases like 'je plaide' (I plead) and 'je milite' (I fight), and proclaims '. . . je souhaite réaffirmer nos objectifs, je veux dire ceux du Gouvernement, dans la négociation' (I wish to reassert our objectives, I mean those of the Government, in the negotiation), suggesting that he is speaking of the French policy-making position. However, it becomes less clear to whom he is actually referring as *nous*, as he widens his discussion to include the protection and promotion of *European* visual culture industries as well as those of France. Toubon argues that the issue affects the whole of Europe as a geographical, historical and cultural entity, besides the political institution of the European Union, when he states, 'And "European" does not only mean European in the sense of the Community. This issue goes beyond the level of the twelve member states.' Mitterrand, too, suggests the idea of only France, amongst the other European countries, daring to speak out, as he states: 'I urge creators and State officials around our continent: we will not build Europe without a European consciousness.'[9]

Perhaps as a result of his presidential status as a politician more removed from the actual level of negotiations, Mitterrand speaks in more abstract terms, arguing for 'une conscience européenne' ('a European consciousness') towards the end of his speech. He, too, advocates European construction through cultural cohesion, citing 'l'esprit de résistance, l'esprit européen' (the spirit of resistance, the European spirit) and the rather mystical idea of the necessity of a European *conscience*. Whilst it is not quite clear what such a *conscience* might be, its juxtaposition with historical references to 'the Middle Ages' and 'the philosophers of the Enlightenment' inspires reflection on the history of the idea of 'Europe'.[10] Like Toubon, Mitterrand envisions a Europe wider than the EU, a vision emphasized when he cites 'the example of Gdansk and Poland' and speaks of 'our continent' and of 'rallying Europe, all Europe, around its founding values', indicating a wider appeal to the *rassemblement* of the countries of Europe in a geographical/cultural sense, besides those of the existing European Union. The sense of history is helped further by his reference to the city of Gdansk as a site of struggle,[11] as he speaks 'in the name of the spirit of resistance and the European spirit that this ceremony symbolizes', and by his appeal to mystical 'valeurs fondatrices', a vague term suggesting the universality of French identity (here disguised as European identity).

Conclusions: From Threats to Opportunities?

The above analysis has shown that both François Mitterrand and Jacques Toubon present the European Union, and also appeal to Europe in a more general sense, as a future opportunity for France's visual culture policy-making following the granting of an *exception culturelle* for the GATT agreements. We can see this in both politicians' continual citation – both overt and more discreet – of issues concerning the need to defend and promote European (including French) cultural products. Whether presented in terms of economic or of cultural liberty, the defence and exaltation of French cultural output is an issue that we know to be clearly related to France's own agenda of long-standing concerns over cultural and national identity, particularly with regard to its fears over US-led cultural imperialism.

Besides the differences noted in the presentation of arguments related to the role of Minister of Culture as opposed to that of President of the Republic, it can be seen that both speakers, from opposing ends of the political spectrum, present European Union visual culture policy-making in their statements on the GATT issue as an opportunity in which France should clearly take part, particularly given its need to compete in an international market. From this we can detect a kind of consensus over the support given by both speakers – including an economic liberal such as Toubon – to the involvement of regulatory bodies in the organization of visual culture, which we would perhaps expect given the French State's tradition of interference in cultural matters. Moreover, a consensus is suggested regarding, first, France and the threat of certain cultural 'others' such as the United States, and second, France and Europe, that transcends any traditional Left–Right ideological cleavage. This is apparent given that Mitterrand was a Socialist, whereas Toubon was from the Gaullist right RPR party. Furthermore, we see the paradox of French elites attempting to use supra-national-level institutions to address what is arguably a national issue for France, whatever various actors may claim. Given France's traditional commitment to European integration and construction, and the support of several other European countries in certain cultural policy areas, it seems likely that the EU, and a wider Europe, may offer further opportunities for the future protection and promotion of French national identity through policy-making on visual culture. The same may be true of other cultural forms such as language, which we have also seen French elites push as policy objectives at the EU level, particularly with regard to the fight against perceived American domination. Yet recent debates concerning the revision of the Television without Frontiers directive have indicated that French policy-makers cannot always have their way as easily as they might wish to.[12]

In addition, French elites finding a louder voice at a European level may present a new diplomatic opportunity for wider influence, and for the re-launch of European construction and integration. This may be of relevance in today's international climate, which may be characterized as 'postmodern', where France may feel a declining influence following the end of the Cold War, and an uncertainty regarding its economic and/ or political 'squeezing' within the evolving European Union. At the same time, it is faced with possible challenges from the USA and the newly industrializing Eastern economies. There are also various threats to identity perceived from within France, such as the presence of different ethnic groups, that may threaten established views of French identity.

Thus, with these issues in mind, we might wonder whether globalization is perhaps the 'wall' that French national identity is currently coming up against, as we see how France attempts to utilize the opportunities of the European Union in order to bolster its identity through policy-making on visual culture. However, as Mike Featherstone asserts (1995: 13–14), globalization may not in fact, as French elites may fear, actually lead to cultural uniformity, but to increased diversity, which both Toubon and Mitterrand would claim to welcome. Yet given the apparent wish of French elites of both the Left and the Right to limit certain cultural influences within Europe, are French policy-makers themselves not open to accusations of seeking to impose a degree of uniformity?

Notes

1. Such a portrayal may seem to be long-standing, but is not immutable. The conception of cinematic creations in France as 'art' rather than

'products' may be comparatively recent, if we consider, for example, the development of the early French cinema at the turn of the last century, led by the highly commercial outlook of the Paris company Pathé-Frères (Abel 1995). The notion of the film as artistic creation arguably developed later, during the 1950s and 1960s, alongside the birth of the journal *Cahiers du cinéma* and the development of the *auteur* school of criticism, which and treated cinema as a serious art form, in parallel with novels and poetry. Thus the admission of visual culture to the hierarchy of 'legitimate' culture may be more recent than we may think, and appeals to a 'tradition' of 'artistic creations' rather than products may be employed defensively without real foundation (see, for example, Shore 1993: 792).

2. See also Forest 1993: 115; Gaillard 1994: 8–9; Kelly 1995: 3.
3. Kuisel argues that current concerns in France regarding identity, including cultural policy developments such as the GATT and language controversies, signify that identity is in fact being 'reconstructed around cultural markers' (1996: 46).
4. Toubon held this post from 1993 to 1995.
5. Bruno Mégret (1993) of the Front National, also argues (30 October) against GATT whilst appealing to a nostalgic vision of an 'old' Europe, as he speaks of the unequal balance between American cinematic productions and 'le cinéma de notre vieux continent', and mentions 'des siècles de culture qui nous ont façonnés'. However, whether or not Mégret has the same conception of 'Europe' in the present day as Mitterrand is questionable (even though Mitterrand himself does not clarify his own definition).
6. Interestingly, such a model of domination is also alluded to in Front National discourse on GATT. See Mégret (1993), in which the film *Jurassic Park* and its related merchandise are likened to a commercial invasion from the East, as well as from the USA.
7. Elsewhere, the argument of France's having a more open cultural identity is alluded to by the Front National and the Parti Communiste, although not always in similar terms, or for the same reasons. This would suggest that such feelings have roots that run deeper than a purely party-political level. See, for example, Mégret 1993; also Marest 1994; Ralite 1993.
8. He mentioned similar anti-*mondialisation* arguments in a related speech to the *Assemblée des réalisateurs,* made the previous month.
9. Here, the use of *on* leaves open the question of *who* exactly Mitterrand envisaged as building Europe now and in the future – it could mean a variety of people, for example Mitterrand and Chancellor Kohl, French

EU commissioners, French governments, French voters, or voters in other countries.

10. See similar appeals to a *vieux continent* occurring in Front National discourse on GATT (Mégret 1993, note 7).
11. This may seem ironic in retrospect, since even symbols of struggle have become multi-layered in a post-Cold War economy, in which the Gdansk shipyards have now closed down.
12. See, for example, the opposition mounted by Germany, the UK, the Netherlands and Spain (*Le Monde*, 19 June 1996).

References

Abel, Richard (1995), 'The Perils of Pathé, or the Americanization of Early American Cinema', in L. Charney and V. R. Schwartz (eds), *Cinema and the Invention of Modern Life*, Berkeley, CA, University of California Press.

Commission of the EC (1992), *Treaty on European Union Signed at Maastricht on 7 February*, Luxembourg, Office for Official Publications of the EC.

Conseil Supérieur de la Langue française (1994), 'Le CSA et l'application de la directive « Télévision sans frontières »', *La Lettre du CSA*, January.

Drake, Helen (1994), 'François Mitterrand, France and European Integration', in G. Raymond (ed.), *France During the Socialist Years*, Aldershot, Dartmouth.

Featherstone, Mike (1995), *Undoing Culture: Globalization, Culture, Postmodernism*, London, Sage.

Forbes, Jill (1995a), 'Popular Culture and Cultural Politics' in J. Forbes and M. Kelly (eds), *French Cultural Studies: An Introduction*, Oxford, Oxford University Press.

—— (1995b), 'Conclusion: French Cultural Studies in the Future', in J. Forbes and M. Kelly (eds), *French Cultural Studies: An Introduction*, Oxford, Oxford University Press.

Forest, Philippe (1993), 'Le Concept contemporain de la culture', *Cahiers français*, no. 260 « Culture et société », March–April.

Gaffney, John (1989), *The French Left and the Fifth Republic: The Discourses of Communism and Socialism in Contemporary France*, London, Macmillan.

—— (1991), 'French Political Culture and Republicanism', in J.Gaffney and E. Kolinsky (eds), *Political Culture in France and Germany: A Contemporary Perspective*, London, Routledge.

—— (1993), 'Language and Style in Politics', in C. Sanders (ed.), *French Today: Language in its Social Context*, Cambridge, Cambridge University Press.

Gaillard, Jean-Michel (1994), 'L'ennemi américain 1944–1994', *L'Histoire*, April.

The Guardian (1995), 'EU Seeks cut in American films', 23 March.

The Independent (1995), 2 February.

Kelly, Michael (1995), 'Introduction: French Cultural Studies', in J. Forbes and M. Kelly (eds), *French Cultural Studies: An Introduction*, Oxford, Oxford University Press.

Kuisel, Richard (1993), *Seducing the French: The Dilemma of Americanization*, Berkeley, CA, University of California Press.

—— (1996), 'Modernization and Identity', *French Politics and Society*, vol. 14, no.1, Winter.

Le Monde, 26 July 1991; 19 June 1996; 12 December 1996.

La Lettre de Matignon (1992), supplement 'La France au coeur de l'Europe', July 1992.

—— (1995), supplement 'La Présidence française de l'Union européenne 1995', January 1995.

Libération (1993), 22 September.

Looseley, David (1994), 'Cultural Policy and Democratization under Mitterrand'', in G. Raymond (ed.), *France During the Socialist Years*, Aldershot, Dartmouth.

—— (1995), *The Politics of Fun: Cultural Policy and Debate in Contemporary France*, Oxford, Berg.

Marest, Lucien (1994), 'GATT: quand le bras droit de Balladur se met à table', *Libération,* 4 January.

Mégret, Bruno (1993), 'Pour un protectionnisme culturel', speech at 'Colloque du conseil scientifique du Front National', 30 October.

Mitterrand, François (1993), 'Allocution prononcée par le Président de la République à l'occasion de la remise du diplôme de docteur Honoris Causa', 21 September.

Morley, David (1996), 'EurAm, modernity, reason and alterity: or postmodernism, the highest stage of cultural imperialism', in D. Morley and K.-H. Chen (eds), *Stuart Hall – Critical Dialogues in Cultural Studies*, London, Routledge.

Ralite, Jack (1993), 'Laissons la culture hors des conséquences du GATT', *Libération,* 20 April.

Ruby, Christian, Nouvel, Kevin and Simonet, Julie (1993), 'La Bataille du culturel', *Regards sur l'actualité*, no.189, March 1993.

Shore, Chris (1993), 'Inventing the "People's Europe": Critical Approaches to European Community 'Cultural Policy'', *Man*, vol. 28, no.4.

Taylor, Peter (1997), 'Historical Geography of Modernities', inaugural lecture given at Loughborough University, 30 April 1997.

Terzian, Alain (1993), 'Il n'y a rien à négocier au GATT', *Le Nouvel Economiste*, 3 September.

Toubon, Jacques (1993a), speech at 'Assemblée des Réalisateurs à Venise', 6 September.

——— (1993b), speech at 'Rencontres cinématographiques de Beaune', 30 October.

Part II
French Civilization and its Discontents

—5—

Jewish Myths and Stereotypes in the Cinema of Julien Duvivier

Simon P. Sibelman

In *L'Histoire du cinéma*, Maurice Bardèche and Robert Brasillach refer to Julien Duvivier as one of the most artful, talented and conscientious film-makers of his day, a reputation frequently echoed in such inter-war French cultural journals as *Marianne, Vendredi, Esprit* and *L'Illustration*. Other critics labelled Duvivier a 'Catholic film-maker', whose films afforded a sense of hope and intense spiritual inspiration during a particularly turbulent period. And, for his part, André Bazin ranks Duvivier among those four French masters whose works exemplify the stark cinematographic images now identified as 'poetic realism'. In our own era, however, Duvivier's significance in the history of French cinema remains little understood. True, some do realize Duvivier directed two of the more prominent films dealing with the exotic and politically charged theme of colonialism in Northern Africa: *La Bandéra* (1935) and *Pépé le Moko* (1937), perhaps his lasting masterpiece. But there is a collection of other films that have bequeathed a uniquely abiding and troubling significance.

Unlike other film-makers of the 1930s whose cinematic corpus evolved and established particular directorial hallmarks, Duvivier's cinema tends to lurch from project to project demonstrating no profound cohesion, no progression. Though massed among a host of diverse film-makers of the 'golden age of French cinema,' Duvivier's work does not altogether adhere to accepted criteria defining the cinematographic poetic realism of the generation. Could this presumable lack of full maturation and direction have resulted from Duvivier's 'motivation for profit'? (Turk 1989: 158– 9). Diverse and compelling questions arise when one seeks to define Duvivier's cinema. How, for example, could Bardèche and Brasillach – rarely champions of poetic realism – confer even limited praise upon Duvivier's work? Might their accolade represent a positive consequence of Duvivier's not having *comprehensively* identified himself with the leading directors and studios of the poetic realist movement? Or, might their critical laurels have reflected certain anti-Jewish issues raised in specific Duvivier films? I would maintain that in certain Duvivier films of the inter-war period one can discern distinct elements that provide a sense of evolving continuity in his work. One group, which provide the critical focus of this essay, are Duvivier's formulaic representations of Jews, most conspicuously in what I shall label his three 'Jewish films', *David Golder* (1930), *Golgotha* (1935) and *Le Golem* (1935). His stereotypical imagery emerged during a disquieting moment in French history, since the decade of the 1930s witnessed a shocking growth of anti-Semitic manifestations. Close analyses of Duvivier's 'Jewish films' elicit a multitude of serious questions concerning his motives. For example, in creating these particular films, had Duvivier consciously sought to contribute to the rising waves of anti-Jewish discourse disseminated throughout France in the wake of the First World War and of the political chaos of the 1930s? In his efforts to produce popular and engaging films, had Duvivier merely permitted prevailing cultural forces to influence his own creative processes, or had he pandered to a particular mentality? Had Duvivier simply been unconcerned in his application of those negative images and characteristics attributed to Jewish characters in his film and to actual Jews themselves?

In *L'Image-Mouvement*, Gilles Deleuze submits that the cinematographic image possesses a protean nature whose instantaneity creates a commanding phenomenological, ontological and symbolic significance. The projected image appears without conditions for the spectator; the representation lives. 'Is not the cinema at the very outset obliged to imitate natural perception?' Deleuze asks (1983: 12). And yet, early French filmmakers desirous of interpreting Jews for the screen did not draw portraits conforming to reality, but ironically expropriated two-dimensional stereotypes that constituted integral components of historic discourses of anti-Semitism. Though Pierre Sorlin maintains that prior to 1936 the French cinema practically ignored minority groups of all sorts, in 'Jewish Images in the French Cinema of the 1930s' he does affirm that the traditional stereotype emerged as the primary means for directors to portray Jews:

> Jews were presented to French audiences in such a way that they might be identified. This identification was necessarily dependent upon the projection of *accepted stereotypical features instantly recognizable by the audience*. [. . .] Stereotyping is an essential cinematic shorthand allowing the film to concentrate its dialogue and visual images upon the development of its central themes

and characters. [. . .] The specific cinematic forms and images which were central to identification of French Jews were physical characteristics, attitudes, names, accents, direct reference, and finally *connections with finance/business.* (Sorlin 1981: 140; my emphasis)

By pandering to images of what society believed the Jew to be and then enabling the public to perceive those conceptions, film-makers of the 1930s abdicated a degree of their moral *and* artistic responsibilities.

Robert Bresson proposes an intriguing image when he speaks of 'la force éjaculatrice de l'oeil' (The ejaculatory power of the eye) (Bresson 1975: 19). This striking metaphor evokes both interior and exterior movement: an impression penetrating by way of the eye elicits a vigorous, even visceral reaction that, in turn, effects an explosive emission. Bresson's evocative figure undoubtedly affords an intimation of the highly significant impact that stereotypical representations wrought on the general public. The legacy of anti-Semitism and its accompanying formulaic portrayals of Jews appeared confirmed. As primary visual impressions of seemingly diabolical Jews merged with a variety of cinematographic techniques – in both staging and montage – viewers were subsequently aroused to summon latent or ignored cultural recollections concerning the Jew, thereby reintroducing the myths into society's active collective memory.

Directors similarly drew upon a potent position explicitly expounded in Edouard Drumont's *La France Juive*, which experienced a revival during the 1930s. Drumont had suggested that the acculturated Jew, the *Israélite*, posed the greater danger for France, since this unidentifiability permitted effortless integration into French society, a phenomenon Drumont likened to infection. France's purity was menaced by Jewish feculence; France's moral and political decadence resulted directly from the inserted Jewish element. Inter-war films treating Jewish themes or introducing Jewish characters would gradually visually articulate aspects of Drumont's ideas, though none of the cinematographic representations would ever descend to Drumont's vile, incendiary rhetoric. Nevertheless, the visual images the cinema offered undeniably did little to alter preconceived opinions concerning the Jews.

This, then, was the historical and cultural context in which Julien Duvivier matured as a film-maker. The sundry aspects of anti-Semitism and casual stereotyping of Jews would have undeniably formed part of his cultural consciousness, though no direct evidence arises from his notes, letters or personal papers that would indicate that Duvivier himself maintained anti-Semitic beliefs. The lack of such evidence necessitates a restatement of those pertinent questions previously posed: why in filming his three 'Jewish films' did Duvivier resort to using those negative stereotypes preferred by anti-Jewish/anti-Semitic groups and individuals? Had Duvivier been unaware of, or worse, unconcerned with the profound repercussions such an exploitation could effect given the politically charged environment of the period, and might he have been insensitive to the increasingly vulnerable position of Jews in France and across Europe? In order to approximate responses to these queries, the ensuing section of this chapter will offer an extended analysis of Duvivier's three 'Jewish films.'

David Golder (1930)

The advent of the cinema's sound age furnished film-makers with a host of inventive possibilities. One of the first films of this new era was Julien Duvivier's *David Golder*. The scenario, written by Duvivier himself, was loosely based on Irène Nemirovsky's 1929 best-selling novel. The Nemirovsky narrative focuses upon a circle of highly assimilated Jews, sketching portraits of their familial and socio-economic milieux. The text explored what Jean-Paul Sartre would in his essay, *Réflexions sur la question juive*, label the conflict between Jewish authenticity and inauthenticity (1947: 108–12.). Nemirovsky's novel scrutinizes David Golder's bitter existential recognition that by ignoring his actual Jewish origins, by opting to acculturate himself and his family into a seductive French culture, he has transformed himself into a solitary, meaningless, superfluous being. That powerful psychological crisis ultimately draws Golder back to a sense of his Jewishness; yet before effecting a complete return, he dies alone and abandoned.

Like Nemirovsky's text, Duvivier's scenario and indeed the film itself are layered with a naturalist patina that expedites the establishment of an atmosphere of isolation, decadence and moral repugnance. No character elicits any audience sympathy, save perhaps the dying Golder during the film's final scenes, though even those moments of pathos are tainted by the expiring financier's obsession with money. As in many subsequent films, Duvivier imbues *David Golder* with a profound sense of pessimism, something one would certainly expect of a naturalist film. In the course of achieving that precise environment, however, Duvivier's cinematic language intimates that the general moral decadence and vulgarity being portrayed are the effects of Jewish interlopers. Though the Jewish characters may appear similar to their French counterparts, Duvivier does present them in a radically different manner. The camera effortlessly reinvents and even insists upon promoting anti-Semitic clichés already active in French culture. Given that *David Golder* represents the first French film to depict Jews as principal characters, perhaps Duvivier's cinematic shorthand sought to facilitate the public's identification of particular characters as Jews. Moreover, Duvivier's presentation of the Jewish images tends towards monstration, an effective filming tool of the silent era, which presented a relatively two-dimensional depiction of a person or object rather than more fully exploring that subject. The ultimate impression imparted by stereotypes projected in this manner simplistically seduces the viewer, the *image-mouvement* suggesting its own veracity. Consider the following examples.

In the film, Duvivier recurrently resorts to what in 1930 was already considered an outmoded, unrealistic cinematic technique: superimposition. Dudley Andrew remarks that this convention implies 'that the supernatural was present in early films' (Andrew 1976: 147), though this cannot be the case in *David Golder*, since the story is firmly rooted in the realistic/naturalist vein. And yet Duvivier's recourse to this technique could indeed imply a belief that Jews enjoy some degree of unnatural power, which appeals to established anti-Semitic prejudices. The film's credits and opening narrative sequences are all filmed using superimposition; and Duvivier opted to resort to it again in order to introduce the film's penultimate series of scenes. Given the revolutionary nature of the sound feature-film in 1930, the repeated application of this technical procedure perhaps signifies nothing more than Duvivier's limited technical possibilities. Yet, a closer reading of these particular scenes, taking into account their *découpage* together with their suggested meaning in the film's overall montage, suggests that they may still merit further attention.

As the credits roll, the screen explodes with a variety of images depicting long-distance, possibly trans-global, transportation: boats dock at berths in unspecified, international ports; rapid trains criss-cross an anonymous countryside; planes buzz overhead. This flood of visual images establishes a keen sense of global connections converging upon a common genesis that is ultimately clarified in the film's opening scene: the façade and trading floor of the Paris Stock Exchange. Over these images, Duvivier superimposes the faces of individual traders in various stages of agitation, while their voices provide a voice-over soundtrack to the chaotic background shouting of nervous investors: 'David Golder is selling shares at 81!'; 'Beware of Golder . . . he'll finish us all!'; 'Golder, my friend, is quite a man!' And, as this information is related, Duvivier's *découpage* has spliced additional scenes of trains, planes and boats that renew the impression of some type of extended web emanating from the

Bourse. Thus, prior to viewing Golder himself, Duvivier has skilfully initiated a succession of striking images that establish suggestive linkages between: (1) travel/an implied global network and the Paris Bourse; and (2) the stock exchange's apparent domination by a single individual whose financial dealings drive other investors and, hence, the national economy.

By the conclusion of these inaugural sequences, the word Jew has yet to be articulated; Duvivier's visual imagery has not provided a single formulaic representation of a Jewish character. The opening sequences nevertheless transmit an indirect anti-Semitic message, namely that a certain Golder – a surname of Jewish, not French, origins and metonymically suggesting wealth/gold/money – possesses the authority to dominate the Stock Exchange. Moreover, the *Bourse* represents the central hub of that multitude of 'lines' emanating into the broader world. The subtle point Duvivier suggests here would not have been lost on the French viewing public. They would undoubtedly have been familiar with various anti-Semitic discourses widely circulated and accepted in French society concerning cosmopolitan, Jewish financiers, their imagined power and presumed plans for world domination. Those audiences might similarly have recalled the Panama Affair (1888–92) when an Alsatian Jewish banking family, the Reinachs, had been accused of duplicity in the financial/political scandals, or analogous accusations of Jewish control of French financial markets that had resounded during the Dreyfus affair (1894–1906).

Given what I consider to be the underlying significance of Duvivier's use of superimposition and the subsequent juxtaposed scenes, one would presume that the technique's repetition conveys an analogous meaning. As in the film's earliest scenes, the primary focus here features the *Bourse* with superimposed images of anxious investors' faces. The clipped, frantic dialogue discloses that David Golder's financial machinations have cornered various markets. Duvivier's use of superimposition would therefore appear to propound an identical message to that suggested at the film's beginning, namely that Jews commanded France's financial markets and had woven an international web to promote their designs. At this point in the film, however, the ensuing sequences do not further accentuate signs and symbols of Jewish capitalism but proceed to reveal Golder employing his fortune to secure petroleum drilling rights in the Soviet Union. The innocuousness of this visual image is not particularly surprising. But, by relating Golder, the capitalist Jew, to substantial financial dealings with the Soviet communists, Duvivier has evoked another anti-Semitic view: that Jews represented the fountainhead of both capitalism and socialism/communism.

Figure 6. *David Golder* (1930), Julien Duvivier. Courtesy Museum of Modern Art, New York.

I believe it imperative at this stage to underscore a troubling fact. *David Golder* is the first major feature-length sound film concentrating upon Jewish characters. As director, Duvivier would have been establishing important precedents concerning the representation of Jews, laying down elements of a formal cinematic 'language' that subsequently would be employed by other directors to depict Jewish characters. Thus, by relying upon particular anti-Semitic myths clearly articulated in all major anti-Jewish publications of the late nineteenth century and by honouring propositions ardently espoused in the twentieth century by Action française and other groups, Duvivier's cinematographic, stereotyping shorthand tends to legitimize the anti-Semites' claims. Moreover, Duvivier's work in *David Golder* would have unwittingly aided in the fostering of public acceptance of certain racist views concerning the Jews.

The film's initial sequences articulate a definite ideological and ontological position that is further elaborated in the ensuing scenes. Focusing upon a luxurious interior, the camera tracks Golder's arrival.[1] An imposing, sartorially elegant figure, Golder regally strides into his home returning from his trip to London, a detail not alluded to in

Nemirovsky's novel. For most contemporary viewers, this relatively banal point woven together with Golder's demeanour does not signify. Such details appear inconsequential or even superfluous. And yet, by exploiting these elements, Duvivier further links Golder to prevalent anti-Semitic images of the well-dressed Jewish capitalist and fantasy-theories of the international/cosmopolitan/Jewish financial web focusing upon universal Jewish conspiracies for world domination. As the camera moves in for a close shot of Golder, what it reveals is a rather ordinary man, not particularly Jewish. And yet, upon closer examination, this portrait does reveal irrefutable aspects of the traditional 'Jewish type': the high forehead, the thick-arched eyebrows, slightly frizzy hair. Such physical manifestations, though only insinuated at the film's beginning, will gradually become emphasized by the conclusion when, parallelling Charles Swann's ultimate metamorphosis into 'an old Hebrew' in Marcel Proust's *A la recherche du temps perdu* (1956: 690), Golder will die resembling the stereotypical Jew. Duvivier further manipulates this scene's imagery by juxtaposing the acceptably acculturated *Israélite*, Golder, with one of his agents, Monsieur Soifer, who does possess all the physical hallmarks of an anti-Semitic caricature, together with stooped posture, fawning nature and bizarre gesticulating, traits that subsequent films would indeed utilize to identify Jews. Duvivier establishes a striking spectrum when Soifer dines with Golder. Waited on by the butler, who casts condescending glances at the two men connected by an elegantly set table, the viewer effortlessly associates Soifer with Golder. The two characters fuse: the traditional depiction of the identifiable Jew, Soifer, and his *doppelgänger* 'Other,' Golder, the assimilated Jew who, Drumont believed, represented the more prodigious peril to the French nation.

Duvivier concludes these opening scenes by offering the audience evidence of Golder's moral character. Returning home from his secretive international travels, Golder discovers his business associate, Marcus, awaiting him. Marcus proceeds to announce his own imminent financial ruin from having engaged in a series of faulty investments. He begs Golder to advance him a relatively nominal sum that would safeguard him. While Marcus delivers his pathetic yet impassioned speech, Golder has occupied himself reading an assortment of telegrams delivered during his absence. When eventually pressed by Marcus, Golder bitterly chides him for his lack of prudence, and then blandly declines to tender any monetary assistance, thereby assuring Marcus's ruin.

The paradigmatic Jewish portraits Duvivier offers in these inaugural scenes confirm certain preconceived notions of Jews in general. The audience, guided by Duvivier's script and his cinematographic techniques, have identified the principal characters as Jews either through specific physical characteristics, language/gesture, or their professions. As if relying on Drumont and other anti-Semitic writers, Duvivier has unquestionably, though subtly, established a frank relationship between Jews and global, financial empires that appear to govern the *Bourse* and the French economy. Finally, in the last sequence analysed, Golder is demonstrated as heartless and lacking all moral acumen. In a manner of speaking, the balance of the film emerges as nothing more than increasingly intricate 'variations' on this initially articulated theme. Several of these variants merit analytic attention.

Drumont and other anti-Semitic writers had frequently portrayed the Jewish family in highly contemptuous terms, a pattern Duvivier embraced to characterize the Golder clan. Nemirovsky's original narrative similarly delineates a rather repugnant nuclear family group in which Gloria Golder emerges as obsessive in financial matters as her husband, and their daughter, Joyce, is portrayed as conniving, materialistic, coarse and uncaring as her mother, and as morally bankrupt as her father. Duvivier effortlessly translates Nemirovsky's depictions to the screen, though the two female characters loom as more vicious and venomous in their cinematographic incarnations. Their pernicious cupidity and moral perfidy repel the viewer. Gloria strives to impersonate *la grande dame*, though she cannot escape her Jewish origins, reinforced visually by an olive complexion, wiry hair and a prominent nose. Duvivier portrays Joyce, however, in a radically different light – fair skin, blonde hair, 'Aryan' nose – traits that hint at her high degree of assimilation. Golder's own demonstrated flawed moral degeneracy echoes in the female characters: self-possessed; obsessed by an aberrant craving for material wealth; absolutely indifferent to the torment of others; prepared to sacrifice friends and loved ones in order to satisfy their own desires. These reprehensible traits are commandingly rendered in perhaps the film's most explosive scene.

Having travelled to Biarritz in order to relax, Golder suffers a heart attack. The interest in this succession of scenes and their association with Duvivier's utilization of anti-Semitic myths and stereotypes lies in the two visits Golder receives from his wife and daughter while recuperating. Joyce demonstrates no genuine filial interest in her father's health, but rather believes that by playing the 'little girl' and coquettishly asking for money, she will receive whatever she desires. Duvivier underscores the fact that these characters are Jews, whose behaviour and demeanour, if not their physical appearances, adhere to conventional 'Jewish traits' proposed and disseminated by diverse anti-Semitic sources. And, if the audience required conclusive proof of the profoundly different natures of the Jews and the French, Duvivier provided it in the encounter between husband and wife.

While Golder sleeps, Gloria sneaks into the sick-room. Duvivier first uses a subjective shot to suggest an omniscient viewer, then unexpectedly shifts to a point-of-view shot from Gloria's perspective. The viewer follows as Gloria's 'eye' lingers briefly on the figure of her husband before abruptly turning aside to focus on his discarded dinner jacket. Her hand extends into view, reaches into the inner pocket and extracts the cash from Golder's wallet. As Golder moans, the camera resumes its former role as omniscient eye, thus engaging all aspects of the ensuing scene.

In a manner reminiscent of Joyce's coyish request for money, Gloria wonders how she is to survive if anything should happen to Golder. Her feigned concerns do not convince her husband, but rather precipitate a vicious encounter between the two. Barely able to speak, Golder rises in order to drag Gloria to his level. Clutching her pearl necklace, he launches upon a verbal assault during which the word 'Jew' is uttered for the first time. The acid recriminations and abhorrent behaviour mount in intensity, conveying the antithesis of familial devotion or love. Had Duvivier not initiated a host of signs and symbols harkening to pre-established anti-Jewish antecedents, this scene would merely stand as a commanding example of naturalist cinema. But the underlying representational system Duvivier has established provides the audience with sufficient confirmation of its own pre-judgements concerning Jews, their heartless nature, and their utter 'otherness'.

Golgotha (1935)

In *David Golder*, Duvivier strove to construct an innovative cinematic shorthand for representing Jews on the screen. In that film, he focused upon a contemporary topic evoking a variety of myths concerning Jews and their real and imagined roles in the worlds of finance and politics, as well as views about Jewish conduct in public and private. When he assumed the directorial responsibilities for this second 'Jewish film', Duvivier faced the intimidating responsibility of filming a subject heavily laden with scenes of Jewish treachery that constituted a primary image in the Christian consciousness. The public similarly possessed fixed notions of Jewish physical types, of how images of twisted, near-inhuman physiognomies reflected the damned essence of the Jew.

As with Léon Poirier's *L'Appel du silence* (1936), Catholic co-operatives and the Catholic Church itself sponsored the filming of

Figure 7. *Golgotha* (1935), Julien Duvivier. Courtesy Museum of Modern Art, New York.

Golgotha. [2] The archbishopric of Paris directly supervised the filming and would seem to have insisted upon Duvivier's adhering to the anti-Jewish statements that a film version of the Gospels would present. The Canon Raymond penned the script, basing the action and the bulk of the dialogue on scriptural texts (*Matthew 26; 27:1–3; Mark 15:1–5; Luke 22:54–71, 23:1–6; John 18–19*). Duvivier's directorial efforts animated the characters and the action of the biblical narratives; but most especially he brought the image of the Jew to life and through his art rendered the Jews plausible menaces.

The egregious 'Jewish types' Duvivier represented emerge directly from the pages of medieval manuscripts, or descend from the façades of churches and cathedrals. Sorlin writes that 'the Jews are very convincing as their physical appearances, voices and faces fill the antagonistic role chosen for them, and this is what the French Catholic audiences expected to see as a reinforcement to centuries of sermonizing on the horrible crimes of the Jews as the murderers of the Son of God' (Sorlin 1981: 147). Duvivier provided the viewing public with what it knew it should perceive: threatening Jewish faces dominated by large, bulbous or hooked noses, sinister eyes staring out from beneath enormous eyebrows and unnaturally high foreheads. To enhance such negative features, Duvivier opted to shoot and illuminate most Jewish characters from below. The resulting portraits depict impressions of human deformity, diabolic imperfection and chilling evil.

In the Western imagination, the ultimate image of Jewish malevolence is the figure of Judas Iscariot, who, as Hyam Maccoby stresses, 'has been the archetypal traitor in legend, art and literature. Wherever the charge of betrayal has been raised [. . .] the name of "Judas" has surfaced. He is the symbol of motiveless evil that is always ready to destroy the good' (Maccoby 1992: 4). This critical proposition is extended when Maccoby adds: 'Judas is not an allegory, but a symbol, which must be allowed to work its magic in darkness' (Maccoby 1992: 5). Significantly, Duvivier filmed Judas in shadows in order to heighten Judas's physical and moral alterity. And Judas alone of all the disciples possesses the traditional hallmarks of the Jew, which, when compared with medieval representations of the Jew or with nineteenth-century anti-Semitic images, offer interesting insights into the living archetype Duvivier chose to project on the screen. These formulaic images of Jews portray virtually identical human types, physically deformed and with a general demeanour suggesting diabolical purpose. The permanence of this archetypal image also echoes the message conveyed by the medieval myth of the 'Wandering Jew', whose very presence signified evil and a Divine curse. Moreover, extending beyond this particular seme, Duvivier adroitly establishes convincing visible links between Judas and other Jewish conspirators (priests, Pharisees, Herod *et al.*), producing a potent suggestion, namely that Judas and the Jews are indistinguishable, all manifesting the same malefic nature. By ultimately placing these stereotypes in glaring opposition to an Aryan Jesus played by Robert Le Vigan, Duvivier provides another means for his audience to gauge Judas's/the Jews' 'otherness'. [3]

Golgotha may have provided Duvivier few creative options, given the film's Catholic sponsorship. Assessing the film, however, the particular images Duvivier has created profoundly discomfort the contemporary viewer. I recognize that this film was made long before Vatican II and that Duvivier's chosen style and imagery reflect particular cultural realities of that era. And yet, how could Duvivier not have recognized the penetrating and contrary impact his 'Jewish images' would have on French audiences, especially in the light of the cultural and political chaos following the Stavisky Affair and the resulting anti-Semitic rhetoric? *Golgotha*, with its vulgar anti-Semitic stereotypes, its promulgation of anti-Jewish calumnies and its resurrection of myths concerning past Jewish iniquities, unquestionably facilitated the public's willingness to suspect the Jews of real and present crimes against the French nation.

Le Golem (1935–6)

If *Golgotha* offered a conventional illustration of imagined Jewish crimes against God and humanity and through that representation suggested to audiences the prospect of Jewish plots against the French people, then *Le Golem* broadened those impressions by projecting visions of nefarious Jewish kabbalistic powers. The Golem, a clay figure reputedly fashioned by the eminent Jewish mystic, Rabbi Judah Loew of Prague, who endowed the creature with life in order to protect the Jewish community, resurfaced in late-nineteenth-century anti-Semitic literature, especially in those texts dealing with imagined plots of Jewish world domination. The Golem similarly figured in the occult preoccupations of the Nazis, especially Hitler, who exhibited a grotesque obsession with it.

The legend of the Golem had already earlier been treated in the cinema when, in 1920, the German director Paul Wegener had produced an expressionist film. Wegener's radical use of sharp, sheer camera angles would be replicated by Duvivier in only one sequence: a presumed impression of a Jewish seance endeavouring to resurrect the spirit of the defunct mystic Rabbi Loew. Otherwise, the two films share nothing in common.

Of all of Duvivier's 'Jewish films', *Le Golem* ironically provides viewers with the most authentic portrayals of Jewish life. Costume designers meticulously recreated late-medieval Jewish dress, even down to such minute details as the coloured, circular identification badge (*tabula* or *rota*) Jews were required to wear before emancipation. Amidst this realistic background, Duvivier nevertheless resorts to stereotyping shorthand in order to advance the narrative. In *Le Golem*, Duvivier calls upon a host of formulaic representations to depict and to differentiate the proverbial 'good guys' and 'bad guys'. With reference to the Jewish images, authentic Jews physically appear quite Jewish, though relatively benign. The overblown conventional portrait of 'Jewish evil' is reserved for Lang, an apostate Jew who through complete acculturation has insinuated himself into positions of power. As the Emperor Rudolph's prime minister, he symbolizes an extreme menace to the state, since he encourages the Emperor in his occult preoccupations. Lang exploits and abuses his power in pursuit of satisfying his own ambitious desire. Though Duvivier has achieved a degree of balance in his depiction of Jewish characters, the impression imparted by his characterization of Lang again evokes the more hostile opinions espoused by many and expressed in anti-Semitic literature.

Aside from the images described above, Duvivier has painstakingly endeavoured to imbue this film with nightmarish qualities that reflect both the misery of the Jewish ghetto and the threat of persecution, and that similarly invoke the theme of the occult permeating the film. The dramatic tale becomes an obsessive pursuit of the clay colossus. Jews and non-Jews search for the Golem in the hope that, by giving it life, each group will achieve its own ends: protection for the Jewish community, and political and military invincibility for the Emperor and his forces. In order to achieve the Emperor's goals, Lang arrests and tortures Rabbi Jacob, disciple of the late Rabbi Loew and the only person thought to possess the knowledge that would animate the Golem. Throughout the scenes of the frantic and occasionally comic quest for the Golem, Duvivier's direction encourages sympathy for the endangered Jewish community and its spiritual leader while simultaneously depicting the apostate Lang in the most reprehensible light.

Audience empathy abruptly comes into question, however, during the masterfully photographed scene depicting the cabal. Duvivier effectively constructs this sequence by employing expressionist cinematic techniques, such as vertical camera shots or sixty- to seventy-five-degree camera angles. Further intensifying the occult nature of the scene, Duvivier illuminates the characters with severe, sharp shafts of light from beneath and above that sculpt grotesque, unearthly shadows on the walls. Duvivier casts Rabbi Jacob and the respected elders of the Jewish community into a bizarre ceremony that derives no validity from Jewish ritual, but could effortlessly have originated from the pages of Drumont's *La France Juive* or the anonymously authored *Protocols of the Elder of Zion*, itself set in Prague. The scene could similarly presage views later expressed in Céline's *Bagatelles pour un massacre*. As a result of Duvivier's camera work and montage, the Jewish spiritual leaders unexpectedly appear more Jewish, the images' new reality having been assured by the film-maker's manipulation and by the final editing of those images. As in *Golgotha*, the Jews emerge as menacing figures, swords in hand, diabolical figures swaying rhythmically as they chant in fiendish cadence. This malevolent surreal ballet produces an impression of Jews as maniacal demons capable of calling upon the forces of Evil in order to obtain the appropriate kabbalistic formulae necessary to achieve victory over their enemies. Even when the Golem comes to life and Samson-like pulls down the Emperor's palace, killing all and sundry, two critical images persist in the wake of the destruction on screen: the Emperor, though obsessed with the occult, is subverted by his malignant minister, Lang, a Jew; and the Golem's existence is assured only through the diabolical intercession of the elders of the Jewish community, who engage in seemingly unholy kabbalistic rites that summon the forces of dread to resurrect the soul of the Golem's creator so that he might impart the magical life-rendering formula to Rabbi Jacob.

Some critics view *Le Golem* as nothing more than a lavish period-costume drama that enhanced its own unsubstantial *jeu de l'amour et du hasard* scenario through the integration of a supernatural component. Unlike Duvivier's other historical drama, *Golgotha*, this final 'Jewish film' does insist upon a degree of historical authenticity. Costumes accurately reflect fashions worn by Jewish men and women living in late-sixteenth-century Prague. Cinematic settings representing the Jewish ghetto or the *Altneuschul*, the great thirteenth-century synagogue forming the focal point for the story of the Golem, are meticulously accurate. And yet, despite such precision, closer critical scrutiny reveals that Duvivier persists in resorting to accepted stereotypical representations in order to depict the Jewish characters. His Jews are nefarious creatures who impart a sense of betrayal and contagion. Therein lies a gruesome irony, for not only would the film have entertained the general public, but its potent formulaic depictions of Jews would have unquestionably bolstered anti-Semitic prejudices espoused by a particular segment of the public.

Conclusions

These readings of Duvivier's three 'Jewish films' propose a number of troubling problems that I do not believe disappear when one turns to other films in his corpus. For example, after the war, Duvivier's 1947 feature-film *Panique* would again present images reminiscent of those he had articulated in the 'Jewish films' (see, for example, Wild 1996). Even in his inter-war masterpiece, *Pépé le Moko*, Duvivier demonstrates a variety of techniques and implementations of cinematographic language that suggest that particular characters in the film are not truly French, but, like Duvivier's Jewish incarnations, 'outside the "group", total strangers, some sort of half-breed' (Sorlin 1980: 205), roles that also happened to be interpreted by Jewish actors. But can such realizations offer command-ing evidence that Duvivier himself was anti-Jewish? I have yet to uncover any definitive evidence in his papers to confirm such a hypothesis.

Although Duvivier seems not to have expressed any personal antipathy for Jews, in the course of the 1930s he would aid in the development of a cinematic shorthand that would be employed by the industry in order to depict Jewish images. That language takes possession of the audience and effects a process of collaboration. Duvivier's images are not mere pedestrian incarnations, but powerful signifers drawn from a powerful collective cultural memory concerning the Jews. Those images then tumble from the screen back into the tenebrous mass from which they arose.

Duvivier constructed his Jewish images and the corresponding cinematographic discourse in accordance with accepted anti-Semitic antecedents. But his decision to do so merely reflected a cultural reality: the arts represented Jews in specific ways, employing accepted techniques. Duvivier simply translated those sanctioned modes of representation to the screen. The precise social impact of those images as assessed by both critical and political responses in diverse journals, reviews and newspapers of that era, as well as the continuing stir *David Golder* and *Golgotha* would create during the Second World War, do suggest that these troubling conventions helped to prepare the French public for the imposition of Vichy's official anti-Semitic policies of exclusion that would lead to the tragedy that ultimately befell French Jewry during the Shoah.

Notes

1. The role of David Golder was interpreted by the superb character actor Harry Baur. Though arrested and tortured to death by the Germans in 1943 for being a Jew and a member of the resistance, during the inter-war era Baur *never* acknowledged his Jewishness. In remarks made in the December 1936 number of *Pour Vous*, a Paris-based movie magazine, Baur spoke of his Alsatian origins and took pains to stress his Catholicism. This admission did not deter such anti-Semitic writers as Lucien Rebatet, who, in articles in *Je Suis Partout* (November 1941) and later in his book *Les Tribus du cinéma et du théâtre*, denounces Baur as a Jew.

2. Working under the patronage of the Roman Catholic Church, Poirier produced an anti-Jewish masterwork. The film's primary locus treats the life and spiritual itinerary of Charles de Foucauld, a French aristocrat who became a Trappist hermit in the Sahara desert, where he was eventually murdered by fanatical Muslims. Ostensibly relating a pious, inspiring tale of Christian martyrdom, Poirier's script included

representations of Jews whom the director chose to depict as dark, menacing figures seeking to thwart Foucauld from his spiritual itinerary. Not only do the Jewish characters exhibit traditional anti-Semitic physical hallmarks, but their invidious behaviour conforms to accepted Christian teachings concerning Jews in general.

3. Robert Le Vigan was a noted anti-Semite who repeatedly spoke out against Jewish influences in France and the negative sway they exerted. He opted to remain in France during the Occupation, openly collaborating and openly continuing his crusade against the Jews. After the war, he was forced to flee to South America, spending the remainder of his life there in exile.

References

Andrew, Dudley (1976), *The Major Film Theories: An Introduction*, Oxford, Oxford University Press.

Bresson, Robert (1975), *Notes sur le cinématographe*, Paris, Gallimard.

Deleuze, Gilles (1983), *Cinéma 1: L'Image-Mouvement*, Paris, Les Editions de Minuit.

Maccoby, Hyam (1992), *Judas Iscariot and the Myth of Jewish Evil*, London, Peter Halban.

Proust, Marcel (1956), *A la Recherche du temps perdu*, Paris, Gallimard.

Sartre, Jean-Paul (1947), *Réflexions sur la question juive*, Paris, Gallimard.

Sorlin, Pierre (1980), 'Présence des Juifs dans le cinéma français à la veille de la Seconde Guerre Mondiale', in Myriam Yardeni (ed.), *Le Juif dans l'histoire de France*, Leiden, E. J. Brill.

—— (1981), 'Jewish Images in the French Cinema of the 1930s', *Historical Journal of Film, Radio and Television,* 1(2): 139–50.

Turk, Edward Baron (1989), *Child of Paradise: Marcel Carné and the Golden Age of French Cinema*, Cambridge, MA, Harvard University Press.

Wild, Florianne (1996), 'L'Histoire ressuscitée: Jewishness and Scapegoating in Julien Duvivier's *Panique*', in Steven Ungar and Tom Conley (eds), *Identity Papers: Contested Nationhood in Twentieth-Century France*, 178–92, Minneapolis, University of Minnesota Press.

6

National Cinemas and the Body Politic
Susan Hayward

Cinema is not a pure product. It is inherently a cross-fertilization (a hybrid) of many cultures, be they economic, discursive, ethnic, sexed, and more besides. It exists as a cultural miscege*nation* – and is, therefore, a deeply uncertain product as to its heritage. In its hybridity it cannot help but challenge modernist (binary) thought, however implicitly. Cinema is a product whose makers are widely scattered. It is not a single, unified voice, nor is it the product of a single patriarchal discourse. Thus, whilst some cinema may reproduce the myth of a unified nation (obviously propaganda films, films produced at times of national emergency), the greater bulk of its production will not be able to do so, however hard it may strive to conceal this fact. To 'frame' national cinema, to read it against the grain, is to delimit the structures of power and knowledge that work behind the scenes to assemble its scattered and dissembling identities, its fractured subjectivities and fragmented hegemonies, which in their plurality stage the myth of a singular and unified national identity.

What follows is an attempt to address the multiplicity of questions that embody, both literally and figuratively, the idea of 'national cinema'. This questioning of concepts of national cinema is composed of two parts. The first will look at national cinema through the historical optic of capitalism, which will provide a backdrop to the second part, which will look at the politics of the (necessarily gendered) subject and its relation to cinematic expressions of nationhood – what I shall term, by way of shorthand, the corporealism of national cinemas.

Capital Goes to the Movies

Cinema is an industrial invention. It is a product of the nineteenth century, invented to make capital. The huge 'rivalry' between France and the United States as to who first invented the *cinématographe* and who could hold down patents to it started as early as 1896 (a year after cinema's invention). This celluloid war is not without its interest in the context of the analysis being put forward in this chapter. After initial successes in major US cities, representatives of the Lumière brothers were met with attempts to thwart their plans to demonstrate their new invention. Screenings were inexplicably cancelled, the equipment was boycotted by the Americans and was even confiscated by customs under the pretext that it contravened customs regulations. This struggle for dominance so soon after the cinematograph's creation attests to the fact that economic and nationalist considerations were foremost, and were closely aligned with cultural concerns. Although the first cinematograph was conceived by the Lumière brothers as having primarily scientific applications, as public screenings increased, film proved to be a big attraction to the general public. From that point on, in order to attract a variety of audiences, cinema expanded by means of product differentiation.

Within capitalism – whose guiding motor is the principle that 'more is more' – not only products, but processes are commodified. This means that industries are vertically integrated (controlling investment, exchange, production, distribution) so that they can maximize market outlets and consumption. In the Western world, only a few nations' film industries have practised vertical integration, including, most famously, the United States and what has come to stand as *the* American film industry, Hollywood. Curiously, however, Hollywood's system of vertical integration did not survive, lasting approximately thirty to forty years (falling away in the 1950s after the effects of the anti-trust laws passed, in 1948, against the studios' monopolistic practises). Since then, the Hollywood model has shifted, first in the 1970s and 1980s, to bolster its ailing industry as a result of heavy competition from television channels and, secondly, in the late 1980s through the 1990s to adapt to global economics – but always with an aim to dominate as many markets as possible. As a result of the strategy developed in the 1970s, most of the studios are now owned by conglomerates (with massive investment from Japanese companies) and they target consumption groups through what is known as the total concept approach, presenting the film as part of a total package including books, T-shirts, Happy Meals, etc. In the face of globalization, Hollywood has adopted a fourfold strategy: first, horizontal integration, whereby studios partner with other producers and distributors (Balio 1996: 27); second, down-sizing to 'concentrate on a core of group activities' (Balio 1996: 28); third, partnering with independents, television companies, and other industrial complexes both within the USA and outside; and finally, exploiting overseas markets and economies by going for overseas co-productions and overseas pre-sales (to exhibitors and, in a more widespread fashion, to television channels). In this way, the financial risks are diminished because they are spread further. But more significantly, in the final analysis, more still remains more: more is sold and the spoils get shared out amongst the investors.

Immanuel Wallerstein informs us (1983: 29) that vertical integration and historical capitalism date back to the sixteenth century. Thus Hollywood's model should not surprise us. What should surprise us is why other national cinemas never truly managed to adopt it. If we look at the historical contexts closely and take Europe as our example we can find clues to this mystery. When, by 1920, Hollywood was fully established as a vertically integrated industry, it became extremely aggressive in its export strategy. Europe attempted to fight back – but rather ineffectually. It sought to seal alliances between countries and to create a pan-European cinema that could stand up against the USA and its drive to conquer foreign markets. However, the various efforts to establish a coherent international trade organization failed because of a lack of true co-operation. European Film Congresses may well have met and hoped that, by bringing European film-practitioners and producers together, some policies would be implemented. But this was never to be, for the simple reason of the uneven development, in capitalist terms, of the various nations' film industries. In the 1920s, Germany was the most important of the European industries and had a vertically integrated system. It might have been willing to team up with other European countries in order to compete as a block against Hollywood, but not at the risk of sacrificing its own economic interests. For Germany, as with Hollywood, size matters, as well as confidence in the market. Thus, France's film industry, in the 1920s and 1930s, was far less structured and financially less secure than that of its neighbour Germany. Indeed, it endured a fairly erratic existence. The two major producers, Pathé and Gaumont, frequently got cold feet and changed tactics, shifting emphasis from production to distribution and exhibition, leaving the smaller production companies to perform the functions from which the larger companies had turned their attentions away. During the 1920s and 1930s, the fate of the smaller production companies was thus more or less dependent on the strategies favoured by the larger producers. Furthermore, Germany and the former Soviet Union have known periods of what could be termed a state monopoly, through nationalization. During the Third Reich, Germany's cinema was nationalized (1936–45) and put to the service of its political ideological machine; the Soviet film industry, too, was strongly controlled under nationalization (begun in 1922, completed in 1924 and lasting until 1990). During those periods no, or very little, co-operation between these nations and the rest of Europe was possible. What we can conclude from these two examples is that economic, political, and nationalistic considerations have meant that Europe, in terms of its film industries, has always been far from a fortress.

In capitalism, the producer seeks to accumulate. So it is not only markets that will be of concern, but also the cost of labour (and its availability). Major companies of all kinds have long gone outside their own countries to seek cheaper labour costs, moving on to yet other countries once the cost of labour becomes 'too high' (see the examples of Nike and Reebok). Within the film industry, too, the search is always on for lowering costs. Thus increasingly, films in part or in their entirety are being made outside the country that produces them. The labour force involved in a film product is often international. Financing is increasingly multinational. And yet the final product will most likely be identified as emanating from one country – primarily by association either with the director, the stars or, in the case of literary adaptations, the original text. The case of *The English Patient* (Anthony Minghella, 1996) is a good illustration in this context. Although it smacks of 'Britishness' (author, director, some of the stars), it is in fact an American-financed product. The profit made from this film will fill American coffers first, smaller amounts going to the other parties concerned. What this tells us is that America is willing to back a winner (no matter its provenance) and to exploit talent outside its own borders. And once it has made that commit-ment, it will back it all the way from pre-production to distribution and exhibition. Hollywood/USA, therefore, does still practise a form of vertical integration, only not within a single studio complex, as before, but *by means of* a kind of horizontal, or multinational, integration. If we compare this kind of cross-national success with European co-productions and their less-than-successful outcomes, we can see how poor investment at pre-production level first and subsequently at the distribution level dooms these so-called Euro-puddings to sink without a trace.

What this also helps us to understand is how national cinemas expose the contradictions of capitalism, starting with the fact that the product value of a film is often less than the expenditure of making it. Most national cinemas run at a loss, yet they survive. They forge alliances with their own indigenous television companies, they attempt co-productions, they look to national and international financing to back their products– but even with all this mixed economy, they still manage to run at a loss. Capitalism cannot function if it does not find a market. But these cinemas do survive, even if they lack a strong enough market to make a profit. How is this possible? There are three possible answers to this question, all interlinked. First, within capitalism, selling and buying is always based in unequal exchange. Thus supply and demand will work both for and against the product (for example, a film may flop at the box-office, but its pre-sale rights to television may help it recoup most of the loss). Second, and still within this notion of supply and demand, Hollywood's/ the USA's monopolistic drive is always going to be to some degree at odds with the push for product differentiation. Hollywood likes to capitalize on a known formulaic success, but there is a limit to how many *Aliens* or *Rambos* audiences will want to consume. It therefore has to search for something new, and it may not be different enough to attract audiences –or it may be too different. Looking for the new product costs money; it may be necessary to search for cheaper production venues. Getting the new product right takes time; during these gaps, indigenous cinemas have some breathing space and their own products are able to attract audiences for a time. Conversely, the decision may be to play safe and not go forward, which can lead to stagnation and the opening of the market once again for indigenous products to flourish. Third, even though Hollywood seeks to dominate through monopolistic practises (by decreasing demand for foreign films and by invoking strong legal and state mechanisms), total domination is not sought. Competition, however uneven, is necessary. Without it, there are no markets, and therefore no profit. In the first two answers proposed, we can see how cinema is about product and market instability, not only for the minority non-monopolistic cinemas, but for Hollywood's own. Cinema, all national cinemas, makes visible the very thing capitalism seeks to eradicate: economic instability within its own practise. In the third answer, other gaps open up and challenge capitalism differently. The dyad of dominant/non-dominant cinema cracks open; and, simultaneously, the idea of a singular national cinema with it.

We are talking here of the permeability of borders: national borders, clearly, but also intra-national borders. Thus, on an intra-national level, differently structured economies, such as those pulled together by an independent producer, can bleed through the borders of a nation's dominant cinema, practising an economism that defies the workings of capitalism. This cinema often gets referred to as 'artisanal' cinema (particularly within France) or art cinema, or independent cinema. Or, again, minority groups of radical film-makers can attack monopolistic practises in a 'big' way at certain moments in the indigenous industry's history (think of the *cinema nôvo* movement in Brazil, for example). These practises – of economics and aesthetics – leave indelible traces and are always already co-present with the dominant national cinema. Whatever their label, their presence forces a pluralism within national cinema. Thus, by the very nature of their co-presence, these alternative cinemas (such as, for example, women's cinema, or the Black cinemas emerging from France, the UK and the USA) become national cinemas – scattered hegemonies – in their own right. These cinemas, too, are performing the nation. But, significantly, they perform it differently. On an international level, we note also how 'minority' national cinemas can seep effectively into markets controlled by the dominant monopolistic one (as in the West, Hollywood), either because they play them at their own game and 'win' (for example the French film-maker Luc Besson), or they break through via the film festival circuit (Turkish and Iranian cinemas are recent examples – including films made by 'dissident' film-makers or films that have not passed censorship at home).

Thus the study of the question of national cinemas within the model of historical capitalism helps us to see what some of the problems of the definition are. It helps us problematize the concept of national cinema at the same time as it enables us to speak more clearly about it – at least in terms of paradoxes and possibly more. And this leads us to one further paradox that must be raised in the context of economism before going on to the second section of this chapter. This paradox is one that is raised by national cinemas in relation to the labour market and capitalism, particularly the way in which they both do and do not reflect the gender bias of historical capitalism. The division of labour and valorization of work that patriarchal capitalism has endorsed for at least two hundred years meets with some interesting contradictions here. If we think about how the film industry manufactures its products, then it is clear that, in terms of performance, gender bias in favour of male labour is less in evidence on screen than behind it. The producers of meaning behind the screen still reveal a heavy tendency to follow traditional gender bias (i.e., male). The point is that those who visibly perform the national cinemas' narratives (the stars and actors) seem to come at us in reasonable amounts of gender parity. The invisible producers of meaning, however, remain predominantly of the male sex. This gender parity on screen opens up another set of issues around race and age and physical ability – areas where representation is in deficit. Performance in national cinemas exposes this lack of representation in the labour force by visibilizing its own lack (i.e., its colour-age-and ability-blindness). For its part capitalism deliberately seeks to disguise or pay no heed to the truth about its labour force. (For example, capitalism seeks out the cheapest labour cost but glosses over this fact at the point of sale – would we continue to buy expensive running shoes if we knew they only cost the company a twentieth of the price they are charging us?)

No national cinema can be an autarky, although Hollywood comes the closest. Whilst it has no need of imports in terms of keeping its own market buoyant, in economic terms it has to call on other nations to help finance its industry (either through international conglomerates, co-productions or partnerships). It is content to bleed through into other nations' representations of their own history. Its economy finances another nation's narcissism (again, *The English Patient* is an excellent example of this). The reverse, however, does not occur. Thus in this respect economism shows us how disparate the concept of national cinema is. Some national cinemas, including France's, are 'forced' into a kind of nationalistic Malthusianism because of the monopolistic practises of others (in this context we can think of Indian cinema as well as Hollywood; and, to a lesser degree, Egyptian cinema can be seen in this light). A number of national cinemas – particularly France's – depend on the interpenetration of the state in terms of policy and economism to sustain a viable level of revenue and production. Or, because they are nationalized (as is the case of, say, China), interpenetration brings with it an obligation to represent the nation according to specific laws of censorship. Other cinemas (primarily Hollywood) aim at the capitalist practise of autarky mixed with free trade (but only if it favours their market). And in this regard they will go to any length to get the support of their government to win their perceived rights to practise free trade (see, for example, the role of the United States in the GATT dispute over the status of cinema).

So, even if we wanted to wish national cinema away as an idea, it simply – if only for economic reasons – will not disappear. But what the above analysis also makes clear is that national identity is an integral component of cinema, necessary to its survival. The relationship between national identity and cinema is more symbiotic than we might at first believe (America/Hollywood needs competitors). The monopoly effects do not in the end drown out resistances. Indeed, they may even provoke them. These resistances in turn generate other models of production that challenge and break boundaries. Crucially, this suggests that these borders are permeable. As the next section will suggest, this permeability is an essential key to our questioning, and our problematizing, of the notion of national cinemas.

Corporealism of National Cinemas

Elsewhere (Hayward 2000), I have discussed in some depth how the nation, through its nationalist discourses, cannot be conceived of without reference to the body, in particular the female body and even more specifically the maternal body (for example, the 'Mother-Nation' that we fight and die for, the 'Mother-Country' to which the colonized referred, the 'Mother-Land' that is violated/raped when invaded by the enemy, etc.). I am aware of course that certain nations refer to the 'Fatherland', and yet would argue that a similar desire for bonding, although this time with the father (the 'Symbolic Other'), is at play here. I now want to broaden these earlier considerations, using as part of my framework, first, the concept of Mother-Nation (although I will make one or two points about the Fatherland, a context for which there is more work to be done) and, second, Lacan's psychoanalytic concepts of the Imaginary and the Symbolic. As soon as we speak of the body, we are immediately also speaking of the subject; and once we are speaking about the subject then we are in the realm of identity, subjectivity and, ultimately, the sexed subject and, of course, desire – and this necessarily brings us into considerations of the interrelationship between the key psychoanalytic concepts of the Imaginary and the Symbolic. If, when we speak of the nation, we refer also to the body (as we have argued we do), then we are immediately within this same context of issues concerning subjectivity. Let us take this a stage further and think about nation and desire, and what it might mean. We know that the nation (in its discursive mode of nationalism) dreams of itself as a unified entity. Its desired image of itself is as a unified subject of history. If we were practising a Lacanian analysis here we might tentatively propose that the nation is in denial – lying as it does in a false sense of the pre-Symbolic, that is, in the first two stages of the Imaginary.

For the nation to possess a discursivity about itself (let alone anything else), it has to enter the realm of the Symbolic, in the Lacanian sense. Thus the nationalist discourses that it generates have also to be read as the subject-nation's attempt to enter into and maintain the social order of things. But to do so, the subject-nation must repress desire, in short the libidinal drives experienced during the Imaginary phase. It can be repressed but not lost. And this repression, as we know, founds the unconscious. Thus the subject-nation, which within the Imaginary is both the idealized image and the desiring subject, is now also, within the Symbolic, a split subject (between the conscious and the unconscious) – and this has consequences. The subject-nation is a divided subject because as it seeks to represent itself in the world (in the Symbolic order of things, in language) it does so at the expense of coming after the word. In other words, when the subject-nation (as the conscious subject) seeks to represent itself – gives itself a discursive form – by the time it has done so the subject-nation (as the unconscious subject) has already moved on and is becoming something else. Thus there is a gap that opens up between the two states (between the conscious and unconscious subject). This in turn means that any notion of the wholeness of the representation (image, text, etc.) is false. What is left, as the image, is that of a fading subject, because the original subject has moved on, leaving behind an utterance (an enunciation) that is no longer representing the true self. It is this gap that interests us here. It shows us perhaps what the subject-nation is trying to hide (to answer our earlier questions of motivation) – its split subjectivity. It tells us that it is deeply troubled by the lack of an idealized image or sense of unity. And it helps to explain why it would spend so much energy repressing difference (as in, for example, differently desiring bodies, such as the queer body). In repressing difference it denies the gap, it attempts to meld (or merge) the two subjects (conscious and unconscious) together, erasing its own dividedness and implicitly the fading subject. This opens up a huge arena for investigation for us in which image-constructions of the subject-nation can be taken to task (including, in this context, ideological representations of the nation-state).

Bearing this outline in mind, what now follows is a three-part examination of this question of nation and representation, which attempts, through a series of problematizations, to open up the complexities of writing about national cinema.

Nation and Representation (1)

Cinema is one of a nation's many means of representing itself to itself. Clearly the mirroring is not a one-to-one relationship (however much certain nations at certain periods in their histories would like it to be); the mirroring offers a set of images of the nation unto itself. Nationalism (as a discursive strategy of the nation – *a* Symbolic Order) may well be about belief in the nation as a unitary-totality in and of itself but, as we know, it is not the only ideology floating around within a nation-state. What I am proposing here is that the concepts of nation, nationhood and nationalism need to be considered in a dialogic fashion. As the above made clear, the nation is not a unified subject. It is a sum of scattered subjectivities, therefore of scattered identities, therefore of scattered bodies. Implicitly, concepts/principles of nationhood and nationalism are equally scattered. This helps us to look towards creating our dialogic model. For, as R. Radhakrishnan argues, if we try to establish a model to articulate the multiple determinations (of 'a nation') that is based in relationality we would get into serious representational problems. It would become impossible to establish 'boundaries and limits to a relational field' (1992: 81). Relational politics lead us into a chain (or domino) effect, one set of categories generating another, which in turn generates another, so that it becomes massive, dispersed and unmeaningful. Scattered hegemonies is a better term (the term is from Grewal and Kaplan 1994). Better, because it points to a number of useful possibilities. First, there is a limit to the scatteredness of these multiple voices/hegemonies/ideologies; second, there may or may not be links between them; third, there is no presence of the concept of 'other'; fourth, it does not exclude an overlapping with other scattered hegemonies; finally, it does not oblige us into all-embracing but ultimately unuseful terms such as heterogeneity, hybridity and so on. This term, scattered hegemonies, helps us to offer a way forward from Bhabha's (1990: 4) proscription for the discussion of a national culture whose 'locality' cannot be seen as unified or unitary in relation to itself, and whose cultural product cannot be seen simply as 'other' in relation to what is outside or beyond it.

To think in terms of the subject-nation as scattered hegemonies means that binary or bi-polar constructions of the nation evaporate (centre/ margin; included/excluded). It means also that the subject-nation can be differently desiring, not singly desiring. As the next two sections go on to argue, cinema, national cinema(s) are a forceful function in exposing, in just this way, the subject-nation's masquerade as an idealized image or unified subject.

Nation and Representation (2)

In considering nations and representation we cannot help but observe that ideology is used to construct the nation-state. If we accept this premise that ideology is a political-cultural manifestation of a nation-state, then we cannot fail to note that ideology serves to enforce a certain set of priorities – all of which have at their heart the suppression of constructions that challenge that of the nation-state. Thus, in China since the Revolution, in Pakistan since Partition, or more closely to hand, in France until the 1960s, and in the Soviet Union from 1920 to 1990, cinema has functioned as an integral part of nation-building. This has occurred at the level of the industry as well as that of production (through a centralizing of industrial practise and of textual discourses that valorize cultural hegemony). Nations that repress difference and contradictions cannot in the end suppress the pathological cultural artefacts this repression produces. Thus other constructions emerge and make visible the contradictions inherent in the prevailing conceptualization of the nation-state. Difference in the end seeps through and does so through images (be they televisual, filmic, digital, etc.) expressing the desire of other bodies.

What we do not understand – no matter what location we are looking or desiring from – we simplify. We reduce to stereotypes. We conflate other nations. For example, we still see Europe as two separate entities even though it is one continent. We speak of Asia, or the Orient, or Latin America or Africa. We do this so we do not have to see them. The ideology of mainstream cinema works in a similar fashion. Comedy and gangster films – which are the two top generic types of films produced by the French film industry – are redolent with stereotypes and expose difference as either amusing or threatening. The comfort of such genres is 'we are not like that'. What goes on, of course, is a form of comfort in denial (of difference). Do straight people ever ask themselves how gay people respond to the often foolish stereotypes (of camp) to which they are reduced? Do white people wonder at the dominant images of black people (often focused around their sexualness)?

Elsewhere, I have explained how the ideology of nation-states functions to create a homogeneous society (Hayward 2000). As such it excludes (or denies) concepts of gender. It also, since it represses gender and therefore the sexed body, necessarily represses desire. This results in a first set of repressions of difference. In certain nation-states it 'eliminates' class. In other nation-states – as history shows – it erases other embodiments of difference (Jews, communists, homosexuals, political dissidents). It gets rid of what it considers contradictions or flaws. AND YET – as we might suspect – the nation falls into its own trap. It does this because it is in contradiction with itself (as we explained above). That is, its ideology – in the form of nationalist discourses – has repressed its own knowledge of itself as a subject-nation. How can a nation remain gender-blind if we know and see all around us example after example of the interpenetration of sexuality and the nation-state? We need only think of the always ongoing social discourses around teenage pregnancies. In this example, we can see how we are right in the centre of a politics of gender in which the nation-state blames the female (as cunning, trying to obtain 'free' accommodation) and deresponsibilizes masculinity (poor family background, lack of sex education at school). The nation-state contradicts itself here as it is clearly practising a politics of gender (and of course sexuality – it is the female sexual reproductive system that must be controlled, not the male phallus) whilst disguising it as a politics of control. Politics is ineluctably about sex and gender – the term itself refers to the civil function of government, the etymology of the word confirms that the 'civil' refers to the citizens of the *polis* (originally the city, but also the body politic, that is, the complex aggregation of people in society). Politics then is about administering (controlling) the subjects of the nation; and all subjects are sexed and, in one way or another, gendered. But the politics of gender have got swept away and (as in the above example), thanks to the ideological discourses of control, have been reappropriated into a politics of repression. Because if nation (as an ideology) did recognize gender then it would be obliged to recognize the sexed subject. It would mean that the nation stopped mis-recognizing itself and recognized itself as a subject-nation – a diverse, multiple set of subjectivities (something it constantly represses). To recognize the sexed subject would be to 'let all hell break loose' – in the form of (recognition of) excreting bodies, disseminating bodies, fluids moving untamed from bodies, and so on.

Thus gender and more precisely the sexual subject (because of course it does exist despite the subject-nation's lies to itself) has to be controlled, repressed. The split subject we spoke of earlier offers the subject-nation an unacceptable, un-idealized image to itself. The gap in-between profoundly destabilizes the homogenized unified nation-body. And this brings me back to my comments on the erotics of nationhood. If, as I argued above, the subject-nation can be located in the pre-Symbolic (particularly at times of great stress), then it is occupying a double-desiring position (it is libidinally motivated toward itself and towards its mother). To a lesser and greater degree these are taboo positions; they are positions of mis-recognition; the target for libidinal expression is 'wrong'; finally, and crucially, in desiring the mother, the subject-nation invites the wrath of the castrating father. Thus the subject-nation is torn between desire for unity and denial of difference. Which is why when a nation invades another nation it does so in a way that forefronts the erotics of a nation. The terms are rape, pillage, plunder, genocide, ethnic cleansing. If we don't believe this analysis then my question would be: why do women get raped by invading soldiers? Why is mass rape an integral part of a militia campaign of genocide (or ethnic cleansing)? Why, to take only one example, that of Rwanda, did Tutsi women get raped by Hutu soldiers who deliberately infected them with the AIDS virus? The newspaper reports tell us that 'propaganda pouring out from government radio stations in the months leading up to the (planned) genocide taunted Hutus with the mythology of the Tutsi women: they were taller, more beautiful and arrogant. They had to be tasted and humiliated before they were killed' (*The Guardian*, 14.9.99, p. 6). Hutu soldiers assailed, violated and infected the 'enemy' in the embodied form of Tutsi womanhood to bring down the Tutsis (that is, the entire Tutsi minority ethnic group) from their haughty ways and ensure (should any women survive their ordeal) that any new generations of Tutsis would be infected.

Gender-blindness, linguistic homogeneity, repression of difference, mythologizing or banishing to the boundaries bodies that threaten – re- couping (through stereotype and trivialization) or denying the presence of bodies that hegemony wants not to matter – this is the generic cultural practise of mainstream Western cinema. What is the thriller or the western about if not the fear of (white) phallic inadequacy? What is the sci-fi film addressing if not the relationship between national space and ideas of race (the invasion of the healthy body politic by aliens)? In westerns and sci-fi movies, difference is written on the body (Indians in the former, aliens in the latter). These bodies threaten the national fibre of a country either by raping the white woman and pillaging the white man's land (westerns) or by spreading disease and terror into the civilized state (sci-fi movies). Sci-fis are about the fear of the corruption of the body politic by impure and imperfect bodies. Westerns are about the fear of miscege*nation*, of a nation's ethnic purity (read whiteness), of its blood- line (its own bodily fluids therefore) being sullied and infected by an- other's impure fluids.

Nation and Representation (3)

The question now becomes (since repression inexorably leads to patho- logical representation) when does cinema problematize the nation? And a *first* and primary answer (the only one this chapter has space to focus on) has to be in its performance of gender issues – in other words, when cinema challenges the short-sighted economy of nationalism. This has to be read as a first example of when cinema can get away with 'it' (which it does more often than we might at first suspect). What has to interest us here is that if national cinemas perform the nation then this performance is ineluctably linked to the concept of masquerade. The concept of masquerade in film studies is closely aligned to the representation of the female body. It is a useful concept that might help elucidate how cinema can problematize the nation. This concept has a double value in that it is differently inscribed according to practise and effect. By that I mean masquerade has been identified within feminist film theory as a strategy practised by the male viewer/voyeur in relation to the female body (it is also of course a practice of mainstream cinema in terms of its construction of femininity). But, secondly, feminist theory has pointed out that there is an effect of this construction when it comes to reading the image (by reading against the grain as it were) – for if the woman is masquerade, masked (as in: to conceal her true identity), then there must be another place behind the mask where the woman might be (Gledhill 1980: 17). The concept of femininity and masquerade is closely attached to the concept of fetishism. The purpose of fetishism is to contain woman, to make her safe. It is a strategy of disavowal of difference (sexual difference). The male seeks to find the hidden phallus in the woman. Thus he fragments off parts of the body (or clothing) and over-invests them with meaning, perceiving those parts as perfection themselves, making those parts figure as the missing phallus. The effect is a peculiar form of transvestism. Woman as a constructed image of femininity performs, masquerades in excess of and in denial of her own sexuality. But, and this is the crucial point, behind this mask, there is another woman at work. Added to which, there is also a gap in meaning between the mask and the woman. What is being argued here is that woman performs the very contradictions that the nation tries to conceal – that is, the nation as a sexed subject and non-hegemonic entity. She also problematizes the nation in that the image construction of her femininity seeks to contain her but can only do so at the price of 'agreeing' to her being double-gendered performatively speaking (as feminine and as phallic). Once that is 'agreed', gender is on the table for all to see – but so too is the mask and what lies behind (and the 'lies' behind the construction) as well as the space in-between. This fissuring makes it possible to occupy three locations when peering upon the cinematic artefact before us. The politics of location become scattered, which in turn suggests a scattering of hegemonies.

This example of femininity and masquerade is not an isolated one. Far from it. As soon as we consider examples of masculinity we can find similar practises in which a play with masquerade can also be unravelled. The male body is differently aestheticized to the woman's, but only to a degree, and often through lighting. The camera roves across the muscularity of the male in not dissimilar ways to its fetishizing effects upon the female body. The body bulges rather than voluptuates. It is hard rather than soft. But the camera is certain that the phallus is present – unlike with the female body, which it voyeuristically investigates and fetishistically attempts to contain as phallic. These hard bodies are as much in excess as their female counterparts, and so they too threaten. Thus, they must be 'softened' (by having a weak point in their character, or by the effect of love), or they must perish, or if they survive they have to have gained some inner wisdom to balance out (atone for) the outer shell of masculine muscularity (Korben Dallas in Besson's *Le Cinquième élément* (1997) is a recent example). The difference of course is that the male is not transvestisized, as is the female. The masculinity perdures through and through (both masquerade and behind the mask). Arguably, this is true even within films that represent male homosexuality, but where the representation is not inscribed within a queer discourse (e.g., Cyril Collard's *Les Nuits fauves* (1991)). The in-between (masquerade and mask) is not about disjunction or gaps in meaning in the way that it is with the female body as constructed by cinema. Nor is the excess about over-determination. Generically the male in this context is constructed as very secure (a unified subject of knowledge and history) and deeply embedded within the Symbolic order of things. He is the Symbolic order. Thus, in this instance, not a lot changes in our peering. The Phallic Law remains intact. But, the crucial point here is that by raising the question of masculine representation in this manner we can find new ways to suggest there is more to the image than pure surface would lead us to believe. If, at first, the kind of viewing/reception analysis of masculine representation does not appear to help us problematize the nation, because in this context the male does not threaten to drop the mask, we still recall that there are gaps in-between the mask/masquerade and the masculine body (in the same way that the split subject experiences gaps). Thus it does allow us to query (queery) the hermetics of the masculine body and the hermeneutics of dominant ideology. It is another first step to locating the nation (the subject-nation) within a politics of gender. It shows us how, on the surface, the politics of the nation-state occupy a single phallic location and will do anything to preserve that location against threats – and that is a start. We are aware of how the artefact is at work for the cultural construction of the nation.

But what happens when the performance *is* based in transvestism? When we have men playing/performing women's parts – let's think about this in both senses of the term 'parts': the role and the ascriptions of femininity. Man performs both being a woman and the woman's bodily being – including her bodily parts, namely, her breasts and genitalia. Or at least he does so at the point of simulacrum. His body as her body is (as simulacrum) a hyper-real body and therefore a hyper-real sex. More real than real. Small wonder transvestites disturb. Performatively speaking, the transvestite's body is doubly-gendered. It is, as Marjorie Garber says, 'a sign of overdetermination'. As an over-determined body, the transvestite's body comes close to the feminine body as described above. But, and here is the twist, and I am grateful to Marjorie Garber's excellent analysis of transvestism for this point, 'the transvestite marks the existence of the Symbolic' (1992: 125). How so? Because the transvestite is doubly-gendered, s/he 'embodies' the Imaginary (as she) and the Symbolic (as he). Thus the transvestite marks the Symbolic order of things, s/he embodies the co-presence of the Imaginary and the Symbolic, and too the dialectics of the true body politic (as s/he).

If we return to our considerations of nation and representation within Western cinema and come back to what we were saying in relation to the representation of femininity as masquerade then we can begin to understand why it suits patriarchy to confine woman to the Imaginary – to a speechless, silent space. If, as Judith Butler explains (1993), the only time that a woman's body 'matters' (counts as matter) is when she is the reproducer of life (as mother), then we can perceive why nations valorize the female body in distinct discourses that represent her as reproducer of the nation. It does not release her from her imprisonment within the Imaginary, however. Yet, paradoxically, cinematic discourses will also construct her as phallic woman, and thus as transvestite. As phallic woman she 'must' assume a position in which she becomes a s/he, a marker (as with the male transvestite) of the existence of the Symbolic. But as we explained above, more happens when s/he has transvestite qualities. We showed how she masquerades as one thing but is different underneath *and* in-between. And she always carries the threat of exposing all of this, by dropping the mask. Surely in her practises of gender and sexual border-crossing she transgresses national boundaries, challenges them just as much as (if not more than) the transvestite male or indeed the queered body? Do these three bodies perhaps occupy a third space – an in-between hyper-real space ironizing (to the extent of possibly shattering and scattering) the nation's simulacrum back to itself? Here I must leave the reader to ponder.

References

Balio, Tino (1996), 'Adjusting to the New Global Economy: Hollywood in the 1990s', in: A. Moran (ed.), *Film Policy: International, National and Regional Perspectives*, London and New York, Routledge.

Bhabha, Homi (1990), *Nation and Narration*, London and New York, Routledge.

Butler, Judith (1993), *Bodies that Matter*, London and New York, Routledge.

Garber, Marjorie (1992), 'The Occidental Tourist: *M. Butterfly* and the Scandal of Transvestism', in *Nationalisms and Sexualities*, London and New York, Routledge.

Gledhill, Christine (1980), '*Klute* 1: A Contemporary Film Noir and Feminist Criticism', in E. A. Kaplan (ed.), *Women in Film Noir*, London, British Film Institute Publishing.

Grewal, Inderpal and Kaplan, Caren (eds) (1994), *Scattered Hegemonies: Postmodernity and Transnational Feminist Practises*, Minneapolis and London, University of Minnesota Press.

Hayward, Susan (2000), 'Framing National Cinemas', in Mette Hjort and Scott MacKenzie (eds), *Cinema and Nation*, London, Routledge (forthcoming).

O'Regan, Tom (1996), *Australian National Cinema*, London and New York, Routledge.

Radhakrishnan, R. (1992), 'Nationalism, Gender, and the Narrative of Identity', in A. Parker, M. Russo, D. Sommer, and P. Yaeger (eds), *Nationalisms and Sexualities*, London and New York, Routledge.

Wallerstein, Immanuel (1983), *Historical Capitalism*, London, Verso.

Zhang, Yingjin (1994), 'From "Minority Film" to "Minority Discourse": The Questions of Nationhood and Ethnicity in Chinese Cinema', paper delivered at the East Asian Colloquium at Indiana University (September 1994).

7

Heritage, Nostalgia and the Woman's Film: The Case of Diane Kurys

Carrie Tarr

Diane Kurys is one of the best-known and most successful French women directors of the generation that began making films in the 1970s. She gained an international reputation with her first semi-autobiographical film *Diabolo menthe/Peppermint Soda* (1977) and has since made another six feature films, including the highly successful *Coup de foudre/At First Sight* (or *Entre Nous*, as it was known in the US) (1983). Despite, or perhaps because of, her popular and commercial success, however, Kurys does not enjoy a high reputation as an *auteur* within French critical circles, and her films have often been dismissed in terms that denigrate women's film-making or the pleasures of popular fictions aimed at female audiences.

Kurys herself has regularly refused to acknowledge that she makes films as a woman film-maker or that her films provide particular viewing pleasures for women spectators. Certainly her films are rooted in her own experiences – she has declared that she makes films about what she knows best. But in an interview with Ginette Vincendeau (1991), she pointed out that her ethnic background (her parents were Russian-born Jews) and her personal history (the break-up of her parents' marriage when she was five years old, the specificity of her bourgeois upbringing and education in Paris) were likely to have been as influential as her gender in informing her individual identity. The need to avoid being contained within a ghetto of women's film-making is understandable as a strategy for access to funding, distribution and recognition within a male-dominated French cinema industry, but this refusal of any gendered specificity makes the thrust of her films curiously ambivalent. Her films draw closely on girls' and women's experiences (specifically those of girls and women of Jewish origin), yet ask to be understood as films in which the matter of gender (and ethnicity) is incidental.

It is precisely this equivocation, however, that makes her films interesting for assessing the extent to which women's experiences can feed into and inflect the construction of national identity in mainstream cinema. The focus of this paper will be the four films she has made that are set in the past: *Diabolo menthe, Cocktail Molotov* (1979), *Coup de foudre* and *La Baule Les Pins/C'est la vie* (1990). All four films are based on autobiographical elements: the everyday story of two sisters growing up as rebellious adolescents in the 1960s in *Diabolo menthe* (which could be the prototype for the recent series of films sponsored by Arte under the umbrella title of *Tous les garçons et les filles de mon âge*); teenage rebellion in *Cocktail Molotov*, set against the background of the events of May 1968; and the break-up of the parents' marriage in the 1950s, seen in particular from the point of view of the mother in *Coup de foudre* and the young daughters in *La Baule Les Pins*. The autobiographical sources of these films are revealed to the spectator through press interviews rather than through specific markers in the texts themselves, since these are not primarily first-person, subjectively narrated films. Rather they reconstruct the lives of the director and her family through third-person narratives that focus in particular, if in a fragmented fashion, on the points of view of the various female characters, but do not ignore or dismiss the points of view of the male characters either. The films thus invite a complex response from the spectator, who can read them as representations of both individualized and more generalized female experiences, and/or as representations of a more collectively-experienced past.

As fictions that are set in the past, these films draw on the pleasures of nostalgia through the carefully researched use of period décor, costumes, props and music. In this respect, they can be seen as a subset of, or an alternative to, films belonging to the more general set of heritage or *rétro* films that have formed such a significant part of French cinematic production in the 1980s and 1990s (Vincendeau 1995; Austin 1996). Unlike the more commonly featured literary adaptations, historical epics and biopics that constitute the heritage genre as it is generally understood, these films, along with other thinly-veiled semi-autobiographical films such as *Louise l'insoumise* (Charlotte Silvera, 1985), *Rouge baiser* (Véra Belmont, 1985), *Le Grand chemin* (Jean-Loup Hubert, 1987), *Au revoir les enfants* (Louis Malle, 1987) and *Les Roseaux sauvages* (André Téchiné, 1994), use the recent past to represent relatively ordinary childhood and/or adolescent experiences that relate the narrative of self-discovery to the narrative of nation. These films can be seen on one level as self-indulgent exercises in narcissism that allow the film-maker to explore and exorcize childhood traumas. Certainly, Kurys's films can be read in terms of a psychodrama through which she aims to settle old scores with her sister and parents, particularly her mother. On another level, they explore the permeability of the social and the individual, the ways in which identities are produced at particular moments in French social history. But they also raise the principal issue that has dominated debate over the heritage genre to date, that is, the tension between *mise-en-scène* and narrative (Higson 1993). To what extent, then, are these films aesthetic exercises in nostalgia, dependent on stable visual and aural surface pleasures to construct a safe, escapist world, far removed from the problematic present; and to what extent are their surface pleasures contested and disturbed by their foregrounding of women's issues and women's history? Do Kurys's nostalgic representations of the lives of members of a particular secular Jewish family in 1950s and 1960s France invite more general reflection on the constitution of identity in ways that take gender and ethnicity into account?

Before analysing the various ways in which these four films, taken as a group, articulate the elements of heritage, nostalgia and the woman's picture (understood here not as melodrama, the Hollywood woman's genre *par excellence*, but rather as film by and about women), I want briefly to situate Kurys, a member of the baby boom generation who participated in the events and debates of May 1968, within the context of two particular influences on French cinematic production in the 1970s. On the one hand, as Forbes has argued (1992), a new kind of history film emerged after May 1968, indirectly inspired by the work of Foucault, the New Left and the Annales school of history. These films sought to challenge dominant representations of the past by exploring the lives of ordinary people, rediscovering lost or forgotten moments in history and giving a 'voice' to the oppressed. Examples include *Lacombe Lucien* (Louis Malle, 1974), *Souvenirs d'en France* (André Téchiné, 1975), *Moi Pierre Rivière* (René Allio, 1976) and *Le Juge et l'assassin* (Bertrand Tavernier, 1976). On the other hand, a wave of women's film-making, inspired by the women's movement of the 1970s, was raising issues regarding women, gender and representation in documentary and avant-garde film as well as in mainstream cinema. Significant films include *Histoires d'A* (Marielle Issartel and Charles Belmont, 1973), a documentary about abortion, *Jeanne Dielmann, 23 Quai du Commerce, 1080, Bruxelles* (Chantal Akerman, 1976), a hyperrealist avant-garde film that takes the life of an ordinary (alienated) housewife as its subject-matter, and *L'Une chante l'autre pas* (Agnès Varda, 1977), a mainstream film organized around the lives of two women friends. All these films have been made after second wave feminism provided the theoretical bases for an analysis of women's position in society and in representation, the desire to retrieve and represent female voices and female narratives that had been hidden from history (inflecting the new history), and an audience for women's films about women.

Although Kurys herself does not acknowledge any particular debt to the feminist movement, and studiously avoids any direct representation of the period of the 1970s, her films do overtly challenge the male-centred bias of dominant cinema. *Diabolo menthe* was the first French film to engage with adolescence and schooling from a girl's point of view, and it cocks a snook at *Zéro de conduite* (Jean Vigo, 1933) and *Les 400 coups* (François Truffaut, 1959), first in the scene where Muriel screams 'Je vous dis merde!' ('Shit on you!'), echoing one of the boy rebels in *Zéro de conduite,* and then in the use of the freeze frame shot, which imitates the famous concluding shot of *Les 400 coups* but substitutes the face of the young girl protagonist, Anne, for the more familiar Antoine Doinel. *Cocktail Molotov* is a bold (but unfortunately unsuccessful) attempt to rewrite the road movie with an active central female protagonist, Anne, in response to the misogyny of Blier's *Les Valseuses* (1974). The film could also have represented the events of May 1968 from a female perspective, but Kurys chooses instead to have her protagonists (and the spectator) miss out on any political action. However the foregrounding of Anne's drive for independence and sexual liberation does suggest the significance of May 1968 in the history of the women's movement to come. *Coup de foudre,* with its story of two women's self-discovery and growing independence, builds on the success of French women's films of the 1970s, like Yannick Bellon's *La femme de Jean* (1974), and on Hollywood's new women's cinema of the 1970s and early 1980s, such as *An Unmarried Woman* (Paul Mazursky, 1977) and *Girlfriends* (Claudia Weill, 1977). The decision to begin *Coup de foudre* in the Occupation period can also be seen as a move to inscribe women into this period of history, pre-dating other French films evoking women's roles during the Occupation, like *Blanche et Marie* (Jacques Renard, 1985) and *Une Affaire de femmes* (Claude Chabrol, 1988). *La Baule Les Pins*, her last *rétro* film to date, is remarkable mainly for its placing of children (both male and female) at the centre of the summer holiday film. Thematically, it reworks the by now familiar ground of child/adolescent rebellion, female rites of passage and the breakdown of a marriage, established in *Diabolo menthe* and *Coup de foudre*, but this time in an explicitly heterosexual mode. In this respect, it is the least innovative of the four films under consideration.

Andrew Higson argues that the aural and visual pleasures of period reconstruction in heritage films generally work to override or negate any disruptions provoked by narrative 'content' (Higson 1993). Pleasure in period atmosphere is enhanced by the use of art cinema-style narratives that depend on episodic rather than dramatic action, and fluid camera movements that show off the décor to best advantage, often at the expense of character and certainly at the expense of plot. Typically, Kurys's narratives work through short, often apparently unrelated scenes to develop atmosphere and characters and enable the spectator to piece together the relationships between them. They are loosely organized around a chronological period of time, which evokes a collective bourgeois or petty-bourgeois French heritage: the 1963 school year in *Diabolo menthe*, a few weeks around May 1968 in *Cocktail Molotov*, a summer holiday at La Baule in 1958 in *La Baule Les Pins*. Only *Coup de foudre* offers a more tangible dramatic progression, opening during the period of the Occupation and then concentrating on the years 1954–6 in the lives of its two central women characters. However, though the episodic narrative structures facilitate spectatorial pleasure in the details of the *mise-en-scène*, the camera rarely lingers on them or presents them to the spectator without focalizing them through the characters' points of view. Kurys's films do not so much privilege a 'museum aesthetic' and heritage space as provide a narrative space that is the site, not only of nostalgia, but also of dramatic tensions between the characters.

The 'look' of a film is to some extent a function of its funding. While *Diabolo menthe* and *Cocktail Molotov* were made on low budgets and shot on location or using inexpensive sets with a cast of amateurs or unknown actors, *Coup de foudre* and *La Baule Les Pins* benefited from much larger budgets, used star actors (Isabelle Huppert and Miou-Miou in *Coup de foudre*, Nathalie Baye and Richard Berry in *La Baule Les Pins*), were shot in CinemaScope, and involved loving and elaborate reconstructions of places and costumes. The additional production values produced by increased funding and the fact that these two films are set further back in the past make them more obviously eligible for the label of heritage films. The spectacular *mise-en-scène* of *Coup de foudre*'s opening sequences set during the German Occupation and then the Liberation of France allows Kurys to demonstrate her virtuosity as a director, but the film then concentrates on the construction of period authenticity through the display of 1950s fashions and domestic interiors. *La Baule Les Pins*' devotion to *mise-en-scène* is even more explicit, with its reconstruction of the model 1950s seaside resort, complete with beach-huts, beachwear and leisure pursuits. This film occasionally presents scenes direct to camera that are not necessarily motivated by considerations of narrative or characterization, as in the credit sequence that establishes the seaside setting, or the scene when Odette, the nanny, settles down in bed, allowing the spectator to admire her nightdress and hair curlers and the period wireless and alarm clock. *Diabolo menthe* also pays careful attention to period detail in the costuming of the girls and the *mise-en-scène* of home and school, though the fashions displayed are distinctly less glamorous. However, the *mise-en-scène* of *Cocktail Molotov* is less obviously available for heritage pleasures, perhaps because the gap between 1968 and 1979 was too close for nostalgia, but also because Kurys uses the *mise-en-scène* expressively to underscore the uncertainties of the central protagonists, exemplified by the scene in which Bruno throws away the Molotov cocktail of the title by the side of the road and it simply fizzles out.

Apart from *Cocktail Molotov*, the films invite spectators to experience nostalgia by basing settings and situations on memories that can be collectively shared, organized as they are around school, the family, and the summer holiday by the sea. Nostalgia is enhanced by the use of music, not just the diegetic and non-diegetic period music, but also the incidental music that accompanies key moments of emotional pathos, and the specially composed, sentimental songs, 'Ma petite Anne' in *Diabolo menthe,* 'Dearest Anne' in *Cocktail Molotov,* and 'La bouche pleine de sable' ('A Mouthful of Sand') in *La Baule Les Pins*. Nostalgia is also evoked through certain visual motifs that are repeated from film to film: panning shots of the bedroom where the lonely child/teenager is to be found; shots of the distressed child/teenager framed in a doorway or window, contemplating the parents' quarrelling or the mother showing affection to someone else; photos and freeze frames to fix particular characters (the father, the boyfriend, the lover) and particular moments in time (the school holidays that punctuate *Diabolo menthe*, the escape from Anne's home at the end of *Cocktail Molotov,* the night out in *La Baule Les Pins*).

Furthermore, in the first three films, Kurys's fleeting authorial presence provides a guarantee of the emotional authenticity of these representations. *Diabolo menthe* is dedicated 'A ma soeur qui m'a toujours pas rendu mon pull-over orange' ('To my sister who still hasn't returned my orange pullover'); *Cocktail Molotov* ends with the lines, 'C'était presque l'été et l'essence était revenue / Et on voulait nous faire croire que tout était fini / Pour nous le voyage venait de commencer' ('It was almost summer and petrol had come back/And they wanted us to believe that it was all over/ For us the journey had just begun'), implicating her in the film's narrative; and at the end of *Coup de foudre*, the epigraph dedicating the film to her father, mother and mother's friend Madeleine makes clear that the little daughter who witnesses the events of her parents' marital breakdown is

Figure 8. *Diabolo menthe* (1977), Diane Kurys. Courtesy Museum of Modern Art, New York.

to be understood as Kurys herself. These statements confirm the films' intention to produce a sense of loss and nostalgia by making the spectator aware of a double time, the past of the films' diegesis and the present of the film-maker's attempts to reconstruct the past.

However, despite the pleasures of period reconstruction and bittersweet nostalgia in relation to everyday life in the 1950s and 1960s (pleasures that also work as a visual record of the development of France as a consumer society), the historical references and emphasis on the lives of girls and women in these films mean that they cannot simply be dismissed as intimate chronicles of family life that are over and done with. The films make reference, either visually or verbally, to certain significant background events that still have a resonance in contemporary France: the Occupation of France and the deportation of Jews, the French presence in Algeria, the Charonne massacre, the arrival of the *pieds noirs* in France, the events of May 1968. These references, like the references to the characters' Jewishness, are often oblique and undeveloped, but form part of the mosaic of images and sounds that constitutes the texture of the films. Taken cumulatively, they draw attention to those moments in recent

French history that are the most troubling to the formation of national identity, and so situate the crises in the lives of the characters in relation to crises in French national life. Furthermore, the films privilege female points of view and female narrative agency as they trace the struggle of first the daughters, then the mother, to establish their identity against the constraints of the family and an oppressive French society. This foregrounding of female subjectivity produces specific viewing pleasures that in various ways and to varying degrees subvert both dominant cinema and the heritage aesthetic and reinscribe girls and women into the social history of the 1950s and 1960s.

First, shots of girls or women simply talking together, enjoying each other's company and focusing on girls' and women's experiences, however problematic, without being constructed as the objects of a voyeuristic gaze, are comparatively rare in French cinema. In *Diabolo menthe* there are repeated shots of Anne and Frédérique talking with their schoolfriends, speculating about sex, men's penises and white slavery in the case of Anne (aged 13), or sharing ideas about boyfriends, sex and politics in the case of Frédérique (aged 15). *Coup de foudre* explores the intimacy between Léna and Madeleine, the two bourgeois housewives and mothers, with repeated two-shots of them simply enjoying being together, be it sewing and reading, going swimming, or spending the night together in Paris. *La Baule Les Pins* also foregrounds the role of friendship between women through the confidences exchanged between Léna and her half-sister Bella.

Secondly, the films take as their subject-matter rebellion against the social order, and the rites of passage of young girls and teenagers. In *Diabolo menthe*, both Anne and Frédérique rebel against the petty rules and regulations that govern their lives at school and at home. Anne also experiences envy of her older sister, longs for and eventually has her first period, wants to wear tights instead of socks, goes to her first surprise party, and gets caught shoplifting. Frédérique has her first boyfriend, gets involved in political groups at school (the peace movement, combating anti-Semitism), loses one girlfriend but makes others, and has a crush on an older man. *La Baule Les Pins* focuses less on female rebellion (all the children are naughty) than on the daughters' growing disturbance at the rift between their parents, but it does address their awakening sexuality, Sophie playing doctors and nurses with René, while Frédérique develops a crush on cousin Daniel but then gets bored with him. In *Cocktail Molotov,* the action is motivated by Anne's violent revolt against her bourgeois mother, which leads to a series of rites of passage typical of the late 1960s: she runs away from home, starts to take the pill, makes

Figure 9. *Coup de foudre* (1983), Diane Kurys. Courtesy Museum of Modern Art, New York.

love with her boyfriend Fred, throws away her bra, gets pregnant, questions her lack of sexual pleasure and finally has an abortion (at a time when abortions were still illegal in France, requiring her to ask her father to pay for it to be done in Switzerland).

Third, and most important, the films tackle the issue of women's emancipation. In *Cocktail Molotov*, Anne's attempts to emancipate herself from her bourgeois family upbringing are rendered problematic by her age and her lack of economic independence. In both *Coup de foudre* and *La Baule Les Pins*, however, the women are victims and survivors of the Occupation and then victims and survivors of an inadequate marriage. *Coup de foudre* traces Léna's growing awareness of the constraints imposed by marriage: not having an income or a cheque-book, having to get her husband's permission to learn to drive or get a job. She reacts by putting her friendship with Madeleine before her marriage (the film has a lesbian subtext), having non-penetrative sex with a soldier on a train, setting up a fashion boutique and leaving her husband. *La Baule Les Pins* similarly shows Léna's assertion of her personal, sexual and economic independence. She has an affair with a younger man, gets herself a flat in Paris and a car, symbol of her new independence, and starts to teach herself to type. Both films provide a critique of male behaviour, the husbands being either comical and incompetent (Costa in *Coup de foudre*, Léon in *La Baule Les Pins*) or affectionate but violent (Michel in both). However, if the men are insensitive to women's oppression, they are also shown to be the victims of their gendered expectations.

Typically, the issues raised by the foregrounding of female subjectivity, like the socio-historical references, are touched on but not explored in any depth, available for the spectator to pick up on or not. The question is, then, the extent to which these issues are also smoothed over by the films' visual style. In most instances, the *rétro* visual pleasures of films are integral to the construction of character and plot rather than used to subsume them. However, in *Coup de foudre* and *La Baule Les Pins* the *mise-en-scène* quite literally becomes the site of patriarchal violence. In *Coup de foudre*, Michel's discovery of Madeleine's presence in Léna's newly opened boutique drives him to smash the wonderfully reconstructed boutique to smithereens. In *La Baule Les Pins*, he crashes Léna's new Renault Dauphine and threatens to strangle her, smashing up the furniture in the holiday villa and driving Frédérique to hold a shard of the broken mirror to her neck and threaten to kill herself. These scenes of violence, constructed through a troubled, fragmented editing style that highlights the isolation of individual members of the family, undoubtedly call into question the heritage of the 1950s as the unproblematic site of social and domestic harmony.

Conclusion

Kurys's films do not break new ground in terms of feminist theorizing with regard to either content or form, nor do they analyse women's condition (or the position of second-generation Jewish immigrants in French society) in any depth. Her choice of topics, as in the more general category of heritage films, avoids the complex issues that preoccupy contemporary feminists and focuses on issues that have, to some extent, become taken for granted in a more liberal society – access to contraception and abortion, acceptance of divorce and single parenting. Nevertheless, her films propose structures of feeling that, despite their *rétro* setting, are still relevant to contemporary female audiences – friendships between girls, friendships between women, female sexual desire, relationships with men, the need for economic independence.

Furthermore, Kurys's films are important for feminist cinema historians because in varying degrees they inscribe female points of view and female issues into representations of post-war France for a popular cinema audience. As Claire Duchen argued as recently as 1994, 'Women are remarkably absent from historical accounts of the Fourth Republic (1946–58) and even from accounts of the early years of the Fifth . . .' (Duchen 1994:1). Kurys's films work through narratives that put women at the centre of the story of everyday French life and open up France's post-war social history to gendered readings. The women in these films are not peripheral, they are not dutiful daughters and passive wives and mothers, but active agents in their own history and rebels against the dominant social order of the period. Even if the films' visual pleasures accommodate nostalgia for the period, the impressionistic accumulation of short scenes, sounds and images rarely simply gives way to the 'museum aesthetic' of heritage cinema, but rather works to validate women's often painful memories and experiences. The audience may be free to draw its own conclusions about the significance of the events being depicted, but it would be difficult to appreciate the films only for the pleasures of their scenic display and ignore the way they call into question the dominance of male-centred narratives of nation and identity.

References

Austin, Guy (1996), *Contemporary French Cinema, An Introduction*, Manchester, Manchester University Press.

Duchen, Claire (1994), *Women's Rights and Women's Lives in France 1944–1968*, London, Routledge.

Forbes, Jill (1992), *The Cinema in France after the New Wave*, London, bfi–Macmillan.

Higson, Andrew (1993), 'Re-presenting the National Past; Nostalgia and Pastiche in the Heritage Film', in Lester Friedman (ed.), *British Cinema and Thatcherism: Fires Were Started*, pp.109–29, London, UCL Press.

Vincendeau, Ginette (1991), 'Like Eating a Lot of Madeleines', *Monthly Film Bulletin*, March, Vol. 58, no. 686: 69–70.

—— (1995), 'Unsettling Memories', *Sight and Sound*, July, Vol. 5, Issue 7: 30–2.

8

Nation, History and Gender in the Films of Jean Renoir

Martin O'Shaughnessy

Despite the considerable body of critical work on his films, Renoir has received insufficient serious socio-cultural analysis. The predominant auteurist approach to his work has tended to cut him off from socio-historical and discursive contexts by seeking authorial thematic constants (nature, theatre, water, Impressionist painting etc.). Extreme variants of this approach suggest that Renoir has made and remade one master-film, while more nuanced versions account for evolution in his films by an individualistic model of apprenticeship leading to secure self-knowledge and mastery of the medium. The other main body of analysis has been generated by critics of the left who focus above all on Renoir's Popular Front period, which tends to be framed in narrowly political and class terms. These critics tend to see the pre-Front period as a time when Renoir moved to a discovery of the social, while inserting post-Frontist films into a narrative of betrayal, decline, corruption or even senility. Both accounts are distorting and fail to engage with the complex interplay of representations of gender, nation, history and class in the films.[1]

Part of the importance of Renoir's work lies in its historical scope. The twentieth century has been a time of multiple crises for France and 'Frenchness', and responses to these crises can be traced through his films. The aftermath of the First World War saw a crisis of civilization that, as Mary Louise Roberts (1994) has demonstrated, crystallized around a perceived crisis of gender. The 1930s saw a deeply fractured national community obsessed with decadence and loss of historical agency, while the Second World War brought a collapse of the nation and a subsequent crisis of representation due to the impossibility of inserting the period into what Paul Yonnet calls the *roman national*.[2] The *Trente Glorieuses*, although a time of rapid and sustained growth, also brought a crisis of identity as French society and France's place in the world were radically transformed in the way described by Kristin Ross in her important study,

Fast Cars, Clean Bodies (Ross 1995). What I examine in Renoir's films are responses to these crises: attempts to rebuild community and renew the social contract; efforts to deal with a difficult present or uncertain future by linking with a rewritten past; struggles to find certainty in times of extreme uncertainty by stabilizing gender and other hierarchies.

The first film I wish to consider is *Charleston* (1926), which presents itself as a *divertissement* and is usually analysed as such, but in fact perfectly illustrates Mary Louise Roberts's comment that 'postwar hedonism provided an escape from a world where the war was both everywhere and nowhere' (Roberts 1994: 1). This short piece shows a scantily clad white woman teaching an erotic Charleston to a black African explorer who has come to chart a post-catastrophe Parisian wasteland. A man-sized ape companion looks on jealously but impotently. Beneath the playful surface of the *années folles* we can see a world turned upside down, with gender and racial hierarchies under threat. Western historical agency and cultural superiority have traditionally been given a male face, so it is significant that it is the woman's ape-mate who loses his humanity as civilization collapses. Broad socio-historical crisis thus condenses around a destabilizing of gender (and at times racial) hierarchies, and above all around the sexual uncontrollability of women.

Hierarchies are violently reasserted in *Le Bled* (1929), a melodrama with documentary elements set in Algeria and made for the centenary of French conquest. This story centres on a young upper-class Frenchman who has squandered his inheritance (and has thus symbolically lost contact with the values of the past), travelling out to Algeria to ask his uncle, a colonial patriarch, for money. He meets a young woman who is coming to claim another inheritance, but her decadent, unscrupulous cousins stand in her way, especially the woman, a classic *femme fatale* who dominates the weaker-willed male cousin. The film ends when the female cousin is killed and the heroine is rescued and married by the hero. The crystalliza-tion of a broader sense of disorder around gender paves the way for the restoration of order by the domestication of women and the reassertion of male virility. The way in which a decadent and socially divisive elite can rediscover collective national purpose is figured in the film by the retying of the dislocated family bond between uncle and nephew, for the young man will follow in the patriarch's footsteps and farm the large, colonial estate. One key shot further reaffirms the link between national past and present by showing the original army of invasion fading into a line of tractors, thus sanitizing the past (conquest is figured as the subjugation of a wild land for productive purposes) while suffusing the present with the heroism of conquest. The colonial context is a site where disorder can be played out and order restored as turbulent melodrama is tamed by national epic.

Le Bled is usually seen as an unimportant Renoir film, a piece that he had been commissioned to make and thus less likely to be the expression of his 'unique' authorial personality. Yet it helps to establish a pattern that will reappear in some of the canonical films. Fears of decadence and historical dislocation are repeatedly figured and contained by narratives that domesticate or otherwise remove turbulent women and restore the broken link with a virile project of national history. However, there is a key difference between *Le Bled* and the later films. The male bonding that serves to anchor national community in it is between the patriarch and his adopted successor. In Renoir's films of the Popular Front era, the male bond is fratriarchal, as French egalitarian traditions rather than colonial dominance are made central.

La Grande Illusion (1937) is often seen as expressing a desire for communion and peace beyond class and national boundaries. Beyond this apparently simple humanist message, it is traversed by multiple tensions, such as those between nationalism and internationalism or between antifascism and pacifism. What will be considered here is the specific tension between a search for universal community and the need to maintain boundaries, specifically those of gender, in order to safeguard identity.

The film begins in a French airforce mess with a vision of non-hierarchical male-bonding whose potential homoerotic component is made safe by the sharing of the prostitute that Gabin is about to visit as the film begins.[3] French camaraderie is linked to a specifically national myth of equality and fraternity by the immediate contrast with the formal, hierarchical, and militaristic German mess that a captured Gabin soon finds himself in. However, when the camera pans to give a close-up of a woman's picture on the wall, there is a clear suggestion that what may bring all the men together, above and beyond other divisions, is the exclusion of women from both communities and their constitution as objects for shared male pleasures.

Although set in an apparently all-male world, the film presents itself and is read as dealing with the social and national divisions that fissure humanity. Men figure all the possible social differences and conflicts beyond which commonality can be sought, there being little room for women in the prisoner-of-war camp narrative. Yet, paradoxically, the film is obsessed with these absent figures. The men talk about them, their short hair and skirts, their sexual uncontrollability and the venereal diseases they pass on. They sing about them and surround themselves with female images. They even cross-dress.

Figure 10. *La Grande Illusion* (1937), Jean Renoir. Courtesy Museum of Modern Art, New York.

Beneath the surface pleasure of this comic transvestism a deeper anguish can be felt. The film shows a threat of a collapse of masculinity as major pillars of its construction are removed. The men in the camps are dominated, denied heterosexual contact and locked into the private, domestic space of the hut. Lacking the usual seal of seriousness that comes from public purpose, their games threaten them with infantilization. 'Men playing at being children', comments de Boïeldieu. They are feminized by their passivity and through the homoerotic component of bonding that is rendered more intense by a desire for solidarity beyond difference and a search for community in adversity. These 'fighting' men feed, comfort, nurture and tend each other. They cry for each other and yearn for each other. If in the first half of the film their bonding is dispersed within the group, within the smaller community of the final prison camp couples begin to form and the film increasingly becomes a love story.

The threats of feminization that accompany the domesticity and emotional intensity of the prison hut are defused by the purposive, outward-directed activity of escape and by the defiant reclaiming of soldierly identity. But this reclaiming is undermined by the film's sense of the absurdity of war in a way that is perfectly illustrated by the famous theatrical sequence. The cross-dressing that had created anguished silence when it was realized that, stripped of his uniform, a man could arouse erotic thoughts in other men, is initially recuperated as an act of virile national defiance when wigs are pulled off and postures pulled erect in a virile rendition of the *Marseillaise*. The anthem, celebrating the recapture of Douaumont from the Germans, is led by a combative Gabin. Yet Gabin is punished and goes a little mad, and Douaumont falls again, as Verdun, that ultimate symbol of the futility of war, blocks any simple salvage of masculinity through militant patriotism.[4]

Tensions in the end are contained rather than resolved when Gabin is incorporated into a heterosexual couple and a family, allowing the return of reassuringly gender-demarcated spaces and roles while at the same time bringing together the warring groups. When the two escapees arrive, tired and bedraggled, at a German peasant-woman's house, she washes Rosenthal's feet and feeds Gabin. The latter fills the place of her dead husband by carrying out the heavier, outdoor, 'masculine' tasks (chopping the wood, fetching the water). Domesticity and nurturing are thus returned to the woman, while the Frenchman can now reconcile international harmony with the maintenance of masculinity. The Christmas celebrations offer the Holy Family as a model of human bonding that stabilizes gender, promotes peace and safely incorporates the Jewish outsider as Jesus' *frère de race*. Yet the ending of the film, which reasserts the primacy of the male bond by showing the two men heading back to the war together, suggests that the tensions in the film have been temporarily contained rather than resolved.

It could of course be argued that beneath this narrative of threat lies a story of illicit desire. The film offers the male spectator the pleasures of gender transgression, homoeroticism and nurturing. It can moreover be seen as a return to a maternal space – its trajectory from denied coitus with the prostitute to the nurturing protectiveness of a mother figure inverts the male coming-of-age narrative. The film offers enjoyment of that which must be abandoned to attain adult masculinity, within the 'safe' context of a male war narrative. It is multi-layered, ambivalent and even contra-dictory, yet tensions and illicit desires are ultimately and predictably channelled into a reaffirmation of the status quo through the locking of women into private space and the positioning of male bonding at the centre of national and international community.

The portrayal of Rosenthal is also revelatory of the tension between the search for open communities and the need to retain boundaries. On the one hand Renoir courageously takes on prejudice by deliberately giving Rosenthal many stereotypically Jewish traits (clearly non-French origins, great wealth, and 'usurping' of lands) yet placing him at the centre of the prison camp community and pairing him rather than the historically rooted aristocrat with Gabin for the final escape bid. Indeed, Rosenthal destabilizes essentialist visions of the nation by suggesting that rootedness in the land and attachment to culture and tradition can all be acquired, and thus that 'natural' nationality is a fiction. His cultural and linguistic mixity and fluidity seem to point the way to de-essentialized and open identities. Yet, on the other hand, more obviously feminine traits are born by him, not by the 'true' and virile Frenchman, Maréchal (Gabin). He cries and plays the role of the weaker partner in the escaping male 'couple', so that the film ultimately draws back from the complete destabilization of identities that it at times points towards.

La Marseillaise (1938), a film in preparation while *La Grande Illusion* was being shot, is usually seen as a coded Frontist text, part of the left's reclaiming of the symbols of the nation in an attempt to build a broad anti-fascist alliance. It is also cited as an example of Renoir's famed humanist tolerance, as manifested in the clearly sympathetic portrayal of Louis XVI. Like *La Grande Illusion*, it is better seen as fraught with tensions inherent in the French republican tradition and exacerbated by fears of decadence, rising xenophobia and external threats. The chief tension that will concern us here is that between generous egalitarianism and a social contract built on male bonding; but we will also refer to that between universalism and exclusionary nationalism.

The film can be seen as two conflicting stories uneasily welded together, with one eventually enclosing the other. In one story women are seen to play an assertive, powerful and violent role in the revolution, claiming the right to a voice and an active role in the public domain. But this more radical story is encased in a male narrative of coming of age, bonding and nation-building, which begins when the country is geographically joined by the all-male march on Paris, continues when it is endowed with a suitably virile and warlike anthem, and ends when the citizen-soldiers defend its frontiers and their own right to citizenship at Valmy. Within this latter narrative, gender hierarchies and male occupation of the public arena are strongly affirmed.

In its early stages the film reaffirms the founding myth of the gendered social contract.[5] Two Marseillais, Bomier and Arnaud, have fled to the hills to avoid arrest, and unite with Cabri, a peasant fleeing persecution by the local noble. In this rediscovered state of nature, the three outlaws bring together city and country to form an ideal, non-hierarchical proto-community.[6] Their heterosexuality is affirmed by their desire for a woman to do the cooking and, it is implied, cater for sexual needs; but Cabri, the older man, warns that such a presence would cause jealousy and disrupt the communitarian ideal. The rest of the film can be seen in part as an attempt to deal with disruptive women.

Bomier, perhaps the most important character, is initially dominated by women. He is prevented from joining the male band that will march on Paris by his attachment to his mother and the debts he has contracted to give money to a duplicitous woman who has exploited his attraction to her. Accused of imitating the King's subordination to a woman and of sacrificing his honour and dignity, Bomier is temporarily threatened with exclusion from the fraternal band. 'It's as if my brother had just died', says Cuculière, one of his companions. It is, ironically, with his mother's permission that he becomes head of the family, clears his debt and rejoins his 'brothers'. As he departs singing, the women are left behind with their emotions and shut the window, reinforcing their confinement within the circular time of domestic space, while the men set out to shape the nation's contours and write its history.

Bomier, the generous 'heart' of the Revolution, will never quite free himself from female influence. Even as he marches to depose the King, his thoughts are with Louison, the woman he has met in Paris and his 'reward' for breaking out of protective maternal space. After his death, it is left to Arnaud, the 'head' of the Revolution, the man who is always in control of his emotions and who continually exercises a rational, calming influence on his more spontaneous comrades, to complete the male monopoly of public space and historical time by attributing to women a purely symbolic role in a male narrative of liberation and coming-of-age:[7]

> You see, before we changed things, peoples stood facing liberty like a lover might face a woman to whom he had been forbidden to speak . . . Of course, she is not yet his mistress and he'll have to work hard to conquer her fully. But now that they know each other, even if others separate them, they will find each other again one day.

The film shows the passage from the patriarchal system of the monarchy to the fratriarchal system of the Revolution. To become autonomous adults the brothers have to kill the father. The ensuing male guilt is transferred to Marie-Antoinette, the foreign woman. It is because she strays into the public domain and subverts the King's authority, or because she manipulates his emotions to make him betray his people

Figure 11. *La Marseillaise* (1937), Jean Renoir. Courtesy Museum of Modern Art, New York.

that the monarchy must be overthrown to replace a decadent father with more virile sons who can better defend France. Yet the famously sympathetic portrayal of the King suggests that, above and beyond divisions of class and political choice, the King and the Marseillais could potentially come together, most obviously through the shared love of food that seems to offer a potential site of reconciliation for Frenchmen.

Ultimately then, the story of active female participation in history, nation and public space is contained and made safe by enclosure in domestic or symbolic spaces, or in the case of Marie-Antoinette, the chief symptom of disorder, by exclusion from the nation and scapegoating for internal disorder.[8] The contradictory stories told by the film come most openly into conflict when the progressive revolutionaries defend a woman's right to participate in public debate, which is then used for a violent attack on Marie-Antoinette (Madame Veto), an astonishing blend of xenophobic misogyny and female assertiveness: 'Madame Veto betrays because she is Austrian! Because she is proud! Because she hates France . . . She is forgetting that you can't push a people around like you can a husband and that we women are here.' *La Marseillaise* reactivates key republican myths to reassert a sense of nation and national purpose at a time of crisis and division, and is thus part of the Frontist project of the reclaiming of national symbols; but the film must also clearly be read in the context of the discourses of decadence (expressed as unmanning) and xenophobia that were so prevalent in the 1930s. Left-wing critics would do well to go beyond a simple assertion of the film's progressive credentials.

Links between *La Marseillaise* and *La Règle du jeu* (1939) can clearly be made. The latter film at once echoes the former (references to hunting and poaching, the presence of an unruly Austrian wife, scenes of aristocratic frivolity), and reverses it (the poacher, for example, becomes a servant of the marquis rather than an outlaw, while the people imitate their decadent masters rather than providing an invigorating alternative). The clear implication is that France has lost contact with its national myths and its role as a progressive maker of history. Yet, bringing forward some of the insights I have drawn from *La Marseillaise*, I would suggest that *La Règle du jeu* can be seen more precisely as a triple failure of masculinity: a failure of male bonding (despite repeated attempts to come together, the men inevitably fight over women); a failure of virility (the men turn their backs on heroism, and refuse to defend their territory or their wives); a failure by several key characters to maintain the boundary between public and private. Jurieux, the national hero, turns to the private world of love. La Chesnaye, whose social position calls on him to provide leadership, is obsessed with mechanical toys. The General likewise abdicates responsibilities by showing more concern for etiquette than material dangers to the group. Marceau, the poacher with the name of a revolutionary general, prefers domesticity to independence or the defence of the marquis's territory against invading animals. Significantly, it is Schumacher, whose name clearly marks him out as un-French, who

Figure 12. *La Règle du jeu* (1939), Jean Renoir. Courtesy Museum of Modern Art, New York.

embodies strength, determination to defend territory and order, and military-style behaviour. Yet even Schumacher, brought to his knees by the disorderly behaviour of his wife, joins the disunited band of unmanned males by the end of the film.

There is a scene in *La Marseillaise* that prefigures the underlying logic of *La Règle du jeu*. It occurs when the exiled aristocrats are discussing the Revolution and the forthcoming war, and, one of their number, Mme de l'Estrange, interrupts, saying: 'Could you please stop your historical debate immediately. We need you to settle a most important disagreement. At Versailles, in the third figure of the Gavotte, did we look right as we went forward or left?'

The women lead the men away from the serious issues that face them into the frivolity of the court. Aristocratic decadence is thus equated with a failure to maintain boundaries between public and private and between male and female roles. Just such a boundary failure underlies the chaos of *La Règle du jeu*. Such an interpretation is reinforced if we remember the parallel montage of the opening of the film, when the public and modern space of the aerodrome is intercut with visions of the La Chesnaye interior, in the form of Christine's dressing-room, with its make-up, its costumes and its plethora of mirrors. Women are thus associated from the start with narcissism and appearances, and thus with falseness and frivolity. It is into this feminized space that the men will be sucked. The undoing of the national founding myth inevitably destabilizes the gender divisions it is built upon.

Le Caporal Epinglé, possibly the most underestimated of all Renoir films, was made in 1962 but recounts a prisoner of war drama set in the Second World War, thus providing clear echoes of *La Grande Illusion*, of which it is sometimes simplistically seen as a pale imitation. Like the earlier film, it is doubly historically inscribed, depicting a collapse of nation in 1940 but also responding to the need to reinvent Frenchness following the radical transformations of the *Trente Glorieuses*.

The film begins with newsreel shots of the collapse of France. We see the Germans marching on the *Champs Elysées*, thus claiming the centre of France and effacing French greatness. We see also the signing of the armistice in the railway compartment at Rethondes that undoes the victory of 1918 and severs the link with the national past. The individual soldiers who have been taken prisoner are thus stripped of external supports for their identity, ejected from any coherent sense of national community and forced to reinvent themselves and the social bond. There follows a male escape story that relinks with the national past and founding republican values by adding the struggle for liberty to the non-hierarchical comradeship (equality, fraternity) of the camp.

However, as suggested above, the film addresses the realities of 1962 rather than simply looking back to the past. The rigidly ordered, confined world of the prisoner of war camp can clearly be seen as an evocation of what Weber describes as the 'iron cage' of modernity, and echoes more contemporary dystopian visions such as that of Marcuse in *One Dimensional Man* (1964). The prisoners are all salaried workers, and thus representative of the accelerated disappearance of independent labour in post-war France. Moreover, they tend to evoke between them a world of bureaucracy, subservience and surveillance. One reads gas meters, while another character checks tickets in the metro. A third is a waiter and another an insurance agent. The imposition of German labour discipline on the recalcitrant French (with the collaboration of a French *sous-off*) cannot help but evoke the post-1957 Franco-German economic axis and the state-sponsored installation of a Fordist regime.

Faced with the collapse of familiar external supports to national pride and identity, the prisoners fall back on a hollow affirmation of their place and importance in the economy or on French sociability and archetypal cultural values such as love of food, *douceur de vivre* or individualistic resistance to the system. Yet, constant shots of barbed wire and German soldiers will not let us forget an essential lack of freedom that prevents them building an authentically positive sense of self.

Interestingly, male insecurities again crystallize around women, despite their almost complete absence from the film. We hear how the women take the jobs of absent men and are sexually unfaithful. Homosocial bonding is again taken to the limits as the men cry for, nurture and feed each other, even begging to share the same bunk. A Frenchman again escapes dressed as a woman, and receives the attentions of a German soldier, in a way that suggests the feminization that accompanies male subordination. This gender confusion seems again best read as an ambivalent blend of threat and desire channelled by the escape genre into a strong reassertion of the status quo.

Gender hierarchy and roles are fully stabilized at the end of the film when, having finally made good their escape, the *caporal* and his adoring friend *Pater* vow to continue the fight against the occupying army after the former has returned home to visit his wife. Intense male bonding is thus directed outwards into a fight for the autonomy and control of public space that is essential to adult masculinity. Women are again interned in domestic space. The only woman who plays a part of any significance is a German dentist's daughter, who falls for the hero, telling him, 'I love a man who is not a slave.' Her love (which consigns her to the private realm of emotion) is a reward for his refusal of subordination and struggle for autonomy.

The film thus restores the severed link with the past by re-founding the gendered social contract. As the nation collapses, individual males have to relocate freedom at the centre of their identity, so that by linking fraternally with other autonomous males they can restore a highly gendered version of the national trinity of values at the centre of France – the last scene shows the two men on a bridge over the Seine in the heart of Paris. Ironically, the Gaullist founding myth of the resistance of a liberty-loving France is mobilized against the unfreedom and subordination that follow from the drive for productivity and economic modernization that the Gaullist state so wholeheartedly supported.

A world separates the *Trente Glorieuses* from the *années folles* and the 1930s, yet certain features link the very different films that I have looked at. Each addresses some form of crisis – of civilization, of community, of identity, of historical agency or of continuity with the past. Although these crises crystallize around gender in each case, it would be a mistake to collapse them into a 'crisis of masculinity' that is too easily evoked and too rarely analysed. Owing to the gendered nature of public space and discourses of the social, perceived crises, be they of agency, identity or historicity, almost inevitably destabilize naturalized gender boundaries. When films invite us to view such multifaceted and over-determined crises through crises of gender, it is an invitation to replace complexity with simplicity and intractable problems with ritual reaffirmations of order that take the reactionary form of exclusion, subordination and stereotyping. At their best, most obviously in the case of *La Grande Illusion*, Renoir's films radically undermine naturalized identities. But they also show a repeated gendered reappropriation of pivotal national values and stories and a remaking of community and the social contract around the homosocial group. Nor should one ignore the (far from uniform) threads of nationalism that run through the work – from the colonial attitudes of *Charleston* and *Le Bled*, through the xenophobia of *La Marseillaise* and the ambivalent characterization of Rosenthal in *La Grande Illusion*, to the stereotypical portrayal of the Germans in *Le Caporal Epinglé.*

Renoir's famed humanism may indeed express itself in the search for harmonious community, but we would do well not to take it at face value and to remember the words of Chantal Mouffe: 'there cannot be a "we" without a "them"[;] . . . all forms of consensus are by necessity based on acts of exclusion' (Mouffe 1992: 379).

Notes

1. The most recent examples of essentialist auteurism are provided by Haffner (1988) and Bessie and Beylie (1989). Faulkner's incisive Althusserian analysis (Faulkner 1986) is the prime example of left-wing criticism. Buchsbaum (1988) also looks at some of Renoir's Popular Front films from a conventionally framed left-wing viewpoint. More recently, a special number of *Persistence of Vision* (Liebman *et al.* 1996) has opened the way to a more multifaceted account of the committed Renoir.
2. See Yonnet (1993). Chapter VIII focuses particularly on the Second World War.
3. When different men sleep with the same woman, it could clearly be seen as indicative of a displaced desire for male sexual intimacy. An early version of the script culminated in the two escaping males

sleeping with the same German woman, male 'coupling' thus reaching its climax by proxy (Bazin 1989: 179).

4. Gabin, who plays the solid man of the people, Maréchal, has a key role in the film as guarantor of a virile masculinity that feeds off the other roles he plays in the 1930s (see Vincendeau and Gauteur (1993) for an analysis of the star's 1930s persona). Maréchal, we learn, has escaped dressed as a woman and has attracted the amorous attentions of a German soldier, but reassures us, '*Je n'aime pas ça.*' Late in the film he mocks Rosenthal for mistaking a woman for a man. This repetition of gender uncertainty clearly suggests an obsessive return to a site of anxiety.

5. Pateman (1988) provides an analysis of the gendered nature of the social contract.

6. In this ideal community there is no demarcation between the domestic and the public. The men cook and eat together while discussing broader political issues. It is only when women appear that the domestic and the public are separated, thus clearly revealing domesticity's exclusionary role.

7. Mosse analyses the setting in place of firm boundaries between normality and abnormality, and the constitution of bourgeois images of respectability as national norms at the beginning of the nineteenth century. He writes, 'manliness meant freedom from sexual passion, the sublimation of sensuality into leadership of society and the nation' (Mosse 1985: 13).

8. Describing the actual historical period and not Renoir's film, Lynn Hunt writes, 'The queen . . . was the emblem (and sacrificial victim) of the feared disintegration of gender boundaries that accompanied the Revolution' (Hunt 1996: 280). What is noteworthy is that one hundred and fifty years later, the same exclusionary strategy is reaffirmed.

References

Bazin, André (1989), *Jean Renoir*, Paris, Lebovici.

Bessie, Maurice and Beylie, Claude (1989), *Jean Renoir*, Paris, Gérard Watelet.

Buchsbaum, Jonathon (1988), *Cinéma Engagé. Film in the Popular Front*, Chicago, University of Chicago.

Faulkner, Christopher (1986), *The Social Cinema of Jean Renoir*, Princeton, NJ, Princeton University Press.

Haffner, Pierre (1988), *Jean Renoir,* Paris, Rivages.

Hunt, Lynn (1996), 'The Many Bodies of Marie-Antoinette', in P. Jones (ed.), *The French Revolution in Social and Political Perspective*, pp. 268–84, London and New York, Arnold.

Liebman *et al.* (1996), 'Politics and the Cinema of Jean Renoir', *Persistence of Vision*, 12/13 (Special number of the periodical largely focusing on Renoir's Popular Front films).

Mosse, George (1985), *Nationalism and Sexuality*, University of Wisconsin.

Mouffe, Chantal (1992), 'Feminism, Citizenship and Radical Democratic Politics' in J. Butler and J. W. Scott (eds), *Feminists Theorize the Political*, pp. 369–84, New York, Routledge.

Pateman, Carole (1988), *The Sexual Contract*, Cambridge, Polity.

Roberts, Mary Louise (1994), *Civilization without Sexes. Reconstructing Gender in Postwar France, 1917–1927*, Chicago, University of Chicago Press.

Ross, Kristin (1995), *Fast Cars, Clean Bodies. Decolonization and the Reordering of French Culture*, Cambridge, MA, MIT Press.

Vincendeau, Ginette and Gauteur, Claude (1993) *Jean Gabin. Anatomie d'un mythe,* Paris, Nathan.

Yonnet, Paul (1993), *Voyage au centre du mal français; l'antiracisme et le roman national*, Paris, Gallimard.

Part III
Cinematic Communities

9

Framing Dreyfus: Méliès and Documentary Realism

Elizabeth Ezra

In *Imagined Communities*, Benedict (1991) Anderson argues that national identity coalesced in and through the spread of print technology, inaugurated at the end of the fifteenth century: as people read books and, later, newspapers, they imagined others like them engaged in the same activity. But four centuries later, an invention as revolutionary as the printing press prompted another sea-change, as the hegemony of written expression was shattered by the advent of cinema. From that point on, national identities would be forged increasingly by visual means; communities would come to be imagined literally, through images.

It was in 1899, less than four years after the birth of cinema, that Méliès, known then and to this day primarily for his 'trick' films and fairy stories, made a series of eleven one-minute non-fiction films about the Dreyfus Affair as it was still unfolding, portraying sympathetically Dreyfus's arrest, his imprisonment on Devil's Island, and his return to France for a retrial. Georges Sadoul called *L'Affaire Dreyfus* 'the first politically committed film' (1970: 28); apart from his brief stint as an anti-Boulangist satirical cartoonist for his cousin's review *La Griffe* ten years earlier, this is Méliès's only known expression of political engagement. Because the film portrayed Dreyfus sympathetically at a time when everyone had a passionate opinion about the Affair, it could therefore be considered to be pro-Dreyfus. For today's viewers, it is not always easy to discern the sympathetic elements of the films; but the abundance of huffy gesturing and self-righteous facial expressions on the part of Dreyfus make of him a dignified hero who refuses to be degraded by the accusations made against him. (The enormous crucifix in the courtroom, shown in the upper centre of the frame in one film, is, in a more literal sense perhaps than Barthes (1994: 26–7) intended, a *punctum*, the detail that wounds, the stigma evoking at once Dreyfus's similarity to the Christian icon through a shared martydom, and his alienation from Christianity, through his Jewish heritage.)

Méliès's series, however, dramatized much more than the Affair itself. It also dramatized the transition between two modes of documentary representation, the written and the filmic. Méliès's career ran parallel to that of the nineteenth-century *litérateur* to whom the new mass media gave a voice in politics. According to Susan Buck-Morss, the new mass readership engendered by the appearance of the *feuilleton*, or serialized novel, in newspapers drew authors into national politics: 'One has only to regard the format of a nineteenth-century newspaper, in which the *feuilleton* occupied the bottom quarter of the front page, to see, literally, how thin was the line between political fact and literary fiction. News stories were literary constructions; feuilleton novelists used news stories as content. The tendency of mass media is to render the distinction between art and politics meaningless' (Buck-Morss 1989: 140). To a certain extent, the central role of writing in Méliès's film series can be attributed to the importance of written documents in the Affair. The charge of espionage against Captain Alfred Dreyfus, a French army officer from a Jewish French-Alsatian family, hinged on a number of written documents: first, there was the anonymously authored *bordereau*, or note containing state secrets, that was discovered in the German military attaché's office; then, there were the samples of Dreyfus's handwriting, said to resemble the writing on the *bordereau*, including the note containing the words of the *bordereau* that the commander du Paty de Clam dictated to Dreyfus, which led to the latter's arrest. There was also the secret dossier shown to the judges in closed chambers but not to the defence, which contained vague allusions to 'that scoundrel D'. And, in 1896, there was a letter mentioning Dreyfus that appeared to have been written by the Italian military attaché to his German counterpart. This document, which turned out to have been fabricated by the commander Henry, would come to be known as 'le faux Henry' ('the fake Henry'). In addition to these documents, there were any number of texts that, while not central to the case itself, played an important role in the Affair – what Gérard Genette would call paratexts (Genette 1987: 7), such as the flurry of newspaper articles and pamphlets written sometimes to inform but more often to persuade, of which Zola's 'J'accuse' remains the best-known – many of which were read by Méliès before and during production of his film series.

Considering the importance of documents in the Affair itself, it is not surprising that writing and reading feature prominently in Méliès's filmed account.[1] The series opens with du Paty de Clam dictating the contents of the *bordereau* to Dreyfus, who copies them down. In the next available episode, Dreyfus is shown on Devil's Island, first reading a book, and then reading a letter delivered to him by a soldier. In the third instalment, two soldiers read aloud from a piece of paper ordering them to shackle a now prematurely aged Dreyfus to his bed. In the next instalment, Colonel Henry sits at a desk writing a letter, which he seals in an envelope before slitting his throat. The episode ends with soldiers opening Henry's letter upon discovering his body. In the fifth episode, notable for its innovative rain and lightning effects, Dreyfus is shown disembarking in Brittany upon his return from the Ile du Diable for the second trial. Before he is led off the boat, another man emerges who hands a letter and a sheaf of papers to an officer waiting on the dock, and the two discuss the papers.[2] The sixth instalment opens with Dreyfus writing yet again, while sitting at a desk in his cell in Rennes. He then walks across the room and picks up a booklet, which he looks through before showing it to his lawyers, who have since entered the cell. In the next instalment, which depicts the attack on Dreyfus's lawyer, maître Labori (played by Méliès), Labori is shown intently discussing a sheaf of papers with Colonel Picquart and the mayor of Rennes before being shot. The scene ends when, the mayor and Picquart having run off in pursuit of the attacker, Labori's cries for help are ignored by passers-by until a man comes along – reading a piece of paper – who stops and helps. Now, the eighth episode, referred to as 'la Bagarre entre journalistes', which is cited along with the 'attentat contre maître Labori' as an early example of deep staging, is notable for its absence of images of writing – yet writing is certainly implicit in the fact that the whole scene revolves around journalists. The final episode available shows Dreyfus and his lawyers arguing his case at the Lycée de Rennes, the site of his second trial. Here, too, although writing is not depicted explicitly, its presence in the law is implicit. (I'll come back to these two episodes that don't actually show writing or reading taking place, in order to discuss what might be replacing them.)

Méliès's serial film could thus be said to make a spectacle of writing. The film both depicts journalists (as in the famous *bagarre* scene) and is modelled on journalistic accounts and illustrations (Méliès freely copied images and descriptions from *Le Petit journal illustré* and *l'Illustration* for his sets, staging, and costumes, down to the most minute detail). This nostalgia for writing was reflected in film generally, which retained the ghostly presence of writing as an after-image. The first newsreels, created in 1908, were given names like the 'Pathé-Journal' and the 'Eclair-journal' (Deslandes 1963: 66), names that evoked film's writerly origins, as did the term for the Lumières' invention, the *cinématographe*, literally writer of motion, and later expressions such as 'caméra-stylo', cinematic 'écriture', and the 'auteur' theory of cinema.

The Dreyfus films' emphasis on the role of the document in the establishment of truth, coupled with the films' own implicit claim to be a representation of the truth, established film's potential to be a new form of document, in both senses of the word, depending on the context (that is, as a narrative or non-narrative account granted historical validity retrospectively, or as a certificate of authenticity; in the case of the latter, the document would stand up in court as legal testimony; in the case of the former, which would include *actualités reconstituées*, the document would serve as a witness to history. Today, Méliès's serial film would be classed under the heading 'non-fiction film', 'docudrama', or, if it were televised, 'reality programming'. *L'Affaire Dreyfus* is one of the earliest examples of a genre that Méliès invented called *actualités reconstituées*, an oxymoron combining contemporaneity and retrospection, which might best be translated as 'old news'.[3] Some of the events depicted in the films had taken place only very recently. (In fact, another of Méliès's 're-enactment films', the 1902 *Sacre du roi Édouard VII* , was actually a 'pre-enactment', having been made before the coronation.) In this context, the form of the film mirrored – or re-enacted – its subject, because re-enactment played a central role in the Affair itself.

It will be recalled that the series opens with Dreyfus being made to re-enact the writing of the *bordereau*, which leads to his arrest. Dreyfus's second trial was something of a re-enactment of the first: both were conducted in extremely irregular conditions, and both concluded with an erroneous verdict of guilt. Similarly, the trial of Émile Zola, famous for his promotion and practice of a realist literary aesthetic that purported to hold a mirror up to everyday life, could be seen as a re-enactement of the first Dreyfus trial. Even the personal mail sent to the prisoner on the Ile du Diable was copied over, according to Pierre Vidal-Naquet in his preface to Dreyfus's personal account of the affair: 'He would occasionally receive books and reviews in the mail, but this mail, from March 1897 onward, was copied over. The authorities lived in fear of an encryption system' (Dreyfus 1994: 6). Finally, the forged document that Henry produced in order to cover up the lack of evidence against Dreyfus completes the cycle of reproduction inherent in the Affair even before Méliès came along to reproduce newspaper images and accounts of it in his film.

Re-enactment is antithetical to the aesthetics of aura, which Walter Benjamin (1989) describes in 'The Work of Art in the Age of Mechanical Reproduction' in terms of a unique authenticity, precisely that which defies reproduction. It is also at the heart of the oft-cited dichotomy between Méliès and Lumière, or films made *sur le vif* and staged films. The very status of documents as proof, witness to events, evokes an aesthetic of

Figure 13. *L'Affaire Dreyfus*, Episode 3, *L'Ile du Diable* (1899), Georges Méliès. Courtesy Museum of Modern Art, New York.

the aura. The newsreel, for example, subscribes to this aesthetic: you must go 'on location' to capture the unique, authentic event. However, Méliès, in recreating the event, was rehearsing the function of mechanical reproduction itself. You don't need to go to the courtroom, he was implying; you can cobble together a set anywhere, anytime, with anyone, and still produce a (reproducible) image of the event. Méliès's re-enactment films, like all films, are indexical; but what they indicate is theatrical. He was replacing the auratic at the profilmic level, instead of waiting to dissolve it at the moment of its reproduction. As usually turns out to be the case, Méliès was ahead of his time, a practitioner of postmodernism before the rest of the world had even entered the age of modernism.

The Faux Dreyfus, or the Doublier Affair

In 1898, Francis Doublier, a cameraman employed by the Lumière brothers, sought to capitalize on the widespread interest in the Dreyfus

Affair by screening film extracts depicting shadowy images of French soldiers, a building, and a warship. Doublier's running commentary to accompany the film footage, a normal phenomenon before the creation of intertitles in 1903, explained that one of the soldiers shown was Dreyfus, that the building spectators saw before them was the scene of Dreyfus's trial, and that the warship was carrying Dreyfus off to Devil's Island. During one of the showings of the film, a spectator stood up and, although he did not yell 'J'accuse', insisted that the film was not what it appeared. Doublier protested, but was finally forced to admit the film was a fake when the spectator reminded everyone that the first two scenes, which were reputed to show events that had occurred in 1894 and early 1895, would have predated the birth of cinema. The outrage caused by this duplicity (committed, incidentally, by a man whose very name suggests doubling) caused the film to be pulled from distribution.

This incident begs the following question: why, if audiences objected to Doublier's film, did they not object to Méliès's re-enactments (that is, if we set aside the partisan fistfights the films provoked, which led to their censorship in France, and to the censorship of all other films on the subject until 1950)?[4] Perhaps because in documentary terms, like the 'faux Henry', Méliès's films themselves were fake – only there was no cover-up, which is, after all, what sparked the Affair's most heated debates. It was this disengenuousness that Zola contrasted with outright fantasy in order to praise the latter: 'the charm of the fantasy play for me lies in its candid evocation of convention, whereas I am put off by the hypocritical use of this convention in comedy and drama. [. . .] What's more, there is nothing duplicitous about a fantasy play, which cannot be mistaken for anything other than a fable. There is nothing illegitimate about it; it is pure fantasy, in which the author admits the intention to remain in the realm of the impossible' (Zola 1968: 500). If he was going to be lied to, Zola insisted on being told he was being lied to (apparently unconcerned with the resulting aporia). It was the pretence to reality, rather than to realism, that offended film audiences, or, more precisely, the claim of having been there, of co-presence, of eyewitness accountancy (or auratic authenticity). The difference between Méliès's film and Doublier's is the difference between reproduction and forgery, a difference that is in turn based on a metaphysics of presence: a reproduction is not presumed to have been present at the event it depicts, whereas a forgery is a text presumed to have been written by a certain person in a certain place at a certain moment; it claims to be the palpable relic of a particular act of writing or recording. This metaphysics of presence also underlies the opposition between documentary film, with its 'you are there' or *pris sur le vif* aesthetic, and *mise-en-scène*, or what Méliès called *scènes composées* – the traditional dichotomy, in other words, between Lumière and Méliès.

For how can this dichotomy be maintained if the Affair itself already, in many ways, resembled a *mise-en-scène*? First, there were the costumes: Roger Shattuck writes that Dreyfus's uniform was 'visibly padded' – *doublé* – when he returned from Devil's Island for the second trial, so that he would not appear too pathetic and scrawny (Shattuck 1969: 16). Then, there were the comments in the press about the theatrical atmosphere of the proceedings: H. Bourgeois, in his column 'Autour du procès' in the 8 September 1899 issue of *Le Petit journal*, wrote: ''In spite of the serious events unfolding there, which would shape France's destinies, it is difficult not to compare the audience to the masses who crowd into the Moulin-Rouge for the Sunday matinées. It's a scandal.' The day before, Bourgeois had written: 'A cinematographic device was set up in front of the exit to the school on Toullier Street, and is turned on as people are leaving. Everyone wants to be photographed, especially the ladies, who approach the camera while trying to act natural. It's all very amusing' (7 September 1899: 2). There was also the observation made by Zola, who mused, 'Has anyone noticed that this affair, this huge, earth-shaking drama, seems to have been staged by some sublime playwright?' (cited in Drouin 1994: 549). Finally, Dreyfus's own account of his belated discovery of the furore caused by his case describes it as a 'narrative', a 'dramatic story': 'Then Master Demange briefly narrated the tale of the "Affair". I listened, breathless, as my mind gradually pieced together the various sections of this dramatic story' (Dreyfus 1994: 214).

Like the border between reality and *mise-en-scène* in the Affair itself, the opposition between fantasy and realism within cinema has always been difficult to maintain. Georges Sadoul was one of the first to note that Méliès's fantastical tricks would eventually become the standard techniques of realist film-making: 'But these magic spells constituted, in reality, the seeds of the syntax, language, and means of expression that enabled cinema to translate life's reality, probably better than any art before it' (Sadoul 1947a: 26). This point was reiterated by Edgar Morin in *Le Cinéma ou l'homme imaginaire* (1956: 59), and then again by Jean Mitry, who wrote: 'The real is nothing other than a form of the fantastic to which we have become accustomed' (Mitry 1990: 489); Christian Metz then repeated the point in slightly more general terms in 1968: '. . . special effects can at any moment become conventional features of realist cinema' (Metz 1968: 185).

Méliès himself recognized the fantastical potential of the new medium upon viewing it for the first time, as he proclaimed it 'an extraordinary trick' (Malthête-Méliès 1973: 157). In a 1912 piece in *L'Écho du Cinéma* entitled 'Le Merveilleux au Cinéma', Méliès describes the nuts and bolts of technological development in terms that seem to undermine the medium's pretension to reproduce reality: p. 1: '. . . each day brings new inventions, thanks to the *fantastical* development of this industry' (Méliès 1912: 1; my emphasis);[5] and, again: '. . . this *marvellous* instrument, whose unprecedented success stems from the variety of its applications' (Méliès 1912: 2; my emphasis). Similarly, if the documentary side of the equation is predicated on being present at an event in order to capture its unique reality, it is useful to recall that the Lumière brothers reshot the first film, of workers leaving the Lumière factory, three times between 1894 and 1895 (Douchet 1994: 8). Jean-Luc Godard, too, invoked the difficulty of distinguishing between realism and fantasy in *La Chinoise* (1967), when Jean-Pierre Léaud's character lectures his revolutionary comrades on the fallacy of the dichotomy between Lumière and Méliès.

In the midst of all these blurred boundaries, the question arises: If grasping reality is so tricky, how is it possible to tell the truth, or at least to tell the truth from fiction? In the early days of cinema, the truth was something that film alone was not capable of telling. Film was an incomplete medium, which had to be supplemented by something else. In what follows, I will examine the nature of this 'something else'.

The Whole Truth and Nothing But the Truth

André Bazin, discussing the work of Stroheim, once wrote: 'In his films reality lays itself bare like a suspect confessing under the relentless examination of the commissioner of police' (Bazin 1984: 27). Before the invention of intertitles, film did not 'confess' its hidden truths unaided: the services of a *bonimenteur*, or accompanying narrator, were required to shed light on the film's subject, which would reveal itself as if under the glare of police interrogation.[6] But subjects and suspects, be they filmic or judiciary, have been known to 'admit' to things that are not true. There was thus a constant drive to supplement the image, first with speech, and then, once Méliès invented the serial film, with more images. As we have seen, the series format, which anticipated the vogue for episodic serial films such as *Fantômas* and *Judex*, followed in the nineteenth-century realist tradition of the newspaper *feuilleton*, conveying the breathless impulse to supplement and expand on a story told as if spontaneously: 'This happened, and then this, and then this . . .'. If fades, dissolves and irises provide the 'punctuation' between scenes in a modern film, then Méliès's series is a radical form of interfilmic punctuation that anticipated the intrafilmic punctuation that would develop soon afterward in Méliès's own work as well as in the work of others. The lack of a full stop, or closure, in each of the films in the series as well as in the series as a whole, which ends inconclusively, only reinforces the perceived need for a supplementary voice to impose meaning on the images.

Méliès's images were supplemented by speech, as written accounts of the Dreyfus Affair were supplemented by his film, and as writing is supplemented by speech (albeit speech that is silent to the film viewer) in two of the tableaux within the film. The *bonimenteur* is like a lawyer arguing a case, interpreting evidence, imbuing events with meaning, arranging them into a teleologically coherent narrative. Or like a historian, who makes events that occurred in the past accessible to modern-day readers (or viewers, in the case of televised history programmes), and who provides the discourse that, according to Michel de Certeau, 'presupposes a gap between the silent opaqueness of the "reality" that [history] is trying to articulate, and the place where [history] produces its discourse, which is protected by a distancing of its ob-ject' (De Certeau 1975: 9). History, like the *bonimenteur*, would present '. . . a problematic that articulates a knowledgeable discourse on what the other does not say, guaranteeing the interpretive work of a ("human") science by the border that distinguishes this work from a region that awaits it in order to be revealed' (De Certeau 1975: 9). In historical accounts, the subject is temporally absent; in Méliès's re-enactment films, the subject is tempo-rally present (having been plucked from 'current events') but spatially absent (it took place 'there', but we are watching it 'here'). Both historical discourse and the *bonimenteur's* narrative were conceived as ways of compensating for these absences, but they also produced them. In the two episodes of Méliès's series that do not feature written discourse (the 'Bagarre entre journalistes' and the 'Conseil de guerre en séance à Rennes'),[7] spoken discourse serves as an explicit surrogate for the document, as a form of communication that is meant to uncover some truth. In the 'Bagarre entre journalistes', those whose profession it is to put pen to paper substitute canes and umbrellas for their quills and give voice to their inflammatory opinions. In the trial scene, briefs are replaced by the lawyer's oral argumentation, which is so vigorous that it engenders more of the same, as the judge stands and yells back in reply. Here, speech is associated with violent persuasion, with the opposite of reason; sloppy, impassioned, uncontrolled speech seems to overflow the neat boundaries of reasoned written discourse. Speech is equated with propaganda, and thus possibly with bending the truth, like Doublier's spoken account that accompanied a film, which, taken on its own, would have caused no offence. The status of speech in Méliès's films reverses phonocentric assumptions about its authenticity, just as the films themselves question what I will call *photocentric* assumptions about the inherent superiority of unstaged documentary film footage (the 'photo' in photocentrism, of course, being Greek for 'Lumière'). Similarly, an analogy may be drawn between the symbiosis of realism and *mise-en-scène* and Hayden White's rejection of the distinction between history as a story that is 'found', and fiction as a story that is 'invented', because, according to White, 'This conception of the historian's task . . . obscures the extent to which "invention" also plays a part in the historian's operations' (White 1973: 6–7). So, while appearing to re-enact history, Méliès was actually making it.

What the emphasis on written documents in Méliès's series ultimately heralds is a widening of film's functions beyond entertainment to include its use as both historical and legal document, signalling the encroaching influence of the visual media in representing and transmitting cultural values. In the society of the spectacle, the *bordereau* would be replaced by the Rodney King video. Méliès's series is situated at the border not only between two centuries, but also between two modes of perception, two often overlapping but nonetheless different ways of imagining communities.

Notes

1. I refer to the copy at the British Film Institute, which, at nine episodes/ 739 feet, is considered to be the most complete copy available anywhere. This copy is missing the second episode, which depicts Dreyfus's military degradation, and the final episode, which shows people leaving the building where the second trial was held.
2. This episode is notable for the movement of characters (along the camera axis), as the group of soldiers, shown from behind, lead Dreyfus away from the camera. This deep staging has not before, to my knowledge, been pointed out in regard this scene, but it his been discussed in relation to two other scenes, the 'Attentat contre maître Labori' and the 'Bagarre entre journalistes'. See Ben Brewster, 'Deep Staging in French Films 1900–1914', in Elsaesser 1990: 45–55, and Jenn 1984: 20, 24.

3. The first film of this genre, *l'Explosion du Cuirassé Maine*, was made by Méliès in 1898; others include *la Guerre gréco-turque* (1899) and *les Incendiaires* (1902). See Sadoul 1962.
4. For an account of the controversy the film evoked, see Malthête-Méliès 1995: 220.
5. '... each day brings new inventions, thanks to the *fantastical* development of this industry'.
6. Madeleine Malthête-Méliès (1982: 167) affirms that the accompanying texts have never been located.
7. These are the titles used in the National Film Archive (British Film Institute) synopsis. Alternatively, these episodes are referred to as 'La Bataille des journalistes au lycée' and 'Le Conseil de guerre à Rennes' in Malthête 1989: 6–8.

References

Anderson, Benedict (1991), *Imagined Communities* Revised edition, New York, Verso.

Barthes, Roland (1994), *Camera Lucida*, trans. Richard Howard, New York, Hill and Wang.

Bazin, André (1984), *What is Cinema?* Vol. I, trans. Hugh Gray, Berkeley, CA, University of California Press.

Benjamin, Walter (1989), 'The Work of Art in the Age of Mechanical Reproduction', in *Illuminations*, trans. Harry Zohn, pp. 217–51, New York, Schocken Books,.

Buck-Morss, Susan (1989), *The Dialectics of Seeing*, Cambridge, MA, MIT Press.

De Certeau, Michel (1975), *L'Ecriture de l'histoire*, Paris, Gallimard.

Deslandes, Jacques (1963), *Le Boulevard du cinéma à l'époque de Georges Méliès*, Paris, Editions du Cerf.

Douchet, J. (1994), 'D'un réalisme l'autre', in *Retour vers le réel*, [?], Conseil Général de Seine Saint-Denis.

Dreyfus, Alfred (1994), *Cinq Années de ma vie*, Paris, La Découverte.

Drouin, Michel (ed.) (1994), *L'affaire Dreyfus de A à Z*, Paris, Flammarion.

Elsaesser, Thomas (ed.) (1990), *Early Cinema: Space, Frame, Narrative*, London, British Film Institute.

Genette, Gérard (1987), *Seuils*, Paris, Seuil.

Jenn, Pierre (1984), *Georges Méliès cinéaste*, Paris, Albatros.

Malthête, Jacques (1981), *Essai de Reconstitution du catalogue français de la Star-Film*, [?], Centre Nationale de la Cinématographie.

—— (1989), 'Les Actualités reconstituées de Georges Méliès', *Archives* 21, mars, Institut Jean Vigo-Cinémathèque Toulouse.

—— (1995), 'Georges Méliès, de la non-fiction à la fiction', *1895* 18, été, special issue: 'Images du réel: la non-fiction en France (1890–1930)'.

Malthête-Méliès, Madeleine (1982), 'L'Affaire Dreyfus de Georges Méliès', *Cahiers de la Cinémathèque* nos. 35–6, Autumn: 166–8.

—— (1995 [1973]), *Méliès l'enchanteur*, Paris, Ramsay.

Metz, Christian (1968), *Essai sur la signification au cinéma*, Vol. 2, Paris, Klincksieck.

Morin, E. (1956), *Le Cinéma ou l'homme imaginaire*, Paris, Les Editions de Minuit.

Sadoul, Georges (1947a), 'Georges Méliès et la première élaboration du langage cinématographique', *Revue Internationale de la Filmologie* 1, juillet–août: 23–30.

—— (ed.) (1947b), Special Supplement to *Sight and Sound*, August.

—— (1962), *Le Cinéma français*, Paris, Flammarion.

—— (1970), *Georges Méliès*, Paris, Seghers.

Sand, S. (1994), 'Les sosies cinématographiques de Dreyfus', in L. Gervereau and C. Prochasson (eds), *L'Affaire Dreyfus et le tournant du siècle*, pp. 224–7, Paris, BDIC.

Shattuck, Roger (1969), *The Banquet Years*, London, Jonathan Cape.

White, Hayden (1973), *Metahistory: The Historical Imagination in Nineteenth-Century Europe*, Baltimore, MD, Johns Hopkins University Press.

Zola, Emile (1968), 'La Féerie et l'Opérette', in *Oeuvres complètes* Vol. 11, Paris, Cercle du Livre Précieux.

10

The Case of the Undead Emperor:
Familial and National Identity in
Jacques Becker's *Goupi Mains-Rouges*

Florianne Wild

Films made during periods of high historical trauma usually do not or cannot treat the events of the moment in which, as cultural artefacts, they are produced. The French cinema during the German Occupation of France is a case in point. Owing to their general erasure of the political and social realities of everyday life in France, discussion of these films has tended to turn them into allegories of their historical moment, films whose content is seen to reveal a veiled socio-political immediacy, and at the same time, a functional realism. Many films, however, may bring to light a deeper engagement with history, one that transcends the historical moment in which they are conceived. The concept of allegory then becomes, in Frederic Jameson's words, a means to an 'opening up of the text to multiple meanings, to successive rewritings and overwritings, which are generated as so many levels and as so many supplementary interpretations' (Jameson 1981: 35). It is possible, then, to 're-write' certain films as allegories of history.

Evelyn Ehrlich has shown that during the Occupation, the cinema in France actually flourished, owing to the new mode of film-making that became known as the *cinéma de qualité*. These 'prestige' films, many of which were lavish costume dramas depicting moments of France's past military glory, the splendours of the *ancien régime*, or adaptations of cherished literary works, were intended for export as well as for consumption at home. They became identified abroad with 'Frenchness'. These films, and indeed the majority of feature films during the Occupation, remained 'neutral,' not expressing overtly fascistic or even conservative Vichy ideologies. 'In fact,' comments Ehrlich, 'many of the films can be read as having both resistance and collaborationist sentiments,' and what is more, '. . . the debate over the extent of collaboration of one film-maker or another, or the question of whether a given film was "collaborationist" has obscured other more fundamental issues' (Ehrlich, 1985: xii).

One such issue has been brought to the fore by Edward Saïd's contribution to the rethinking of the dominance of Western forms of culture and the ways in which they have rendered imperialism and colonialism transparent. Saïd has enabled us to see 'a history of the imperial adventure rendered in cultural terms' (Saïd 1993: xxiii). As a result of changing cultural politics, a given narrative figure who was seen in the past as marginal now moves closer to the centre.

The film *Goupi Mains-Rouges*, based on the novel written during the thirties by Pierre Véry, serves as an example of a film that may offer an opening onto a broader context in which long-standing issues of French history and identity can be brought into play. A film's articulation of history is often subliminal: even when there is no stated presence of historical events, the past perturbations of history, because they continue to govern the present, manage to push their way to the surface. I will attempt to illuminate some of these issues while avoiding the rather reductive gesture of showing how the film's mimesis might 'reflect' or 'comment on' the period of the Occupation.

An immensely popular film upon its release and winner of the Grand Prix du Cinema Français for 1943, *Goupi Mains-Rouges* was one of fifteen films selected after the Liberation for a film festival designed to demonstrate the French cinema's ideological 'untaintedness' during the Occupation (Bergstrom 1996). The early 1940s of course mark a period in which the official version of French identity and national values took a sharp turn away from *liberté, égalité, fraternité*, and away from the revolutionary, democratic contentiousness of Paris, as official ideology veered toward the *travail, famille, patrie* of the Vichy motto. According to Herman Lebovics's analysis of the period, an essentialist idea of culture issuing from right-wing ideologues posited a 'true France' – the *pays réel* rooted in the soil of rural life – in opposition to the *pays légal* of Third Republic politics (Lebovics 1992: 51).

The characters and setting of *Goupi Mains-Rouges* doubtless encourage the aforementioned kind of allegorization. The Goupi family, deeply rooted on its farm in the Charente, might be seen as a microcosm of rural French society of the time. They appear to be a tightly-knit, autonomous (if not harmonious), self-regulating social cell in which the patriarchal word has always been law. Family clannishness is emphasized by the custom of stating the family name first when referring to a member: Goupi Mains-Rouges (Red-Hands), Goupi la Belle (Beauty), Goupi La Loi (The

Law), and so forth, with the nickname that follows underscoring a personal characteristic of the bearer instead of a given name.

On a dark train-station platform in the dead of night we encounter the first of their number, Goupi Monsieur, 'The Gent' (Georges Rollin), whose mother had escaped the farm – and her husband – some twenty years earlier in order to seek a life in the capital. She took with her the young Eugène, now returning home at the behest of his father, who sees in him a likely match for his cousin Muguet, or 'Lily of the Valley', (Blanchette Brunoy), since the Goupis' wealth must not be dispersed. But Monsieur has deceived the family by exaggerating the importance of his job and the size of his pay cheque. He is not, in fact, a Paris department store manager, as his chagrined father will discover, but a mere tie salesman. When his shameful status is brought to light, his name is abruptly changed to Goupi Cravate ('Necktie').

Upon his arrival, Goupi Monsieur is met by a taciturn peasant whom he takes for a railway employee. It is his uncle Léopold, or 'Mains-Rouges' (Fernand Ledoux), who appears at the outset disquieting and enigmatic. On the way to the farm, Mains-Rouges engineers the break-down of his horse-cart in the middle of a dark forest, obviously intending to disconcert the newly arrived city slicker. The uncanniness surrounding him increases as he ushers Monsieur into his isolated shack in the woods, where, seated across a table from the wide-eyed traveller, he mutters imprecations while sticking pins into effigies of local worthies. Are we to take him for a real practitioner of voodoo? We hesitate as well over his possible criminality when he tells the tale of his beloved Goupi la Belle, who drowned many years before in his well. Neighbours still entertain the thought of a murder for an inheritance.

The Mains-Rouges of Véry's novel, in a kind of parody of Zola's natural-ism, has inherited both his sobriquet and a supposed taint of violence from an eighteenth-century ancestor, the 'original' Mains-Rouges, who had dipped his hands in the blood of Marie Antoinette just after she was guillotined. Eliminated from the film, this bit of guignolesque historical detail is replaced only by a close-up shot of Mains-Rouges' upturned palms, accompanied by a few discordant musical crashes on the sound-track. We learn later that Mains-Rouge's life has been controlled by a tyrannical father who forbade his marriage to Goupi la Belle, making him disabused and distant. This doesn't prevent him from engaging in antics with another family member, Goupi Tonkin (Robert le Vigan), in an attempt to frighten away Monsieur, now Tonkin's rival for the beautiful Muguet. Both Mains-Rouges and Tonkin, a former colonial soldier, semi-outcasts from the rest of the family, live apart from the family homestead and inn.

Eventually we meet the perpetual squabblers who dwell within this inn: Goupi Tisane (Germaine Kerjean), Goupi L'Empereur (Maurice Schutz), aged patriarch of the clan, Goupi Cancan (Marcelle Hainia), labelled 'Gossip' by her grasping and insufferable husband Goupi Mes Sous, 'Pennypincher', (Arthur Devire), the father of Monsieur Eugène, and two servants. Tisane, the hypochondriac unmarried daughter, is established as a tight-fisted shrew when she fires the young retarded servant and his mother, Marie des Goupis (Line Noro). Continuing the family circle is Goupi Dicton, 'Dictum' (René Genin), whose tedious recitation of sayings trotted out for every conversational occasion betrays a lack of mental flexibility, and by extension points to the unchanging mentality of the family down through the generations. Further, like any repetitive tic, it underlines the mechanistic and thus the farcical aspects of human behaviour. Dicton's daughter Muguet is as sweet-tempered, patient, and charitable as Tisane is cruel, cranky, and grasping. Goupi Mes Sous, a Zolaesque type entirely reminiscent of Misard in Zola's *La Bête Humaine*, tallies his meagre profits while inveighing against the profligacy of the others. Like Misard, he expends much effort in searching for the family's *magot*, the time-honoured stash of gold, in this case a purse found (or stolen) by the founding father of the family, one Besace, 'Moneybag', and now presumably hidden somewhere beneath the floorboards of *la France profonde*. Completing the family lineage is the grandfather, Goupi la Loi (Guy Favières), a retired gendarme. Once an agent of the law of state and nation, he is portrayed as ineffectual and deceitful. When the local gendarmes appear at the door following the murder of Tisane, La Loi treats them like nosy intruders and obstructs their investigation, saying 'Les affaires des Goupis se règlent entre Goupis.' (The Goupis settle their family business themselves.) Established legal procedures, then, are seen by the family as a force preventing the carrying out of its normal business and as a threat to its continuity. They would seem to recognize no law beyond the preservation of the family and its property.

The central action of the film takes place when Tisane is bludgeoned to death after she has dismissed the gentle, dim-witted servant and his mother. Since she has been assigned the role of stone-hearted harpy, any possible shock at her murder is considerably diminished, both for the spectator and for the family. There is perfunctory sniffling after the funeral on the part of the women, but the greatest source of anguish among the clan is the possibility that a Goupi might be found guilty of the murder and exposed. Mains-Rouges decides to tell the gendarmes that Tisane fell from a ladder, and La Loi agrees.

Figure 14. *Goupi Mains-Rouges* (1942), Jacques Becker. Courtesy Museum of Modern Art, New York.

Tisane's murder is immediately upstaged by another event, namely, the collapse of Goupi L'Empereur. This 106-year-old patriarch is indeed the family's most permanent feature. A storehouse of history, he can remember all the way back to Charles X, although his precise battles float in oblivion. Was he at the battle of Isly? The Moroccan campaign? Madagascar? The family has tired of his stories, alternately tolerating him and treating him as a nuisance. He is infantilized by Tisane, who refuses him the cookies, the glass of wine, and the allowance he begs for. Left alone on the evening of Monsieur's arrival from Paris, he downs some wine in solitary pleasure and suffers a paralytic stroke. He is thought dead by the others, who discover, along with the body, the theft of 10,000 francs from the linen closet. They blame the deed on Goupi Monsieur, who arrived in the night, glimpsed the body before anyone else, dropped his pocket comb, and fled. As prime suspect, Monsieur is locked up in a stable by his father Mes Sous, who also takes away his cigarettes. So far, he has found cold comfort on the family farm.

The moribund Empereur miraculously revives, but is temporarily unable to speak. The family's greatest concern thus becomes that, in his paralysis, he will not be able to pass on the whereabouts of the *magot*. In one of the film's most comic moments, the Empereur, frozen and immobile, is carried in a straight-back chair from cellar to attic by Mes Sous and La Loi who hope that, in the manner of a divining rod, he will somehow be able to point to the location of the family treasure.

The Goupi family does indeed offer the temptation to see the film as an act of resistance to the official Vichy version of identity and national values. The Goupis are variously grasping, mendacious, schizophrenic, violent or merely odd, a claustrophobically enclosed and contentious tribe in whom other larger ideals or forms of identity, whether religious or secular, have either degenerated or failed to take root. At the very least, such a skewed rendering of *travail, famille, patrie* and of the injunction to 'return to the soil' seems to suggest an indifference or an ambiguity about assigning these notions to either political ideology, be it Vichyist or Resistant. But if the film is *not* a sharp and ironic revelation of the hollowness and bankruptcy of Vichy slogans that glorified the pure and noble life of tillers of the soil and hewers of wood, what is it? Might it be a film-in-dialogue with those of Marcel Pagnol, a deliberate retort in which the local colour is mainly black? (Indeed, nearly half its sequences take place at night.) Or is it an illustration of wicked intent by its director, the Communist Party member Jacques Becker, of Karl Marx's comment on 'the idiocy of rural life'?

Certainly, the portrayal of the aged patriarch, bedridden, infantilized, alternately dotty and cantankerous, most tempts an allegorical reading as Marshal Pétain himself, a similarly beloved but impotent figurehead hovering over the hearth while others carry on the nation's business. Yet the film seems to hint that the most important historical tendencies of *la France profonde* are always buried: deep in the well, like the drowned Goupi la Belle, or hidden, like the gold of the family fortune, in the pendulum of the grandfather clock. The Empereur's name itself obviously points to historical substrata, to layers formative of French political identity. The figure of the Empereur can be seen as encapsulating the persistent military strain in national politics that certainly contributed to the installation of Pétain as nominal Head of State. What indeed seems to be routed through the film is the question of the French *principe impérial*, embodied in the character of the great-grandfather, forever ailing but never quite succumbing. Though he is unconscious and apparently dead through much of the story, a cadaver-like presence around whom the family activity continues, he nonetheless outlives the film, as if he were imperial France refusing to die. To emphasize the 'timeless and eternal' quality of this patriarch, the gold that allows him to remain a figurehead has been recast and hidden as the pendulum and counter-weights of the grandfather clock.

Moreover, in patriarchal fashion, he and his sons in turn dictate to the younger males of the tribe whether or not to marry, and whom to marry, thus controlling their sexuality and their procreative destinies. Though he is physically a barely-functioning shadow of himself, he and his first-born, Mes Sous, keep in place a family dynamic that damages and emasculates the younger men, while keeping all the women except Tisane in their place as well. Tisane, usurper of the control of farm, household, and inn, is conveniently murdered. Yet the Empereur could not remain in power without the complicity of the others. The 'imperial principle', like patriarchy, can be perpetuated by family members of lesser scope and stature, passed on from generation to generation, even should a strong leader prove temporarily non-functional. In the Goupi family, then, generations of males have issued from a military man whose stories of valour in glorious battles once took hold of the family imagination just as the Napoleonic legend once took root in the French national memory. But the Emperor's male descendants have followed a downward trajectory – from La Loi as law officer, to Mes Sous as merchant and innkeeper, to the department store tie salesman, Monsieur, and finally to the alienated failed soldier, Tonkin. In the great-grandfather's nickname, L'Empereur, the memory of Bonaparte has lived on, but it is the staging of a latter-day descending trajectory of the Bonapartes represented by the reign of Louis Napoleon that surfaces most strongly in the film's allegory of history. This becomes strikingly visible in the juxtaposition of the figure of the Empereur to that of Tonkin, the son who had fled the farm to participate in the great colonial adventure, returning afterward addled and abject. Living alone in his bizarre quarters, a bamboo hut complete with hammock and opium pipe – a re-creation of the French fantasy of Indochina in the heart of the Charente – he forces recognition of the consequences of the *principe impérial*. It is Tonkin's appearance in the film that exposes the contradictions of imperialism: he is now considered a degenerate, the family member most marked by difference and con-taminated by the 'otherness' of the colonies, riddled, as Tisane puts it, with *maladies chinoises* (foreign diseases).

During the striking sequence of the local schoolmaster's visit, Tonkin confronts his audience with both a counter-geography and a counter-history to that of the Hexagon, as he feverishly spouts the names of the 'marginal' places that have been important to his life in the colonies. The schoolmaster arrives at the family homestead for a post-funeral visit. He is hoping for an update on the civic glories of the capital – which he has not visited since the Colonial Exposition of 1931 – from Goupi-Monsieur, the closest thing to a Parisian available. Monsieur has been released from captivity in the stable in order to perform for the visitor. In the school-teacher we see the personification of the principle of universal and compulsory education as it evolved during the Third Republic: an institution supremely responsible for uniformity of thought in the population, for dissemination of official ideas about French identity, and indeed, through its main proponent, Jules Ferry, for the inculcation of an ideology of pride in the growth of France's empire. The dialogue that ensues in this rather comic-opera sequence stages a kind of elocution contest between the two rivals for the hand of Muguet. Monsieur Eugène recites a passage on the demographics of Paris retained from his school days. Tonkin encounters him in this verbal duel by means of his own oppositional geography, a sort of 'défense et illustration d'Outremer'. As he spins off his lyrical litany of Asian names, Tonkin's diction detonates in a veritable explosion of otherness, a living reproof to the long-standing belief that, to quote Theodore Zeldin, 'to be a Frenchman . . . meant to be civilized, which required that one accept the models of thought, behaviour, and expression held to esteem in Paris' (Zeldin 1977: 6). Tonkin, the very reverse of the *Français par acquisition*, (Frenchman who has acquired nationality) is rather the *Français de souche* (born and bred Frenchman) who has uprooted himself, turned in his credentials, and rejected his cultural heritage.

The presence of 'poor Tonkin', as the others call him, causes an unexpected surfacing of the Indochina conquest and its consequences for French citizens, making it possible to read the film as a critique of a certain French identity, one that fosters a yearning for the military glory that followed France's Napoleonic and colonial exploits, one that longs for the military leader whatever the consequences. Vichy and Pétain can also hardly be avoided as historical allusions in this film; they are too close. But the 'liberal empire' could be overlooked – its distance in time is remote enough – were it not for the figure of Tonkin. An insistence on the equation 'L'Empereur = Pétain' would prevent us from seeing the Empereur as the lingering and now historiographically repressed tendency of the French attraction for empire. The historian Steven Englund points out that in Pierre Nora's *Lieux de Mémoire,* 'there is almost no study of the myth, tradition or ideology of "empereur," "empire," or "bonapart-isme," even though, of all forms of non-monarchical government, it is the *empire libéral* that has come the closest to imposing itself permanently in the Hexagon' (Englund 1996: 69). Among French historians currently addressing the question of identity, Robert Muchembled, in 'L'Etat et

Figure 15. *Goupi Mains-Rouges* (1942), Jacques Becker. Courtesy Museum of Modern Art, New York.

l'image du roi/président' argues that French identity is inseparable from the State and the Prince who governs it (Muchembled 1989: 146–61) . Michel Winock suggests that both Marshal Pétain, the beloved authority figure in uniform, and General de Gaulle stand in a direct line descending from the plebiscitary authoritarian mode of the liberal empire of the two Napoleons (Winock 1995: 110).

But in the figure of Tonkin, as the 'refusal' of the colonial adventure, the deranged remnant of an epic past, we find an unexpected exposure of the contradictions of militarism and its modern concomitant, imperialism. Supposedly crazed by the sensory excesses of soldiering in the colonies as well as physically diseased – 'C'est le paludisme!' explains Mes Sous (It's the malaria!) – he is also unloved by Muguet and thus socially incapable of generating a succession of further Goupis. As Pierre Maillot observes, as a possible *fiancé de Marianne* (suitor for Marianne), he is unfit (Maillot 1996: 106).

With Tisane's murder, the family has become a community in crisis. Order must be re-established, for if Monsieur, the chosen mate for Muguet, were found to be the perpetrator, the continuity of the family line would be threatened. It is Mains-Rouges, the one who most resembles Tonkin by his self-imposed separateness from the others, who ultimately solves the crime by identifying Tonkin, his companion in pranks and fellow creature in solitude, as the murderer. All that is left now for Tonkin is to eclipse himself so that the family may remain 'unscathed' and unexposed to secular justice.

In the films of Jean Renoir, with whom Becker worked in the early part of his career, there is often a character, usually an outsider, or one who fits uncomfortably into the social group, who comes upon the scene, causes some havoc or is accused of a crime, and then disappears or is killed, leaving the others behind to contemplate what has happened to them, while their corner of society nonetheless continues undisturbed. After the killing of André Jurieu, the aviator in *La Règle du jeu* (1939), the would-be 'dangerous poet' and truth-teller Octave fades away into the night as the family closes ranks in order that the truth not be known nor the family name besmirched. In *Goupi Mains-Rouges*, Tonkin obligingly excludes himself by committing a spectacular suicide, fleeing out the window as the gendarmes approach and climbing rapidly to the top of a towering tree, where he rages about merging with the sun and cries reproaches at the family for their small-mindedness until a branch (allegorically!) breaks beneath him.

With Tonkin dead, the film closes on an affirmation of family normality, a meal whose function is inclusiveness (again, a Renoiresque gesture). Mains-Rouges, the lone poacher, is invited to join the others in celebrating the happy union of Goupi Monsieur and Muguet. The marriage will assure further generations of Goupis as well as the passing on of the family gold, an eventuality confirmed as the film concludes with a shot of the swinging pendulum of the grandfather clock.

References

Bergstrom, Janet (1996), unpublished paper delivered at Rutgers University.

Ehrlich, Evelyn (1985), *Cinema of Paradox*, New York, Columbia University Press.

Englund, Steven (1996), 'History in a Late Age', in *French Politics and Society*, Vol. 14, No. 1.

Jameson, Frederic (1981), *The Political Unconscious*, Ithaca, NY, Cornell University Press.

Lebovics, Herman (1992), *True France: The Wars Over Cultural Identity, 1900–1945*, Ithaca, NY, Cornell University Press.

Maillot, Pierre (1997), *Les Fiancés de Marianne*, Paris, Nathan.

Muchembled, Robert (1989), 'L'Etat et l'image du roi/président: héritages de l'ancien régime', in *L'Identité Française, Colloque à l'Université de Copenhague*, Copenhagen, Akademisk Forlag.

Saïd, Edward (1993), *Culture and Imperialism*, New York, Knopf.

Winock, Michel (1995), *Parlez-moi de la France*, Paris, Editions Plon.

Zeldin, Theodore (1977), *France 1848–1945, Vol. 2*, New York, Oxford University Press.

–11–

Truffaut's Imagined Community
Russell King

Ma patrie, ma famille, c'est le cinéma. (Cinema is my nation, my family).
— Truffaut

François Truffaut seems a quintessentially French director who was in a
constant state of denial concerning his French identity. Such cases lead
us to be at the least curious about how national identity, national character,
and cultural identity are theorized, about how such concepts are attributed
to individual artists, about how they are inscribed into their texts and
described from them. This chapter is exploratory in that questions and
the formulation of problems are somewhat easier than answers. What is
there to the concept of national identity beyond unstable stereotypes,
superficial generalizations, glib platitudes, and subjective impressionism,
worthy of tabloid feature articles? Benedict Anderson argues that it is
difficult to theorize any sense of nation: 'Nation, nationality, nationalism
– all have proved notoriously difficult to define, let alone to analyze. In
contrast to the immense influence that nationalism has exerted on the
modern world, plausible theory about it is conspicuously meagre'
(Anderson 1991: 3). 'Truffaut' too needs breaking down: my concern
here is not really the person or the biography of François Truffaut, his
social and political engagements. Rather it is the discursive Truffaut, the
one who never tired of talking and writing about the cinema, as expressed
particularly in the interviews, speeches, articles that reach us through *Le
Cinéma selon François Truffaut* (1988), *Les Films de ma vie* (1975), and
Le Plaisir des Yeux (1987). The question can be formulated in a multiplicity of ways: is Truffaut a French film-maker, that is, one who is
somehow defined by his sense of being 'French'? Or, quite simply, is he
a film-maker who happens to be French? Is the specificity of his cinema
somehow wrapped up in his Frenchness, in a kind of European 'art-house'
cinema practice, as formulated by, for example, David Bordwell in
Narration in the Fiction Film (1995): character-based, loose narrative
structure, ambiguity, weak heroes, absence of closure? Or, is Frenchness

for Truffaut no more than a geographical tag, a random accident of being that has little or no discernible effect on artistic practice?

Let us continue this tentative exploration for a moment: where else might we look for an *auteur*-director's sense of national identity, especially one in whom there is a close correlation between creative persona and cultural artefact? We could look for it in the way he is integrated into the French film industry, particularly in the areas of production and financing, campaigning for the industry against foreign (that is, American) hegemony. Or, since one of the first principles of identity is naming – the naming of the self and the places in which this self is located – we can look at how, in his films, images and icons of France are specifically named: France, Paris, the Eiffel Tower, the Metro, the provinces, French road or street signs, car number-plates, maps, French films and novelists, French landscapes and architecture, and all the other ingredients of costume and heritage cinema. French location is indeed privileged in this way, for example in *Les Mistons* (1957), with its location in the 'touristy/heritage' sites of the arena in Arles and the Pont du Gard. Or we can examine how ideology informs, or feeds into, his films, consciously or unconsciously, in the form of mimesis, mimicry or imitation. This is a special challenge for a director who so constantly proclaimed the erasure of the socio-political.

What makes Truffaut's sense of national identity such an interesting case is that he constantly and resolutely denied any sense of patriotic Frenchness. He claimed never to have felt patriotic about France and the French, investing instead his sense of nation in cinema itself: 'When I go abroad, I do not have the impression of representing France. I represent my work, that's all' (Truffaut 1988: 413). Elsewhere, in different speeches and interviews, Truffaut repeatedly placed himself in this situation of denial *vis-à-vis* France, French politics and French society: 'The cinema is my religion. I believe in Charlie Chaplin', he is famously recorded as saying (Truffaut 1988: 442). But does Truffaut protest too much? I am not particularly concerned by the fact that witnesses and biographers will wish to argue that at various stages of his life Truffaut was far more politically and socially active and aware than he here claims. Moreover, critics like Mas'ud Zavarzadeh in *Seeing Films Politically* (1991) or Graeme Turner in *Film as Social Practice* (1993) would suggest that films always have cultural and political identities inscribed in them: film can never be nationally, culturally, politically innocent. The above statements made by Truffaut himself, however platitudinous and suspect they may appear to us, will in due course nonetheless provide us with a double point of entry – not a solution – into aspects of Truffaut's 'Frenchness': namely language and the family.

As a preliminary exercise it is necessary to examine briefly that most obvious approach to national identity, namely the one existing along the axis of difference/similarity. French cinema is so often defined by its difference, especially *vis-à-vis* American cinema. The first defining aspect of Truffaut's sense of national difference concerns his extraordinary enthusiasm for American cinema, from his conviction that his career had been shaped by American films (1988: 123), to his enduring passion for Welles's *Citizen Kane* (1987: 276), to his assertion that 'I have seen 1500 American films. In them I liked a certain atmosphere; I was now going to use these things again, in a French way (*à la française*), paying a kind of homage to them' (1988: 120). Everywhere in Truffaut's critical writing we see his interest in, and admiration for, American cinema: in his account of his working with Spielberg as an actor in *Close Encounters of the Third Kind* (1977), his love of Woody Allen, especially *Annie Hall* (1977), his enthusiasm for John Travolta in *Saturday Night Fever* (Badham 1977). The *auteur*-directors of Hollywood whom he admired and championed were numerous. Nor did he decry the 'attractions' of Hollywood's large-scale action-spectacle movies, which he thought were returning to cinema's roots. The main reason he gave for not working in Hollywood was that he believed his kind of film-making, with his anti-heroes, was not compatible with Hollywood's practices.

It is also quite remarkable that Truffaut adapted so many American works, including: David Goodis's *Down There* (*Tirez sur le pianiste*); Ray Bradbury's *Fahrenheit 451*; William Irish's *The Bride Wore Black* (*La Mariée était en noir*) and *Waltz into Darkness* (*La Sirène du Mississippi*); Henry Farrell's *Such a Gorgeous Kid like Me* (*Une Belle Fille comme moi*); Henry James's *The Altar of the Dead* and *The Beast in the Jungle* (*La Chambre verte*); and Charles Williams's *The Long Saturday Night* (*Vivement dimanche*). The major, if that is the word, French writer whom Truffaut used was Henri-Pierre Roché, and both his novels are partly located abroad, namely in Germany and Britain. Likewise several of Truffaut's films starred foreign actors: *Jules et Jim*, *Fahrenheit 451*, *Les Deux Anglaises*, *La Nuit Américaine*, *L'Histoire d'Adèle H*. Location is more problematic: only *Fahrenheit 451* was filmed abroad, in England, and released in both English and French versions. *L'Histoire d'Adèle H* was filmed in the Channel Islands, though the story location is Nova Scotia and Barbados.[1]

Truffaut's own location of Frenchness takes us immediately and unambiguously to questions of language and dialogue:

I feel very French when it comes to dialogue. If you are a film-maker of images alone, you can surely film in any country in the world; but to write dialogue, there are indirect ways of saying things which you can do only in your own language. Many of the film-makers who emigrated to Hollywood could master light, image, working with actors, but I think that deep down they couldn't control what they did because of language. (Truffaut 1988: 413)

This claim is surprising coming from a director who so valued cinemato-graphic communication by visual means. Indeed, much of the enterprise of the early New Wave was to re-invigorate film-making as an independent visual medium rather than allowing it to function simply as the hand-maiden of literature. And yet, paradoxically, Truffaut is, in many respects, a literary film-maker, who valorizes the written and spoken language. It is of course commonplace knowledge that Truffaut, at the beginning of his career, hesitated between writing and film-making. He viewed himself as a person of nineteenth-century sensibility, making his admiration for the century's major novelists such as Balzac explicitly evident in a number of films, most notably *Les 400 Coups* and *Les Deux Anglaises*. His fascination with language is apparent in his reflections on the problems he encountered in making *Fahrenheit 451* in England:

Yes, I suffered in England, obviously because of the problem of language. I missed not being able to modify and tamper with the dialogue while filming. When we talk of films, we underestimate the importance of words. [. . .] Basically, I came to cinema through dialogue, and I'd learn the dialogue by heart. Only later did I hear about 'mise-en-scène', through Rivette. My inclination was always to get intoxicated with films, so I'd know their dialogue and music soundtracks by heart. That's why I never side with those who criticise dubbing. I can quote *Johnny Guitar*, which probably has more importance in my life than in the life of its director, Nicholas Ray; in fact I could even say that I prefer the dubbed version of *Johnny Guitar* to the original. (Truffaut 1988: 178–9)

This same literary tendency is especially manifested in Truffaut's love of the narrator's voice-over. It is as if in the darkened cinema, explains Truffaut, the voice from the screen were addressing the spectactor personally (Truffaut 1988: 436). Books are constantly quoted or referred to, and the written letter is a favoured means of communication.

Like Truffaut, others have made links between language and national identity. For example, Joseph Conrad stated that 'My nationality is the language I write in.' Theodore Zeldin in his book on the French wrote: 'If one forces the French to striptease, discarding one by one all the outward disguises that give them their national identity, the last thing one would be left with would be their language' (Zeldin 1977: 350). Benedict Anderson, without contradicting Zeldin's witty formulation, theorized the problematic equation as follows:

> It is always a mistake to treat languages in the way that certain nationalist ideologues treat them – as emblems of nation-ness, like flags, costumes, folk-dances, and the rest. Much the most important thing about language is its capacity for generating imagined communities, building in effect particular solidarities. [. . .] Print-language is what invents nationalism, not a particular language *per se*. (Anderson 1991: 133–4)

An understanding of issues of language and communication is, then, crucial to any full analysis of Truffaut's films. What is at stake is the equation Truffaut makes, for himself, between national identity and language and dialogue. Is it little more than the fact that he was better able to ensure the way dialogue was written and spoken with his native language than with English? Could it be something more profound, taking on board Anderson's argument that 'the most important thing about language is its capacity for generating imagined communities'? It is through language – that is with the literal language of French, combined with the figurative language of film-making – that Truffaut imagines and articulates his/the world. Language creates and informs knowledge. It is for this reason that at some subliminal level, perhaps, *L'Enfant sauvage*, which, like *Les Mistons*, is quite minimalist in terms of dialogue, and in some ways resembles early silent cinema, is important in our understanding of the Truffaldian world. For Victor, the wild child, to enter the world as a fully functioning human being, he must master language, whether it be the language of words, or the language of pictures. He partially achieves the latter but, having been deprived of maternal or paternal love, example and instruction as a child, his education in a sense more or less fizzles out. The film ends with no clear closure. Victor does not achieve, against the odds, the mastery of written and spoken language, like his instructor/film-maker Truffaut. Victor's socialization, in society in general and in French society in particular, is incomplete.

It is through language too that Truffaut enacts the double axis of difference and continuity: with the French language, he is faced with difference with English, which he never really mastered in the way that Louis Malle and many other French directors did. It is also a matter of continuity in that through French specifically he is able to feel a familial and national lineage back through Renoir to the nineteenth-century French novel. Language is perhaps not what characterizes his sense of French identity, but it arguably has significance as a means of imagining an alternative and substitute community.

This sense of continuity and community brings us to the other equation that Truffaut makes, namely between the family of cinema and national identity. Now, the most widely admired study of Truffaut's cinema is that of Anne Gillain in *Le Secret perdu* (1991), with its analysis of narratives centred around dysfunctional males suffering from foreclosure of the oedipal trajectory, fetishized women, and children. Unlike the conservative narratives of American cinema, which traditionally are located within families and frequently seek to reassert family values, French narratives generally depict the nuclear (father, mother, child) family or couples in the process of imploding or exploding, disintegrating: infidelity or adultery, the theme *par excellence* of the nineteenth-century French novel, is normally the cause. In this crude distinction between radical French and conservative American cinema narratives, Truffaut is typically French.

What Truffaut, consciously or unconsciously, sought to achieve was the creation of an idealized family of the cinema. Constantly he writes about the 'family' of film-makers to which he claims membership:

> Those film-makers [Bresson, Hitchock, Godard, Bergman, Buñuel, Rossellini, Hawks] are amongst the greatest in the world; they are orphans because their fathers are dead: Griffiths, Lubitsch, Murnau, Dreyer, Mizoguchi, Eisenstein, Stroheim, but they've still got brothers, some more fortunate than others, working or unemployed, but brothers who are at the same time colleagues [*confrères*]: Renoir, Ford, Lang, Kurosawa, Sternberg, Walsh, Vidor and others. (Truffaut 1987: 273)

It is a commonplace, in Truffaut studies, to argue that the cinema represented a place of triumphant escape and happiness from both an unhappy family life and from the failures and misery of the world of reality. The family of the cinema, to which Truffaut strives to belong, and which his narratives suggest is unrealizable, is a microcosm of, or substitute for, the large imagined world of society, or France. It becomes his cherished personal, imagined native country. In the world of cinema, in the world of play, the father can cherish and educate the child – literally or figuratively – as we see in two films in which Truffaut chose to play: the bachelor Dr Itard who seeks to educate the wild child in *L'Enfant sauvage*, and the director Ferrand in *La Nuit américaine*. Ferrand is notably one of the few characters who does not seem to be involved in a marital, romantic or sexual relationship – a fact that caused Godard to

Figure 16. *L'Enfant sauvage* (1969), François Truffaut. Courtesy Museum of Modern Art, New York.

accuse Truffaut of hypocrisy. For Truffaut, despising society and politics, the world of cinema becomes a substitute, an imagined community, which reaches back beyond the invention of cinema, to the fiction film's immediate predecessor, the nineteenth-century novel. In this world fathers can be imagined, enacted, idealized, and children can be taught to become functioning adults, under the paternal and loving eye of Truffaut:

I think that things are not good for children in France. It's worse than hostility; it's hypocrisy; it's narrow. *Les 400 Coups* is a criticism of the French way of bringing up children. I didn't realise that until after I had made the film, as, before making it, I had never left France. It was only later, when travelling abroad, that I was struck by the fact that the happiness of children has nothing to do with the material situation of their parents and country. In Turkey, which is a poor country, children are sacred. In Japan, it is inconceivable that a mother could show indifference towards her son. [. . .] When I showed *Les 400 Coups* to Renoir, he said to me 'That's a picture of France.' I liked that, but I didn't know why. I understood only when I went abroad. (Truffaut 1988: 260–1)

So Truffaut's argument seems to be that, through language, literally through the French language and figuratively through the language of cinema, he is able to imagine and create a world, and especially a sense of community and continuity within that playful substitute family, in which he seeks to erase France and specific French identity, in order to occupy a territory rather akin to that of mid- and late-nineteenth-century aestheticism and decadence.

This brings us to *La Chambre verte* (1977), surely the director's strangest film, which might appear to be the one most unlikely to provide any meaningful insight into the director's sense of Frenchness, national identity, or national character. The images of the film, in my view, provide one key to Truffaut's sense of national identity: it is a film – in which Truffaut himself acted the principal role of Julien Varenne – about a provincial obituary writer who builds a shrine most particularly to his wife and, more generally, to the dead. So often notions of national identity encompass cenotaphs, shrines, remembrance, in the pursuit of continuity with the past and a permanent lasting community. As Anderson states: 'No more arresting emblems of the modern culture of nationalism exist than cenotaphs and tombs of Unknown Soldiers' (Anderson 1991: 9). Could this provide us with the most profound sense of Truffaut's search for an identity that either equates with or replaces his sense of Frenchness and French national identity?

The film begins with archive footage of the trench warfare of the First World War, with the image of a solemn Julien Varenne/Truffaut as a fellow soldier superimposed. This superimposition is repeated three times during this opening sequence. This is a major temporal/locational variation of the original Henry James short stories – 'The Altar of the Dead' (1895) and 'The Beast in the Jungle' (1903) – and would suggest a potential for some patriotic identification of France, the First World War, the war dead, and Julien Varenne/Truffaut. The film will proceed to deny this modifica-tion to the plot and make the war dead of First World War trench warfare simply one of the contributing factors to the hero's obsession with commemorating the dead.

Indeed, the first sequence of the film proper, following this initial credit sequence, establishes the primary motivation for the hero, by way of personalizing and individualizing the experience of death. It depicts the 'hysterical' reaction of Varenne's friend at the funeral of his beautiful young wife. His loss of his wife is a repetition of that experienced by Varenne ten years earlier, after just a few months of marriage. Varenne's shrine to the dead, in particular to his wife, occupies a room in his house, and will later, after a fire, occupy a converted chapel, dedicated to a community of the dead, with his wife being the provisional centrepiece. Ultimately, a candle will burn there for him after his death, thus completing the permanent shrine of his 'family' of the dead.

When Julien Varenne invites his friend, Cecilia, who herself is differently obsessed with remembering the dead – she remembers one person in particular who coincidentally had once been a friend of Varenne – and who will be the guardian of the shrine after his death, we are solemnly

Figure 17. *La Chambre verte* (1978), François Truffaut. Courtesy Museum of Modern Art, New York.

introduced to those who represent 'his' dead. They are not the dead of the cinema – fellow directors from the present and past, as we see in the scene in *La Nuit américaine* in which books about them are displayed one by one. Nor is it a patriotic French shrine. It is resolutely international, and only partly relates to cinema. There is an Irishman who had lived in France for many years, an inseparable couple who had fled France to live and die in Holland, a timid man, an American who had become an Englishman (Henry James), a German soldier (Oscar Werner), a musician, and many others. These people, with a candle burning for each of them, transforming their death into life, will constitute the triumph of life over death, in the eyes of Varenne, by creating a community, his community, which will live in perpetuity.

Julien Varenne resembles Ferrand in *La Nuit américaine*, who sees fellow actors and technicians as a substitute for a family, with him alone not involved in any other family/sexual relationship. Like Dr Itard in *L'Enfant sauvage*, Ferrand is unmarried but assumes a symbolic family in the form of Victor and Mme Guérin. Unlike his friend Gérard Mazet, who replaces his first wife, Geneviève, Julien Varenne remains a faithful widower, with an intimate relationship with Cecilia, but one that is never consummated into an affair or marriage. Instead, he has a substitute family in the form of a deaf-mute son – totally absent from James's short stories – and a housekeeper, Madame Rambaud. This self-portrayal in these three films as a bachelor or faithful widower appears a strange self-representation in the eyes of critics (and especially for Godard), in view of Truffaut's serial womanizing in real life; indeed, the hero of *L'Homme qui aimait les femmes* might be a truer representation of Truffaut, this being a role he did not want to play himself. Instead of being interpreted as a gross act of hypocrisy on the part of Truffaut himself – Godard's charge – it might well be that in some other desired way Ferrand/Dr Itard/Julien Varenne suggest profoundly and symbolically the longing of Truffaut to find an alternative family/community that is truly his, to which he truly belongs, and in which he is able to perform and re-present himself as some idealized patriarchal/paternal figure.

There are differences among the families/communities in the three films. In *La Nuit américaine*, the family comes together and soon disperses, to come together again in the future. It is a renewable family. In *L'Enfant sauvage*, the 'story' of Dr Itard and Victor runs out of steam and the film ends, on a most ambiguous note. Dr Itard and Victor, in his education and socialization, have gone as far as they can go. In *La Chambre verte*, Varenne, by dying, and joining in death those he commemorates, gives a kind of permanence to constructed or imagined family/community. One may well wish to follow Anne Gillain, in *Le Secret perdu*, in seeing Truffaut's films as enactments of oedipal crises, resulting from dysfunctional family relationships with a rejecting mother and absent father, and resulting in equally unstable, dysfunctional, fetishized relationships, which Gillain's psychoanalytic approach splendidly elucidates. On the other hand, and perhaps as a result of all this, there is another profound desire in Truffaut's work to create another more stable, more lasting community, which transcends France and all things French at a deeper level, however much we may find the actual films cluttered with iconic emblems of France.

Notes

1. Truffaut's enthusiasm for America did not extend to England. Though he made one film in England – *Fahrenheit 451* – he seemed to exile himself in the Hilton Hotel for six months, moving only to the studio. He disliked the excessively realistic acting style of English actors: 'When I asked for actors who didn't have a British appearance, I was asked: "What is a British appearance?" I was tempted to reply: "It's when you've got a crooked face." In fact it's true: the English have all got crooked, asymmetrical faces, whereas in Hollywood they've all got symmetrical faces; they go to Hollywood thanks to that, because the two sides were the same. The only Englishmen who are successful in Hollywood are people like Cary Grant. As soon as an Englishman becomes idealised, stylised, he leaves for Hollywood. So in London the only ones left are the realists. All their lives they'll have Peter Finch. This English phenomenon is curious; you could go on talking about it for ages' (Truffaut 1988: 178).

References

Anderson, Benedict (1991), *Imagined Communities*, revised edition, New York, Verso.

Bordwell, David (1995), *Narration in the Fiction Film*, London, Routledge.

Gillain, Anne (1991), *François Truffaut – Le Secret perdu*, Paris, Hatier.

Hayward, Susan (1993), *French National Cinema*, London, Routledge.

Insdorf, Annette (1989), *François Truffaut*, New York, Simon and Schuster.

Truffaut, François (1975), *Les Films de ma Vie*, Paris, Flammarion.

—— (1986), *Hitchcock*, revised edition, Paris, Paladin.

—— (1987), *Le Plaisir des Yeux*, Paris, Flammarion.

—— (1988), *Le Cinéma selon François Truffaut*, ed. Anne Gillain, Paris, Flammarion.

Turner, Graeme (1993), *Film as Social Practice*, London, Routledge.

Zavarsadeh, Mas'ud (1991), *Seeing Films Politically*, Albany, NY, State University of New York Press.

–12–

Beineix's *Diva* and the
French Cultural Unconscious
John Izod

Jean-Jacques Beineix's *Diva* (1981) has a particular interest for the Jungian textual analyst in that it invites analysis by two different methods. One very potent element of its diegetic story world – the relationship between the principal protagonists Cynthia and Jules – responds splendidly to a classic reading of the archetypes of the type that Jung himself might have made. However, the diegesis as a whole is cast far wider – and embraces the interactions of a host of colourful and highly differentiated characters. This wider network of diverse characters and symbols is best analysed deploying ideas derived by his successors after Jung's death. The distinctive quality of the post-Jungian work in question is that it seeks to hold the cultural and the psychological in balance, presenting them as mutually influential.

As its title gives notice, *Diva* centres on an archetypal figure, the film's leading woman Cynthia Hawkins (Wilhelmenia Wiggins Fernandez). She is an artist with an extraordinarily fine voice, a hard-working and dedicated professional singer. As an archetypal figure in the Jungian sense, she is the focus of an energy that has the capacity to form powerful predispositions that can, when activated, govern human behaviour patterns. Jung referred to figures that have this power as archetypal images because, as contents just surfacing from the unconscious ('the treasure-house of primordial images'), they dress out the structuring energies latent in it, and make their hidden actuality knowable in the arena of consciousness (Jung 1968 [1954]: 4–5).

Cynthia Hawkins understands the passions that her voice arouses in her audiences. When her singing awakens deep emotions in a young admirer, Jules (Frédéric Andrei), her archetypal qualities are revealed and she takes on the mantle of the diva in an older sense of the word. She has become his goddess, his *anima*, and she soon recognizes that he wants from her more than any mortal woman can give. There are hints that this is not an unfamiliar experience for her. She is practised in dealing with the effect her voice has on others. However, as we eventually discover, she keeps hidden even from herself the feelings that her voice arouses in her own heart.

Jules attends (and secretly tapes) a performance in which Cynthia sings an aria from Alfredo Catalina's *La Wally*. In this, a tragic heroine seeks her death in the purity of mountain snows as the proper restitution for her broken heart. Such episodes of high melodrama are characteristic of the *anima* (no less than the *animus*). First, they occupy a rhetorical register that signals their importance to the recipient. And second, their heightened, overwrought quality (which may be, as with Cynthia, coupled with a distinctive radiance) embellishes the numinous energies – that vitality that appears to spring direct from the gods – to which they give form (Beebe 1992). Beineix prefers the heightened aesthetics of opera to flattened cinematic realism as a method of film-making (Auty 1982), and this style invites the reading offered here.

The *anima* is a contrasexual archetype, its counterpart being the *animus* in women. Frequently encountered in dreams and associations, the contrasexual archetype is often projected outwards upon living people. It represents those aspects of an individual that have the characteristics of the opposite sex and that he or she is unable to acknowledge in daily life. In a man, the *anima* typically presents herself in the form of a woman who stirs the emotions intensely. She does so precisely because she seems to promise an answer to his deeply felt need to complete himself – to find his other half. In representing a man's want to him, the archetype may present itself as a dream image of an imaginary woman; but often its power is projected upon an actual woman, so that she becomes inextricably wound into the man's fantasy life. The energy of the archetype charges her image with a magical force that makes her seem (either benignly or malevolently) divine.

Cynthia Hawkins is a benign *anima* to Jules. At 32, a full ten years older than him, she has a better understanding of what is moving him than he does himself. Nevertheless she is intrigued by him. Since, when seen in a Jungian context, the attraction between them resonates with undertones of incestuous desire, that theoretical context needs to be examined.

The son/mother incest theme concerns the maturation of the adolescent male's psyche. One way in which the completion of this process can be signified is through the young man's successful reframing of the mother image. A boy is drawn to his first and most potent *anima* in the image of the mother; but he has to break free from his fixation upon her if he is to achieve maturity. A straightforward example of such a plot is found in Bernardo Bertolucci's *La Luna* (1979). The dream or fictional configuration of mother–son incest has therefore a double-edged significance. On the positive side, a boy has much to draw from the mother in the nourishing of his feminine side. But on the contrary, negative side, should he not manage to break free, he risks being seduced into a lasting union with the image of his mother. That can bring about a stultification of his own psyche, subordinated to hers. Successful development can be indicated when the *anima* transfers away from the mother and takes a new form: in the heterosexual male, it often settles upon a young woman, who now becomes the object of his desire.

In the hero myth, the completion of a young man's successful transformation into adulthood is often signalled by his returning from the encounter with the mother bearing a trophy. The trophy symbolizes his having faced the danger of a prolonged incestuous union, and, rather than succumbing, having broken free, thereby winning the prize that is his newly made psyche. Jules does indeed hunt for trophies, but, in a variant of the traditional pattern, he steals them before he has earned them. He takes both Cynthia's robe and (by recording it) her voice. That these are sacramental thefts is indicated by his draping the robe around her picture on his wall, making it a shrine; also by the recording, which, whenever he replays it, engulfs both the characters and the audience with its voluptuous beauty. Because Jules has seized the trophies prematurely, far from freeing him, they bind him more tightly in Cynthia's thrall.

This becomes clear when Jules hires a prostitute to model the robe for him and finds it has lost its magical appeal when Cynthia is not wearing it. He takes it back to its owner and confronts her shyly. His odd mix of diffidence and boldness attracts Cynthia and they begin an intimate friendship. However, Jules comports himself more tentatively than might have been expected, largely through shame over his still unconfessed theft of her performance. But eventually this diffidence turns to their mutual advantage. Alerted by his guilty feelings to every nuance in her speech, he intuits that there is something excessive in Cynthia's distress when told by her manager that a good-quality pirate recording of her voice has been made. Refusing to sanction its release, she insists that her singing creates an experience of high art all the more intense because it cannot be reproduced. Jules, however, perceives that she is covering an unspoken fear beneath her anger. It helps him recognize his diva as a human no less vulnerable than everyone else. Risking everything, he plays his recording to Cynthia – and offers it as both his confession and his gift to her. Moved, she reveals that she has never heard her own glorious voice in playback,

Figure 18. *Diva* (1981), Jean-Jacques Beineix. Courtesy Museum of Modern Art, New York.

and this is the cause of her fear. As the determining factor in her life, her voice has become an overcharged *animus* that terrifies her through her certainty that it will eventually betray her when age steals it from her.

The *animus* often manifests (in the way Cynthia's image does for Jules) as the figure of a person of the opposite sex on whom psychic contents are projected. Although a gentle, affectionate *animus* is not uncommon in women's dreams and waking associations, *animus* problems are often represented through images of the overbearing father or brother, or the dominant (and sometimes promiscuous) lover – in short a male power-broker of some type. However, *animus* can equally well be displaced on to other, related phenomena (as can the *anima*); and Cynthia's voice is just such a depersonalized *animus* and has an authoritarian impact on her life. As such, it falls into a class well recognized in the literature of analytical psychology. Ann Ulanov says,

> Typical animus problems arise when there is insufficient conscious differentiation of the 'I' of the ego from the 'Thou,' or 'other,' of the animus. Where there is no separation of ego and animus, there is no conscious personal relationship to whatever the animus symbolizes. The woman opens her mouth, but the animus speaks (Ulanov 1971: 42).

If she becomes fixated in this state of being, the risk to which a woman is exposed is that the ego ends up serving the *animus* rather than the other way round, as should be the case (1971: 254). Then *animus* may take the form of an internal voice, the 'self-hater'. This phenomenon, which feminists believe to be a common internalized source of oppression of women in patriarchal societies, has the capacity to do severe damage to a woman's self-esteem by constantly undermining everything she hopes to value in herself (Wehr 1987: 18–19, 123). Cynthia's dissociation from her *animus* has not reached this stage, but it is a risk to which she would likely be exposed but for the self-recognition entailed in the discovery Jules forces upon her.

At this, its end, the film allows us to reverse perspective and see that from Cynthia's point of view, Jules also fulfils an archetypal role – although he does not complement her *anima* function by being her *animus*. Despite the contrary indications – namely that at his most gauche he is a somewhat inept lad with a romantic sensibility – Jules embodies an element of the divine. This is signalled through his work as a postman. It makes him a type of the messenger god, Hermes, two of whose roles are relevant here. First, he is the trickster: his unstable behaviour unsettles Cynthia, makes it more difficult for her to hold on to her set ideas, causes her pain, but ultimately releases her from her demon. Second, like Hermes, he is her guide, bringing her the revelation of how her own voice sounds to others, and with it access to a degree of self-knowledge she formerly lacked.

> Our egos, protected by the structures of time, space, and causality that hold them in place, can delay the gratification our contrasexuality brings . . . But they cannot hold anima and animus at bay forever.
> Anima and animus demand entry. Their purpose is to open in us a space for interior conversation, where we can consult ourselves about the things we most deeply desire, and those we most dread (Ulanov and Ulanov 1994: 222).

What Jules first stole from the goddess, he has now, asking her forgiveness, restored to the woman. The original theft of the tape and the robe, his attempt to grab a hero's trophies without earning them, was plainly unheroic. By restoring them, Jules shows that he has found another way to attain maturity than that of the embattled hero. Rather, he has come to know and accept the *anima*. As the film ends, the relationship between Cynthia and Jules is newly in balance. So too is the relation between the human and the divine, which is to say that the balance

Figure 19. *Diva* (1981), Jean-Jacques Beineix. Courtesy Museum of Modern Art, New York.

between the personal and the archetypal spheres has been restored in each of them.

So far so good, but in *Diva* there remain vivid features, such as its extraordinary, eye-catching imagery and its characters (for example, the psychotic criminal Le Curé). These are so strange that they cannot adequately be deciphered by reference to the norms of any genre, be it *policier*, gangster movie or romantic comedy – although there are points of reference to each of them.

The symbolic elements in *Diva* reflect a group unconscious centred on youth culture. The film has an obvious predecessor in Jean-Luc Godard's *A Bout de souffle* (1959), but the differences, no less than the resemblances, are informative. Both films show the infiltration of French culture by American iconography, and both feature a young American woman encountering France. In addition, both films are not only peopled by young heroes and heroines (with a few exceptions, the middle-aged characters tending to be outcasts), but they adopt a cinematic style that is fresh and invigorating and proclaims the novelty of youth. However, Godard's heroine Patricia (Jean Seberg) is a white tourist who has almost no knowledge of French language or culture (whether high art or popular).

She is in Paris to enjoy mildly rebellious kicks, and ekes out her itinerary with casual work selling *The Herald Tribune* on the streets. In contrast, Cynthia Hawkins is black, a competent French speaker, and has come to Paris to perform arias from European operas. Through her, *Diva* emphasizes a blending of cultures more complete than the forcible penetration of French ways by American style and values that interested Godard. Indeed, in *Diva* the seamless wedding of French and American culture is only the first symptom of cultural *mélange*. Overall, the film represents Paris as a vivid polyglot scene. Its juxtaposition of radically disparate cultures and styles has the impact of the surreal. The collision of elements runs through its *mise-en-scène*, its characters, the plots that weave them together, its visual and aural styles and finally its symbolism. The effect is to build an energy that the spectator experiences in watching the film and that our account of the contrasexual archetypal images has not fully explained.

As we have said, archetypal images have a universalizing potential, but they must also draw from the culture of a period if they are to communicate through its language and signifying systems. Therefore they take new shapes across the generations. Observation of their slow mutability is one of the factors that encouraged some of Jung's followers to modify his original model of the unconscious by introducing the concept of the *cultural unconscious*. This is thought of as an intermediate realm that links the collective and the personal unconscious. Here is the territory in which *symbols* operate, connecting the archetypal, the cultural and the personal.

At first sight, symbols seem very like archetypal images, and they do indeed partake of their qualities, being, for instance, charged with an intense energy whose source is not within the domain of consciousness. However, they do not share the universal quality of the archetypal image. To understand this, we need to know the specialized sense in which Jung used the term. The figure he termed the 'symbol' presents unconscious contents in a form that the conscious mind cannot immediately grasp, though it may eventually be able to apprehend them, if not without difficulty.

> The true symbol . . . should be understood as an expression of an intuitive idea that cannot yet be formulated in any other or better way (Jung 1966 [1931]: 70).

> It is 'the best possible expression for an unconscious content whose nature can only be guessed, because it is still unknown' (Jung 1968 [1954]: 6n).

Even a brief selection of the figurative components of *Diva* makes the point that it is laden with figures that are symbolic in Jungian terms. Jules's apartment is entered via an industrial freight lift that opens on to an area filled with the wrecks of luxury cars. We are dealing, he remarks enthusiastically, in disaster de luxe, a theme developed in his living space, which is hung with murals depicting cars as they might occur in a teenager's dream. Bulbous, oversexed American autos cruise palm-lined avenues; others hang like dirigibles in the sky; and all of them seem to thrust into Jules's living space. In some of the cars, ecstatic passengers seem to have found their ultimate delight; but a child is spilling out of another to her death.

The actual vehicles of the film's story world are no less strange. Jules's scooter sports a sound system that fills the streets with overtures to the operas. He rides it everywhere – into his apartment and (in flight from the villains) down beneath the streets and on to the Metro. His rescuer, the 'oneiric' Gorodish (Richard Bohringer) has a car that might have sprung direct from the dreams of a hero. It is a vintage Light 15 Citroen, in mint condition, a fitting mode of transport for the white knight that he is. When the villains blow it up, he calmly unveils an identical white car, and drives off in it. Wish fulfilment of a most magical order. Even the corrupt police Inspector Saporta gets around in a fantasy vehicle – a large American coupé. In this milieu, when the hired killer Le Curé (who drives a boring Renault) mumbles, 'I don't like cars,' it simply confirms his psychotic attitude to life.

The symbol frequently links the personal with the social and cultural because (unless confined to the secret dreams of an individual) it usually enters the public domain via one medium or another. And this returns us to the idea of the *cultural or group unconscious*. A number of post-Jungians have posited this concept as a means of refining Jung's model of the spheres of the unconscious. It explicitly opens Jungian theories of the psyche to the recognition that social and cultural pressures conjoin their considerable influence with many other factors in forming all but the deepest psychic images. The cultural unconscious has been described as the site of a collision of psychic energies from two separate origins – archetypal images having their source in the collective unconscious, and repressed contradictions from oppressive social formations. The horror movie is a good example of a site where such cultural repressions surface (Rushing and Frentz 1991: 391; Wood 1986: 75). But the cultural unconscious is also hypothesized as having two other functions. It appears to be both a repository of cultural experience, and the means, already existing as a potential, by which the human psyche gives birth to cultural difference and then reinforces it (Samuels 1993: 328).

In *Diva,* the entire city as *mise-en-scène* becomes a metaphor for the cultural unconscious of French youth. As our brief account of the some of its elements has already suggested, it is clearly a repository of cultural experience. A case in point is the representation of automobiles. In the 1950s, American cars (along with other American icons, none more than the movies) were treated as objects of desire in many French books and films. Godard's *A Bout de souffle* is simply one example among many of the tendency to mythologize the American car and way of life for a heady combination of connotations. They were taken to signify the emergence of a new young generation with a confident taste for speed, personal freedom and independence. And this was the case even when, as in *A Bout de souffle,* these same values were undermined by the romantic expectation that their ultimate outlet was likely to be a James Dean-like immolation of youthful purity in a highway pile-up (Ross 1996: 15–54). Beineix's representation picks up this mythology and changes it. American cars of the 1950s still have a mythic quality about them; but they are associated with death and disaster – both in Jules's apartment and in the fact that the murderous Inspector Saporta drives one. Now the desired dream machine is a pristine 1950s French car which, for the film, combines elegance with the sense of its having sprung from a classic age. Today's domestic product, the Renault, is Le Curé's transport – not only boring, but also battered and rendered largely impracticable by the volume of traffic. It adds to the mythology of the white Citroen that it enjoys a freedom of movement impossible in the Paris of the 1980s. But for mortals who lack the enchanted powers of the white knight, Jules' scooter is an altogether more effective machine for threading (and linking together) the many sectors of Paris that he visits.

Like many narratives that have as a major strand the uncovering of a crime, *Diva* is also a site where the culturally repressed emerges. There are plenty of characters whose disposition illustrates this point. The personality traits of the malicious Inspector Saporta (Jacques Fabbri) are just the opposite of those inherent in 'saporita' – which means tasty or witty. With his saturnine disposition and his ruthless destruction of all those who (whatever their service to him in the past) no longer feed his appetite for the corrupt abuse of power, Saporta survives by deception. He is not as visibly demonic a figure as his sidekick, on to whom his evil characteristics are displaced. But the eye-catching killer Le Curé (Dominique Pinon) displays his boss's monstrosity beautifully. Under his bald beetle dome and with his wrap-around sunglasses like a ball-goer's mask, he could have stepped out of Breughel's vision of hell. His words are limited to the curt dismissal of all things: 'J'aime pas ça!' And his speciality is murder by stiletto. The two Thai audio pirates are equivalent types, their coldness and their eyes blanked off by baleful sunglasses being shorthand ways of signifying that they too belong to the shadow group.

Nevertheless, all that has been said so far does not do enough fully to explain the enticing weirdness of this bewitching film. I want to suggest that there is a further function of symbol play in operation here. Jung argued that symbols have the capacity to initiate change in the psyche: because they compensate for the inevitable biases of the conscious mind, they point 'to the onward course of life, beckoning the libido towards a still distant goal' (Jung 1976 [1921]: 125). This occurs because symbols represent in darkly metaphorical form material that previously was hidden in the unconscious, so that the conscious mind can strive to grasp it and enhance knowledge of the self. Extrapolate this from the personal sphere of the individual to the cultural realm where large groups of people share comparable experiences of symbolic material (as do the fans of film stars), and Jung's observation consorts well with Samuels's suggestion that the cultural unconscious is the means by which the human psyche gives birth to cultural difference and then reinforces it (Samuels 1993: 328).

Figure 20. *Diva* (1981), Jean-Jacques Beineix. Courtesy Museum of Modern Art, New York.

It is possible to point to some of the characters as having this function, their metaphorical role being indicated by their surreal behaviour. When we first see Gorodish, he appears to be a social drop-out dedicating his life to solipsistic pleasures. He passes the first half of the plot (his cool period) in his open-space apartment, which is as big as a warehouse. Enveloped by blue objects and light, he divides his time between meditation, completing a vast jigsaw puzzle, and creating the perfect baguette sandwich. But, called on to rescue Jules from the gangs that pursue him, he shows the skills of a formidable military strategist, and becomes both the white knight who lays waste to evil, and also the young man's mentor. In the event, Gorodish, as a type of the wise older man, contributes his spirituality and his severe practicality as a role model.

However, Gorodish's role would not be profiled so starkly were it not for the counterpoint provided by his Vietnamese lover. Alba (Thuy An Luu) becomes Jules's friend. A common interest in petty larceny brings this pair together, but they also share the experience of being in love with an older person. Their friendship allows them the chance to chatter uninhibitedly and behave like other teenagers, a freedom that is inhibited in their amorous relationships. Alba's role thus counterpoints that of Cynthia. Although a potential *anima* figure for Jules, she does not play that part, being instead the canny assistant who augments Gorodish's magical powers in looking after Jules. Gorodish and Alba teach Jules to look beyond himself. Alba does so through her capacity for joy. And the two together offer Jules their strategic and tactical shrewdness and their wit.

The structure of the film is startling and charged with energy that the narrative itself does not fully absorb. This is one factor triggering the spectator's appetite to explore its symbolism. The action consists of clashing elements, there being four dissonant plot threads. Plot A is that of Jules and Cynthia. Plot B concerns the corrupt chief of police, Saporta, the thugs whom he uses to control his ring of Caribbean prostitutes, and the inept cops he bamboozles so that they fail to identify their boss as the master criminal they are hunting. Plot C features the sinister pair of Taiwanese bent on getting hold of Jules's recording of Cynthia and selling it on the pirate market. The characters in the latter two plots literally get in the way of each other as the two gangs of villains pursue Jules for two quite different tapes – the one he knows he has of Cynthia and another he does not know about that incriminates Saporta. But it is Plot D that weaves the others together: Gorodish, replete with wisdom, knowledge and wry humour, gains entry into all their worlds and succeeds stylishly (almost effortlessly, just like a fantasy knight in shining armour) in eradicating the villains.

Another factor triggering the spectator's appetite to explore *Diva's* symbolism is the element of fantasy. The vivid representation of colliding worlds, both in picture, story and accompanying music, has a great impact on spectators. It frees those representations from old cultural connections and produces new associations to seduce spectators' libido. The latter are deliciously battered by the film's exuberant surrealism; its insistent colour coding through blue and white; its unexpected icons; the overlay of classical music on to pop visuals. All these jarring components cohere in a highly tensioned unity. The factor that tends to pull them apart is obviously enough their extreme diversity. What makes for coherence has two main ingredients. The first is the characters' own acceptance of the fragmented worlds they pass through. The key figure in this is Jules. All the action centres on him, and, despite the boyish excess of his passion for Cynthia, he has a personality as normal as can be imagined in this milieu. The second is the delight in its fantasy world that the film communicates to audiences. It endows the diegesis with a persuasive virtual reality, which can be understood as the beginning of an emerging cultural differentiation.

As Auty says, *Diva* is a traditional morality tale in modern garb (Auty 1982). Its surrealism encourages us to extend our reading beyond morality, through myth, and thence to psychology. All told, what we see and hear is a dynamic psychodrama peopled, lit, coloured, and resounding with motifs that are energized with a symbolic charge. No one character or motif dominates the others – all are present in roughly equal vigour. The bright and the dark elements are locked together in conflict as countertypes producing what Jung would have termed a *conjunctio oppositorum*. Such a conjunction is a classic representation of the psyche in which conscious and unconscious are in balance. In *Diva* it allows those who respond to the film to see and feel that knowledge of all the passions, both noble and ignoble, is necessary to the well-balanced psyche. The *conjunctio* penetrates even into the magic inner circle that Cynthia and Jules inhabit. Jules is not immune from temptation, since he, like several of the villains, indulges in theft (albeit of a special kind). And for her part, Cynthia conceals a terror of her shadow side.

As a vehicle for the cultural unconscious, *Diva* is unusually generous. Through both its characters and its scintillating aesthetics, the film summons the young of heart – the audience with whom it might resonate – as a repository of Parisian cultural experience, both lived and virtual. Audiences are invited to bear witness that full human development demands exposure to many aspects of culture – both light and dark, joyous and potentially murderous. Despite the darker elements it contains, *Diva* is buoyant with an effulgent and emotional optimism that its soundtrack insists upon. In sum, it is not merely about the cultural unconscious of the young, it invites the audience to assimilate the register and to enter, at least virtually in heart and mind, that social group itself.

References

Auty, Martin (1982), 'Breathless: *Diva*', *Sight and Sound,* 51 (4): 302.

Beebe, John (1992), 'The Anima in Film,' on Don Williams's web site 'C. G. Jung, Analytical Psychology, and Culture,' http://www.cgjung. com/films.

Jung, C. G. (1966 [1931]), 'On the Relation of Analytical Psychology to Poetry', in *The Collected Works,* Vol. 15: *The Spirit in Man, Art and Literature,* London, Routledge & Kegan Paul.

—— 1968 (1954), 'Archetypes of the Collective Unconscious', in *The Collected Works,* Vol. 9 (1): *The Archetypes and the Collective Unconscious*, 2nd edn, London, Routledge & Kegan Paul.

—— (1976 [1921]), *The Collected Works,* Vol. 6: *Psychological Types,* rev edn, Princeton, NJ, Princeton University Press.

Ross, Kristin (1996), *Fast Cars, Clean Bodies: Decolonization and the Reordering of French Culture,* Cambridge, MA, MIT Press.

Rushing, Janice Hocker and Thomas S. Frentz (1991), 'Integrating Ideology and Archetype in Rhetorical Criticism', *Quarterly Journal of Speech* 77 (3) (November): 385–406.

Samuels, Andrew (1993), *The Political Psyche,* London: Routledge.

Ulanov, Ann Belford (1971), *The Feminine in Jungian Psychology and in Christian Theology,* Evanston, IL, Northwestern University Press.

—— and Ulanov, Barry (1994), *Transforming Sexuality: The Archetypal World of Anima and Animus*, London: Shambhala.

Wehr, Demaris S. (1987), *Jung and Feminism: Liberating Archetypes,* Boston, Beacon Press.

Wood, Robin (1986), *Hollywood from Vietnam to Reagan,* New York, Columbia University Press.

–13–

Negotiating Conformity:
Tales of Ordinary Evil
Martine Beugnet

Some of cinema's most enduring and popular genres – *film noir*, horror, thrillers – are specifically designed to cater for our fascination with evil; a fascination that feeds on a combination of repulsion and attraction, of abjection and desire. In the *Powers of Horror*, Julia Kristeva defines the abject as that which dissolves the 'I', or 'pulverises the subject', an 'ever present' that 'repels but beseeches', that which 'disturbs identity, systems, order. What does not respect borders, positions, rules' (Kristeva 1982: 4). The compulsion to investigate evil corresponds to this attraction towards that which pushes and destroys the boundaries established by social and moral structures and fundamentally questions the nature of human identity and behaviour. But, as the conclusion of *Dr Petiot* (Christian de Challonges, 1991) emphasizes, it is in vain that one searches for a definite answer: the criminal takes his secret to the grave, and evil remains ultimately incomprehensible.[1] As common systems of thought – logic, ethics, functionalism – fail to grasp it and define it completely, the understanding of evil is endlessly delayed, echoing the patterns of the desiring process (like the strategies of delayed reward and resolution that narrative film exploits so efficiently) and its resulting relations of dependency and power.

Yet, and for all its elusiveness and mystery, in its various manifestations and appearances, evil is never ahistorical, nor is it detached from a wider context of social, economical and cultural realities. As the fragmented narrative of *J'ai pas Sommeil* (Claire Denis, 1994) illustrates, only one, in a group of individuals from the same background placed in similar circumstances, will become a dangerous criminal; but to focus solely on this aspect of the film is to deny an uncomfortable but crucial connection of evil with a social system and its strategies of representation.

The role of the unfathomable makes representations of evil into privileged sites for the projection of deep-rooted fears and frustrations.

As expressions of intolerable yet compulsive impulses, and as ventures into the realm of the forbidden, incarnations of evil necessarily evoke in some way the social and moral anxiety of a particular time. On the one hand, fiction films present us with representations of evil that are informed both by the necessity to attract and entertain an audience, and by the self-referential nature of a cinematic language that relies to varying degrees on established conventions. However, on the other hand, as Robin Buss remarks: '. . . if it seems to overstretch the significance of a 100 min. crime thriller, one can only say that it is more than improbable to suppose that genre films will not reflect something of the morality of their time' (Buss 1994: 145).

In French cinema, where the criminal remains a key figure, this central but changing connection between representation and potential significance in terms of historical and socio-cultural context becomes apparent when looking at the *mise-en-scène* of evil and its implications in terms of power relations and representations of class, gender and race.

In the French cinematic tradition, the incarnation of crime and evil has links with several apparently contradictory trends that are in fact connected by a tendency, both on the level of the narrative and of character development, to focus on the criminal rather than on the representatives and enforcers of law and order. Departing from a long-standing tradition drawing on concepts of evil as a form of human transcendence and provocation, French cinema is rich in representations of evil as banal – the mere expression of the spirit of a particular era – on the one hand, and as manifestation of apparently repressed but ineluctable, deadly traits of the human psyche on the other.[2] Hence, the figure of the criminal traditionally becomes the site of a tension that in turn can generate a greater potential for empathy or for positive identification. In this approach, perhaps best exemplified by the films of Claude Chabrol, but also by the work of Louis Malle – witness in particular the controversies spurred by the portrayal of a serial killer in *Le Boucher*, 1970, and of a young Gestapo member in *Lacombe Lucien*, 1974 – the criminal hero or anti-hero is portrayed both as a victim of a social system and as prey to the primitive, darker drives inherent in human nature.

In the sample of films discussed below, some of these traits are still important, yet, through specific stylistic approaches, all three films display an interest in the figure of the criminal as a manifestation of a lack, and in exploring its potential significance in terms of critical discourse.

Chabrol's 1995 crime drama, *La Cérémonie*, includes many familiar elements of the director's long-standing exploration of evil and crime. In particular, alongside a precise deconstruction of a social system of class-based, banal exploitation, the film plays on the suggestion of the dormant, fundamentally unruly and amoral nature of humanity, which the director famously illustrated in *Le Boucher*, 1970. However, *La Cérémonie* also testifies to a recent shift in the representation of crime and evil: the increasing 'opacity' that surrounds the central characters undermines conventional patterns of 'alignment and recognition' (according to Murray Smith's definition, the processes of identification through the recognition of motives and of expressed emotions (Smith 1995)). Where Popaul, the serial killer of *Le Boucher*, cut a versatile figure – a sometimes threatening presence, but also a sympathetic and charming man, and, ultimately, a tortured soul – the ironically named Sophie Bonhomme, the heroine of *La Cérémonie* and the murderess of a family of four, is an impassive figure devoid of natural grace. The closing image of the film is a close-up on her face as she faces arrest. Her features, delineated against a background of complete darkness, yield no information and little emotion. Stripped of its conventional function as a trigger of identification or recognition, here the close-up becomes synonymous with a glimpse of a void.

The scenario, an adaptation of a Ruth Rendell novel, depicts the arrival of a new maid in the house of a well-to-do family, and progressively builds towards the final showdown, and the collective killing of the Lelièvre family by Sophie and her friend Jeanne. As Frédéric Strauss, writing in *Les Cahiers du cinéma*, describes it:

> *La Cérémonie* is a diabolical film, which, almost silently, and without ever raising the tone of the dialogues, constructs a violent universe, ordered around the beauty and harmony cultivated by the bourgeois *art de vivre*, and created by a perfectly structured mise-en-scène. [. . .] In the mise-en-scène, Chabrol reproduces the ritual of the waiting at the table, in its most coercive sense [. . .] – as Mr Lelièvre humorously comments, 'she must be taught how to *serve*' (Strauss 1995: 25).

The very first scene, the interview and hiring of Sophie by Mme. Lelièvre, already contains most of the elements that are at the core of the film's thematic and aesthetic structure. The first image of Sophie Bonhomme is a silhouette bleached by the outside light, and seen through the window of a café. While across the street the young woman asks the way, like early visual clues of miscomprehension and alienation, the writings on the window, seen in reverse, superimpose themselves on to the image, palimpsest-like. The camera takes the point of view of Mme. Lelièvre who, already settled at a table, observes Sophie's progression, and eventually beckons her, without standing up, to a seat in front of her. The setting – a bar-brasserie – is one of ordinary conviviality; yet, the atmosphere is steeped in uneasiness, as Sophie's awkwardness contrasts with Lelièvre's vague attempts at friendliness, and her spontaneously commanding manner. The shots alternate between transversal, objective views of the two women facing each other across the table that separates them, and a series of shot/counter-shots where Lelièvre's point of view tends to be slightly higher, domineering. The dialogue precisely maps out the tensions (Sophie's abrupt interruption when Mme. Lelièvre starts talking about an art gallery, or her reminder to her forgetful employer about the issue of the wages), each gesture is carefully choreographed, and the images are dotted with small clues to and warning signs of the presence of a threat (Sophie's gloved hands; a flash of the word *noir* written in gold). In the following sequence, when Mme. Lelièvre comes to collect the new maid at the train station, Sophie Bonhomme is not placed 'where she should be' – she appears on the 'wrong' platform.

Sophie cannot read, and her illiteracy, a sign of her deep social and cultural alienation, is not limited to the written word. The characterization suggests that the young woman has not had the opportunity to learn the language of sociability and of emotions. By implication, she has not been given the tools to analyse her situation, and has little means of articulating the frustration and anger that may arise from her condition. Television takes the familiar role of a provider of relief and of a numbing device, but even here, in the realm of traditionally popular mass entertainment, the social gap becomes obvious. For Sophie, the experience of this form of spectacle is hypnotic. Seated too close to the old TV set that has been placed in her maid's room, her viewing is one of undifferentiated captivation. Oblivious of their impending fate, in their expansive living-room, the Lelièvres organize their television evening as a familial event, gathering in front of the high-tech wide screen to watch the live broadcast of an opera. The Lelièvres are not portrayed as 'bad', neither are they unsympathetic characters. Rather, as their occasional patronizing attempts at engaging with their new maid outside the mode of 'service' are nullified by their indifference and blindness, they follow the easier course of unquestioned, 'naturalized' privilege and organized exploitation. The Lelièvres' culpability is *sui generis* – it derives simply from their unquestioning existence as representatives of a particular social hierarchy – hence the ritualistic aspect and symbolic dimension of their final obliteration suggested by the film's title and underlined by its *mise-en-scène*.[3] Jokingly, to watch the opera on television, the Lelièvres (the name derives from 'hare') have dressed as for a night out, unknowingly preparing themselves for the ultimate ceremonial, before they place themselves in front of the camera, on display as in a *tableau.*

Yet, and despite a *mise-en-scène* that functions like a precisely designed metaphor of social inequality and power, the emerging elements of an essentialist discourse work as a counterpoint to the film's critical stance: the film includes aspects of the stereotypical portrayal of female friendship as sexualized and threatening, with Jeanne as a reminder of the 'female *castratrice*'. This aspect of the scenario becomes most strikingly apparent in one of the sequences preceding the murder scene. Laughing hysterically, Jeanne is shown soiling the matrimonial bed in the Lelièvre's bedroom, placing a jug of hot chocolate between her legs to suggest a man urinating.

Such essentialist themes, recurrent and particularly prominent in the work of Chabrol, do not appear to be a dominant element in contemporary French cinema's representations of evil. Films as stylistically different as *J'ai pas Sommeil*, and *Dr Petiot* focus, as does *La Cérémonie*, on the criminal figure as the embodiment of a lack, but resolutely exclude the essentialist component from their portrayal of serial killers.

In Christian de Challonges' *Dr Petiot*, 1990, it is the symbolic function of the criminal character as a cipher, the incarnation of the *Zeitgeist*, that is developed through a defined formal approach. As the film illustrates, the banality of evil, a dominant aspect and almost a cliché in French cinema's representation of crime, often leads back to the experience of the Second World War. The long years of conflict and the advent of the Occupation brought about an atmosphere of suspicion and debasement particularly marked in the occupied countries: anyone could be a traitor, a collaborator, a nazi, or could be accused of having in some way colluded with the greatest horror, that of the Holocaust. The aftermath of the war, with its interminable unravelling of tales of abomination, impressed further a strong feeling of evil's endless depth and, at the same time, of its closeness and ordinariness. *Dr Petiot* interestingly combines such a representation of evil with an aesthetic approach derived from early expressionism. Based on real events, the film centres on the character of a serial killer who, under the guise of smuggling them out of the occupied area, robs and murders Jewish people. Through the characterization, and through significant stylistic choices, evil is doubly represented as a reflection of the mores of the age, with Petiot as an incarnation of the spirit of the period. In its expressive use of a dark colour palette, of lighting, contrasts and shadows, in the privileging of nocturnal scenes, and choice of sets (graveyards, bourgeois houses still clad in the obsolete lushness of the previous century, empty windy streets and expanses of old, disused industrial buildings), the film draws inspiration from the

German expressionist aesthetic in order to conjure up the claustrophobic atmosphere of occupied France during the Second World War and the sinister character of Petiot. The actor's expressionist make-up and his performance – his stare and slightly jerky movements – also evoke the silent films of the pre-war period. The film presents us with a chameleon-like character, a man who seemingly lacks a proper personality, but shows a remarkable ability to take on any guise required for his most efficient survival in given circumstances. Petiot the serial killer is also an efficient and dedicated doctor, an affectionate father-figure to ill children and to his own son, and an apparently trustworthy member of the resistance, before becoming, after the liberation, a respected officer of the French army, in charge of questioning collaborators. As an individual, Petiot is a 'void'; his behaviour and actions are determined by his environment, and his only extra-ordinary quality is this capacity to 'blend in' with a context that calls equally for the ordinary, the heroic and the abject sides of man.

But the style of *Dr Petiot* is atypical. The driving trends of the 1990s have been marked by a return to the realist approach, with crime films often drawing on realism and on the documentary approach while still borrowing from the conventions of established genres. *J'ai pas Sommeil*, for instance, draws upon the *film noir* to explore intricate connections of race and social alienation. Not only does the title suggest its affiliation with the genre, but the film also follows the *noir* conventions of the urban setting and favours artificial light, and scenes shot at night or during the uncertain hours of dawn and sunset. It also features a jazz-mambo score that is both exotic and nostalgic, underlying the desire for escape on the part of some of the characters. *J'ai pas Sommeil* is an equivocal cinematic universe, where secure moral judgement gives way to an atmosphere of social malaise and fatality (the murderers do not take precautions to avoid arrest). The subject of the film is highly controversial, and could be described not only as a 'gift to homophobia', but also to racism. Inspired by a real case, the complex narrative structure of *J'ai pas Sommeil* revolves around the crimes of Camille, a young black man of Martiniquan origins, who is gay and HIV-positive, and who murders old women. In an interview, Claire Denis remarked:

> The terms politically correct or incorrect were constantly present in the idea of the film. I knew I could not follow these concepts, even though they could not be dissociated from a character who kills more than twenty old ladies – amongst the most vulnerable members of society – and who is black, homosexual, and takes drugs. It was the absolute opposite to what black characters should be according to the conventions of the politically correct (Denis 1994: 27).

These remarks about the film's controversial thematic premise echo Richard Dyer's comments on Jean Genet's work as often seen as ' a gift to homophobia, easily appropriated as the living proof of how sick, neurotic and degraded homosexuals are' (Dyer 1990: 75). But the analogy does not hold: in *J'ai pas Sommeil*, the criminal's actions bear none of the provocative overtones that characterize Genet's work. Commenting on the novel *Querelle de Brest* (1953), in which Genet depicts the systematic decline of the young sailor Querelle – a traitor, a criminal and a murderer – Dyer underlines how through such a character, Genet takes the stance of one who 'fully accepts his social designation and lives it out defiantly. You say this is what I am, OK, that is what I am, and I am going to be it to the hilt' (Dyer 1990: 75). Indeed, it is Genet's belief in the existing order of things that gives its force to the provocation: 'The elements of evil, criminality and homosexuality are inextricably entwined in this tradition [. . .]. It is Genet's acceptance of the truth of the Christian moral order that gives his work its special intensity' (Dyer 1990: 61). In contrast, *J'ai pas Sommeil* appears as a complex exploration of a perverted drive to conformity.

Despite its central subject, the film is not constructed like an investigation of a serial killer's case. Although, as a performer (he performs in a nightclub), Camille may offer himself to the gaze of an audience and to the gaze of the camera, in many shots the objective is 'too close', and the young man's body often blocks out part of the frame, becoming obtrusive. Camille remains elusive, an unfathomable, 'opaque' presence. As Denis explains, 'Even when you read reports of the trial, in such cases, the opacity remains [. . .], and it is through the bystanders – witnesses, policemen, and most importantly the family – that the criminal is discussed' (Denis 1994: 27).

'Is Mummy here?': the first sentence uttered by the character is the most innocuous of questions, addressed to a young child. Like the Dr Petiot of the Christian de Challonges film, Camille is a versatile and changing character, occasionally affectionate, a soft-spoken, soft-mannered man, but prone to angry outbursts. While the character's personality escapes definition, the film does not linger on his crimes either. The scenes of the murders are consciously shot in a 'flat', detached manner, in medium, static shots and long takes, so as not to invite a voyeuristic gaze:

> It was impossible to avoid the scenes of the murders, and you could not mask them, hide them behind a door, a table or in a corner; they had to be shot in full view. At the same time, they had to be shot in one take, otherwise it is disgusting, and not very moral: it would be embellishing violence (Denis 1994: 26).

Absence and lack are at the centre of the film's thematic, but are counterpointed by an accumulation of clues – comments, often visual, often implied, on the social, psychological and physical environment of the characters – that are woven together to form the basis of the narration. Like the characterization and *mise-en-scène*, the narrative underlines the elusiveness of the serial killer's personality, but through its multifaceted structure builds an impressionistic and complex picture of the context. Behind a seductive but shallow surface of cosmopolitanism, glittering night-lights and picturesque settings, the Paris of *J'ai pas Sommeil* is also a place of alienation and non-communication, of routine intolerance, implicit racism and hidden domestic violence. Behind the 'buzz', it is a city inhabited by a crowd of isolated individuals, lonely old women and ineffectual, prejudiced policemen, a place where bodies rather than souls are being exchanged and sold, and where churches are tourist attractions.

Camille's first appearance occurs in a short, mostly silent scene, which shows him having a violent altercation with his lover Raphaël. The motif of the argument is never elucidated, but the setting and *mise-en-scène* are significant. The scene takes place in the early hours, presumably at the end of a night out. The fighting is accompanied by the sound of a refuse truck. As the vehicle, with its all-black crew of early morning workers, passes Camille, the national flag, hung on the façade of the local town hall, flaps discreetly in the background. Thus, the composition briefly comes together like a passing comment on Roland Barthes' famous analysis of a *Paris Match* cover, which describes the propagandistic image of a black soldier proudly saluting the French flag (Barthes 1957: 189).

As in *Short Cuts* (Robert Altman, 1993), the story is populated by a multitude of characters whose paths only occasionally cross, but whose experiences are paralleled. Amongst others, the camera follows a young woman, recently arrived from Lithuania and hired as a cleaner in a small hotel, and Camille's brother, a jazz musician and the father of a young child, who moonlights to make a living. Whereas such characters are shown struggling with feelings of entrapment and alienation, Camille conforms to the rules of a Parisian shady world into which he can integrate, provided he can afford a way of life based on expensive pleasures and appearances.

In his 'looks', Camille likes to play on overtones of darkness and evil, and when he buys an expensive, tailor-made suit in a specialized shop, he regrets not being able to afford an all-leather outfit: it is the costume, the appearance, that yields authenticity and value. The propensity to take on guises, the transvestite performances, and the obsessive narcissism all hint at the existence of a basic lack at the core of the character. In contrast with his brother, who, through his music and his desire to raise his son in his country of origin, nurses a nostalgic, perhaps illusory, connection with his cultural roots, Camille appears to have little interest in the past. His ability to 'identify' with the masks suggested by his environment recalls Frantz Fanon's analysis of the black man's neurosis in *Black Skins, White Masks* (1967). In the psychoanalyst's study, the neurosis stems from the contradictory situation of the black man who has to integrate into a white society that largely defines itself precisely in opposition to the 'Other', to himself.[4] By contrast with the deeds of Querelle, Camille's crimes are not acts of defiance. Rather, as with the fashion-obsessed young murderers of Bertrand Tavernier's *L'Appât* (*The Bait*, 1994), they are gruesome but logical expressions of a desire to participate fully in a materialistic system, of an overriding drive to conform.

Death, in *J'ai pas Sommeil*, bears no overtone of transcendence. At the end of film, as the police inspector who interrogates him reads aloud the serial killer's list of crimes, it is the seemingly endless repetition that gives the recitation its horrific quality. The choice of victims, old women who live alone, is symptomatic of a system of social alienation where the most vulnerable members of society are also the most isolated. But it also calls to mind Richard Dyer's suggestion that in white Western cultures, '. . . the suspicion of nothingness and the death of whiteness is, as far as white identity goes, the cultural dominant of our times, that we really do feel we are played out' (Dyer 1997: 217). Significantly, *J'ai pas Sommeil*'s murderer never strikes alone: in spite of his angelic name, his white lover and accomplice Raphaël accompanies him to the end, mirroring Camille's movements like a white shadow.

In Norman Denzin's definition of the postmodern socio-cultural state, the overriding dominance of the late capitalist mode in all aspects of life (materialism replacing other schools of thoughts and codes of morals) is combined with the lack of access, in large parts of the social strata, to a world driven by consumption and the defining role of the image, and logically leads to a culture of violence:

> It is an emotional mood systematically produced by those social structures, including the social democracies, which espouse the equality of rights for all, but permits wide gaps between expectations and what is in fact received. [. . .] Resentment is greatest when self or group injury is experienced as destiny and beyond one's control. In such moments, the other is transformed into an object deserving revenge and violence (Denzin 1991: 55).

Because it is a type of character whose behaviour is not confined to the familiar mode of cause and effect, the figure of the psychotic criminal holds a privileged position in the systems of representation that both exploit and cater for a 'culture of resentment'. For even the violence of a serial killer can be submitted to the visual and narrative treatment needed for the production of such forms of entertainment, which 'build on malice and revenge, and form as a joy at another's misfortune' (Denzin 1991: 54), while avoiding any proper mention (let alone a critical one) of the possible sources of anger and social tension.

Yet, particularly in a cinematic world where it appears in all its elusiveness and versatility, the figure of the psychotic criminal necessarily conjures up questions and doubts. As an evil character who does not offer the safe backdrop of rationality – of fully explained motives – but instead an abject presence that cannot be dismissed as a self-contained pheno-menon, the psychotic criminal becomes the incarnation of a lack, which in turn invites the questioning of a wider context.

It is this present-*absence*, which signals the increasing presence of a 'lack' in the cinematic representation of the evil, criminal figure, and the masking of this void by processed images, pre-existing roles, expressions and attitudes, that arguably give the films their postmodern feel. Yet, again, it is an absence that calls for the questioning of a wider context. Thomas Docherty contrasts previous forms of fiction, which identified 'change as something that always happens at the level of the individual rather than in the wider socio-political formation itself' with a postmodern characterization that 'seeks to return the dimension of history which earlier modes of characterization, or of the theoretical understanding of character as "identity", deny' (Docherty 1996: 59). While dealing with the elusive nature of evil, such films position the characters in precisely depicted environments, and rather than falling back on the portrayal of violence as a spectacle in itself, redirect attention towards the reassessment of the larger social, economic, and cultural context.

French cinema's most recent representations of the evil criminal may still rely on the suggestion of the existence of darker drives inherent in the nature of human beings; but increasingly, the criminal figure takes on the role of a sign, a warning. Its presence has ceased to express defiance, nor does it encourage subversive strategies, or connect with politics of resistance: on the contrary, in the most horrific way, it conforms to the logic of its environment. A symptom of a wider social malaise, the psycho-killer of contemporary French cinema becomes monstrous in the postmodern sense: behind a presence that evokes a lack, the representation of an absence, lurk disturbing forms of hyperconformity.

Notes

1. The concluding caption recounts how, after hearing the verdict of the jury that condemned him to death for the tens of murders he committed, Petiot was asked by the judge whether he had an ultimate declaration to make and replied, 'I always travel with my luggage.'
2. As in the literary tradition set by the work of authors such as Charles Baudelaire, le Comte de Lautréamont, Georges Bataille, and in the writings and films of Jean Genet. Early on, the films of Louis Feuillade also based their appeal on such representations of evil.
3. 'In Marxist terms: it is through its social status (*état*) that it [the bourgeois family] can be attacked': Interview with Claude Chabrol, *Cahiers du Cinéma* 494, September 1995, pp. 27–8.
4. . . . 'himself': as in many founding psychoanalytical studies, the issue of the woman's status (in the case of the black woman, that of a double alienation) is brushed aside.

References

Barthes, Roland (1957), *Mythologies*, Paris, Editions du Seuil.

Buss, Robin (1994), *French Film Noir*, London, Marion Boyars.

Denis, Claire (1994), Interview, *Cahiers du cinéma* no. 479 (April).

Denzin, Norman K. (1991), *Images of Postmodern Society: Social Theory and Contemporary Cinema*, London, Sage.

Docherty, Thomas (1996), *Alterities*, Oxford, Clarendon Press.

Dyer, Richard (1990), *Now You See It: Studies on Lesbian and Gay Film*, London, Routledge.

—— (1997), *White*, London, Routledge.

Fanon, Frantz (1967), *Black Skin, White Masks*, trans. Charles Markman, New York, Grove Press.

Kristeva, Julia (1982), *The Powers of Horror*, trans. Léon S. Roudiz, New York, Columbia University Press.

Smith, Murray (1995), *Engaging Characters: Fiction, Emotion, and the Cinema*, Oxford, Clarendon Press.

Strauss, Frédéric (1995), 'Les dits commandements', *Cahiers du cinéma* no. 494 (September).

Filmography

Abbreviations:
sc: screenplay
c: camera
l.p.: leading players
r: running time
p: producer
col.: colour
b/w: black-and-white

Chantal Akerman
Jeanne Dielmann, 23 Quai du Commerce 1080 Bruxelles
sc: Chantal Akerman − *c*: Babette Mangolte − *l.p.*: Delphine Seyrig, Henri Storck, Jacques Doniol-Valcroze, Yves Bical − *r*: 225 min., col. − *p*: Paradise Films/Unité Trois 1975

René Allio
Moi Pierre Rivière, ayant égorgé ma mère, ma sœur, mon frère
sc: René Allio, Jean Jourdheuil, Serge Toubiana, from a text by Michel Foucault − *c*: Nurith Aviv *l.p.*: Claude Hébert, Jacqueline Millière, Joseph Leportier, Annick Gehan, Nicole Gehan, Emilie Lihou, Antoine Bourseiller, Michel Amphoux − *r*: 125 min., col. − *p*: René Feret/Les Films Arquebuse 1976

Jacques Becker
Goupi Mains-Rouges
sc: Pierre Véry, from his novel − *c*: Pierre Montazel − *l.p.*: Fernand Ledoux, Robert le Vigan, Georges Rollin, Blanchette Brunoy, Germaine Kerjean, Line Noro, Marcelle Hainia − *r*: 104 min., b/w − *p*: Minerva 1942

Jean-Jacques Beineix
Diva
sc: Jean-Jacques Beineix, Jean Van Hamme, from the novel by Delacorta − *c*: Phillipe Rousselot − *l.p.*: Wilheminia Wiggins Fernandez, Frédéric

Andréi, Richard Bohringer, Thuy Ann Luu – *r*: 115 min., col. – *p*: Irène Silberman/Films Galaxie/Greenwich Film Production with the participation of Antenne 2 1981

Yannick Bellon
La Femme de Jean
sc: Yannick Bellon – *c*: Georges Barsky – *l.p.*: France Lambiotte, Claude Rich, Hippolyte, James Mitchell – *r*: 103 min., col. – *p*: Films de l'Equinoxe 1974

Vera Belmont
Rouge Baiser
sc: Vera Belmont – *c*: Ramon Suarez – *l.p.*: Charlotte Valandrey, Lambert Wilson, Marthe Keller, Laurent Terzieff, Gunter Lamprecht – *r*: 112 min., col. – *p*: Vera Belmont 1985

Claude Berri
Germinal
sc: Claude Berri, Arlette Langmann, from the novel by Emile Zola – *c*: Yves Angelo – *l.p.*: Renaud, Gérard Depardieu, Miou-Miou, Jean Carmet, Judith Henry, Jean-Roger Milo – *r*: 152 min., col. – *p*: Renn Productions, in association with France 2/D.D. Productions/ Alternative Films/Nuova Artisti Associati 1993

Luc Besson
Nikita
sc: Luc Besson – *c*: Thierry Arbogast – *l.p.*: Anne Parriauld, Jean-Hughes Anglade, Tcheky Karyo, Jeanne Moreau, Jean Reno, Roland Blance, Marc Duret – *r*: 117 min., col. – *p*: Palace/Gaumont/Cecci/Tiger (Jérôme Chalou) 1990

Le Cinquième élément
sc: Luc Besson, Robert Kamen – *c*: Thierry Arbogast – *l.p.*: Bruce Willis, Gary Oldman, Milla Jovovitch, Ian Holm, Chris Tucker, Lee Evans, Tricky, Mathieu Kassovitz – *r*: 127 min., col. – *p*: Gaumont 1996

Bertrand Blier
Les Valseuses
sc: Bertrand Blier, from his novel – *c*: Bruno Nuytten – *l.p.*: Gérard Depardieu, Patrick Dewaere, Miou-Miou, Jeanne Moreau, Brigitte Fossey, Isabelle Huppert – *r*: 117 min., col. – *p*: CAPAC/Uranus/UPF/Prodis 1974

Claude Chabrol
Le Beau Serge
sc: Claude Chabrol – *c*: Henri Decae – *l.p.*: Gérard Blain, Jean-Claude Brialy, Bernadette Laffont, Michèle Meritz – *r*: 93 min., b/w – *p*: AJYM-Films 1958

Une Affaire de femmes
sc: Colo Tavernier O'Hagan, Claude Chabrol, from the book by Francis Spizner – *c*: Jean Rabier – *l.p.*: Isabelle Huppert, François Cluzet, Marie Trintignant – *r*: 110 min., col. – *p*: MK2 Productions 1988

La Cérémonie
sc: Claude Chabrol and Caroline Eliacheff, from the novel by Ruth Rendell – *c*: Bernard Zitzermann – *l.p.*: Sandrine Bonnaire, Isabelle Huppert, Jacqueline Bisset, Jean-Pierre Cassel – *r*: 111 min., col. – *p*: MK2 Productions 1995

Christian de Challonges
Docteur Petiot
sc: Dominique Garnier, Christian de Challonges – *c*: Patrick Blossier – *l.p.*: Michel Serrault, Pierre Romans, Zbigniew Horoks – *r*: 102 min. col. – *p*: Electric/MS/Sara/Ciné 5 1990

Cyril Collard
Les Nuits fauves
sc: Cyril Collard, Jacques Fieschi, from the novel by Cyril Collard – *c*: Manuel Teran – *l.p.*: Cyril Collard, Romane Bohringer, Carlos Lopez – *r*: 126 min., col. – *p*: Banfilm Ter/La Sept Cinéma/Erre Produzioni/SNC with the participation of Sofinergie 2/CNC/Canal +/Procirep 1992

Claire Denis
J'ai pas Sommeil
sc: Claire Denis, Jean-Pol Fargeau – *c*: Agnès Godard – *l.p.*: Katherina Golubeva, Richard Courcet, Line Renaud, Alex Decas, Béatrice Dalle – *r*: 110 min., col. – *p*: Bruno Pésery 1994

Julien Duvivier
David Golder
sc: Julien Duvivier, from an idea by Irène Némirovski – *c*: Georges Périnal, Armand Thirard – *l.p.*: Harry Baur, Jackie Monnier, Jean Coquelin, Jacques Gretillat – *r*: 86 min., b/w – *p*: Vandal et Delac 1930

La Bandéra

sc: Julien Duvivier, Charles Spaak, from an idea by Pierre Mac-Orlan – *c*: Jules Krüger – *l.p.*: Jean Gabin, Annabella, Robert le Vigan, Pierre Renoir, Margo Lion, Aimos, Gaston Modot – *r*: 100 min., b/w – *p*: SNC 1935

Golgotha

sc: Chanoine Reymond – *c*: Jules Krüger, René Ribault, Marc Fossard – *l.p.*: Robert le Vigan, Jean Gabin, Lucas Gridoux, Edwige Feuillière, Juliette Verneuil – *r*: 95 min., b/w – *p*: Ichtys Film 1935

Le Golem

sc: Julien Duvivier, André-Paul Antoine, from an idea by Gustav Meyrinck – *c*: Vaclav Vich, Jan Stallich – *l.p.*: Harry Baur, Roger Karl, Germaine Aussey, Jany Holt – *r*: 100 min., b/w – *p*: A.B. Film 1935

Pépé le Moko

sc: Julien Duvivier, with Henri Jeanson, from an idea by Ashelbé – *c*: Jules Krüger, Marc Fossard – *l.p.*: Jean Gabin, Lucas Gridoux, Mireille Balin, Line Noro, Fernand Charpin, Gabriel Gabrio, Saturnin Fabre, Fréhel, Marcel Dalio, Gaston Modot – *r*: 100 min., b/w – *p*: Gargour 1936

Jean-Luc Godard
A Bout de souffle

sc: Jean-Luc Godard, from an idea by François Truffaut – *c*: Raoul Coutard – *l.p.*: Jean-Paul Belmondo, Jean Seberg, Daniel Boulanger, Jean-Pierre Melville – *r*: 90 min., b/w – *p*: Georges de Beauregard 1959

Vivre sa vie

sc: Jean-Luc Godard – *c*: Raoul Coutard – *l.p.*: Anna Karina, Saddy Rebot, André S. Labarthe, Guylaine Schlumberger, Brice Parain – *r*: 85 min., b/w – *p*: Les Films de la Pléiade 1962

Histoire(s) du cinéma

sc: Jean-Luc Godard – *c*: Jean-Luc Godard, Pierre Binggelli (video) – *r*: 344 min. col. and b/w – *p*: CanalPlus/La Sept/FR3/Gaumont/JLG Films 1988–98

Jean-Loup Hubert
Le Grand chemin

sc: Jean-Loup Hubert – *l.p.*: Anémone, Richard Bohringer, Antoine Hubert, Vanessa Guedj – col. – *p*: 1986

Marielle Issartel and Charles Belmont
Histoires d'A
sc: Marielle Issartel, Charles Belmont – *c*: Philippe Rousselot – *l.p.*: no credits – *r*: 85 min., b/w – *p*: Belmont and Issartel 1973

Mathieu Kassovitz
La Haine
sc: Mathieu Kassovitz – *c*: Pierre Aïm – *l.p.*: Vincent Cassel, Hubert Kounde, Saïd Taghmaoui – *r*: 95 min., b/w – *p*: Lazennec/Canal +/La Sept Cinéma/Kaso inc. Productions 1995

Diane Kurys
Diabolo menthe
sc: Diane Kurys – *c*: Philippe Rousselot, Christian Backmann, Dominique Brenguier – *l.p.*: Eléonore Klarwein, Odile Michel, Anouk Ferjac, Michel Puterflam, Yves Renier, Robert Rimbaud, Marie-Véronique Maurin, Corinne Dacla, Coralie Clément, Valérie Stano, Darius Depoléon – *r*: 101 min., col. – *p*: Films de l'Alma/Alexandre Films 1977

Cocktail Molotov
sc: Diane Kurys, with Philippe Adrien, Alain le Henry – *c*: Philippe Rousselot, Dominique Brenguier – *l.p.*: Elise Caron, Philippe Lebas, François Cluzet, Geneviève Fontanel, Henri Garçon, Michel Puterflam, Marlène Sveinbjornsson – *r*: 100 min., col. – *p*: Alexandre Films/Antenne 2 1980

Coup de foudre (UK: *At First Sight*)/ (USA: *Entre Nous*)
sc: Diane Kurys – *c*: Bernard Lutic – *l.p.*: Miou-Miou, Isabelle Huppert, Guy Marchand, Jean-Pierre Bacri, Robin Renucci, Patrick Bauchau, Patricia Champagne, Saga Blanchard, Guillaume Le Guellec – *r*: 111 min., col. – *p*: Partner's Production/Alexandre Films/Hachette Première et Cie/Films A2/Société Française de Production de Cinéma 1983

La Baule Les Pins/ C'est la Vie
sc: Diane Kurys, Alain le Henry – *c*: Guiseppe Lanci, Fabio Conversi – *l.p.*: Nathalie Baye, Richard Berry, Jean-Pierre Bacri, Zabou, Valéria Bruni-Tedeschi, Didier Bénureau, Julie Bataille, Candice Lefranc, Alexis Derlon, Emmanuelle le Boidron, Maxime Boidron, Benjamin Sacks – *r*: 97 min., col. – *p*: Alexandre Films/SGGC, Films A2 1990

Louis Malle
Ascenseur pour l'échaffaud
sc: Louis Malle, Roger Nimier, from an idea by Noël Calef – *c*: Henri Decae – *l.p.*: Maurice Ronet, Jeanne Moreau, Georges Poujouly, Yori Bertin, Félix Marten, Lino Ventura, Elga Anderson, Jean-Claude Brialy – *r*: 90 min., b/w – *p*: Irénée Leriche 1957

Les Amants
sc: Louis Malle, Louise de Vilmorin, from an idea by Dominique Vivant – *c*: Henri Decae – *l.p.*: Jeanne Moreau, Jean-Marc Bory, Alain Cuny, Judith Magre, José-Louis Villalonga, Gaston Modot – *r*: 88 min., b/w – *p*: Irénée Leriche 1958

Lacombe Lucien
sc: Louis Malle, Patrick Modiano – *c*: Tonino Delli Colli – *l.p.*: Pierre Blaise, Aurore Clément, Holger Lowenadler, Thérèse Giehse, Jean Bousquet, Jean Rougerie – *r*: 135 min., col. – *p*: Claude Nedjar/NEF/ UPF (Paris)/Vides Film (Rome)/Halleluyah Film (Munich) 1974

Au revoir les enfants
sc: Louis Malle – *c*: Renato Berta – *l.p.*: Gaspard Manesse, Raphaël Fejto, Francoine Racette, Philippe Morier Genoud, Stanislas Carré de Malberg – *r*: 103 min., col. – *p*: Nouvelles Editions de film S.A./MK2 Productions/ Stella Film/NEF 1987

Georges Méliès
L'Affaire Dreyfus
c: Georges Méliès – *l.p.*: no credits – *r*: 11 min., b/w – *p*: Star-Film 1899

Luc Moullet
Brigitte et Brigitte
sc: Luc Moullet – *c*: Claude Croton – *l.p.*: Françoise Vatel, Colette Descombes, Claude Melki, Michael Gonzales, Claude Chabrol, Samuel Fuller – *r*: 85 min., b/w – *p*: Luc Moullet 1966

Jean-Marie Poiré
Les Visiteurs
sc: Christian Clavier, Jean-Marie Poiré – *c*: Jean-Yves Le Mener – *l.p.*: Christian Clavier, Jean Reno, Valérie Lemercier, Marie-Anne Chazel, Christian Bujeau, Isabelle Nanty, Didier Pain – *r*: 107 min., col. – *p*: Arrow/Gaumont/France 3/Alpilles/Amigo 1993

Jacques Renard
Blanche et Marie
sc: Jacques Renard – *l.p.*: Sandrine Bonnaire, Miou-Miou – col. – *p*: 1985

Jean Renoir
Charleston
sc: Pierre Lestringuez, from an idea by André Cerf – *c*: Jean Bachelet – *l.p.*: Catherine Hessling, Johnny Huggins, André Cerf – *r*: 20 min., b/w – *p*: Néo-film 1926

Le Bled
sc: Henry Dupuy-Mazuel, André Jaeger-Schmidt – *c*: Marcel Lucien, Léon Morizet – *l.p.*: Jackie Monnier, Enrique Rivero, Diana Hart, Manuel Raaby, Alexandre Arquillière – *r*: 100 min., b/w – *p*: Société des Films Historiques 1929

La Grande Illusion
sc: Jean Renoir, Charles Spaak – *c*: Christan Matras – *l.p.*: Jean Gabin, Pierre Fresnay, Erich von Stroheim, Marcel Dalio, Julien Carette, Dita Parlo – *r*: 113 min., b/w – *p*: RAC 1937

La Marseillaise
sc: Jean Renoir, with Carl Koch and Nina Martel-Dreyfus – *c*: Jean-Serge Bourgoin, Alain Douarinou, Jean-Marie Maillols, Jean-Paul Alphen, Jean Louis – *l.p.*: Pierre Renoir, Lise Delamare, Andrex, Edmond Ardisson, Nadia Sibirskaia, Edouard Delmont – *r*: 135 min., b/w – *p*: CGT/Société de production et d'exploitation du film *La marseillaise* 1937

La Règle du jeu
sc: Jean Renoir, with Carl Koch – *c*: Jean Bachelet – *l.p.*: Marcel Dalio, Roland Toutain, Nora Grégor, Mila Parély, Paulette Dubost, Jean Renoir, Julien Carette, Gaston Modot – *r*: 112 min., b/w – *p*: Nouvelles Editions Françaises 1939

Le Caporal Epinglé
sc: Jean Renoir, Guy Lefranc, from the novel by Jacques Perret – *c*: Georges Leclerc – *l.p.*: Jean-Pierre Cassel, Claude Brasseur, Claude Rich, Cornelia Froeboess – *r*: 105 min., b/w – *p*: Films du Cyclope 1962

Alain Resnais
Hiroshima mon amour
sc: Marguerite Duras – *c*: Sacha Vierny, Takahashi Michio – *l.p.*: Emmanuelle Riva, Eiji Okada, Bernard Fresson – *r*: 91 min., b/w – *p*: Anatole Dauman 1958

L'Année dernière à Marienbad
sc: Alain Robbe-Grillet – *c*: Sacha Vierny – *l.p.*: Delphine Seyrig, Giorgio Albertazzi, Sacha Pitoeff – *r*: 93 min., b/w – *p*: Pierre Coureau/Raymond Froment 1961

Yves Robert
La Gloire de mon père
sc: Jérôme Tonnere, Louis Nucera, Yves Robert, from the novel by Marcel Pagnol – *c*: Robert Alazraki – *l.p.*: Philippe Caubère, Nathalie Roussel, Didier Pain, Thérèse Liotard, Julien Ciamaca, Victorien Delamare, Joris Molinas, Paul Crauchet, Jean-Pierre Darras – *r*: 110 min., col. – *p*: Palace/Guamont International/La Guéville/TF1 1990

Charlotte Silvera
Louise l'insoumise
sc: Charlotte Silvera – *c*: Domininque le Rigoleur – *l.p.*: Catherine Rouvel, Roland Bertin, Myriam Stern, Joelle Tami, Deborah Cohen, Marie-Christine Barrault – *r*: 95 min., col. – *p*: Les Film Epoc 1984

Bertrand Tavernier
Le Juge et l'assassin
sc: Bertrand Tavernier – *c*: Pierre-William Glenn – *l.p.*: Philippe Noiret, Michel Galabru, Isabelle Huppert, Jean-Claude Brialy – *r*: 110 min., col. – *p*: Raymond Davos/ Lira Films 1976

André Téchiné
Souvenirs d'en France
sc: André Téchiné, Marilyn Goldin – *c*: Bruno Nuytten – *l.p.*: Jeanne Moreau, Michel Auclair, Marie-France Pisier, Claude Mann, Orane Demazis, Aram Stephan, Hélène Surgère, Julien Guiomar, Michèle Moretti, Pierre Baillot – *r*: 95 min., col. – *p*: Stephan Films/Buffalo Films/Renn Productions/Belstar Productions/Simar Films 1975

Les Roseaux sauvages
sc: André Téchiné, Gilles Tauraud, Olivier Massart – *c*: Jeanne Lapoirie – *l.p.*: Elodie Bouchez, Gaël Morel, Stéphane Rideau, Frédéric Gorny, Michèle Moretti, Jacques Nolot – *r*: 110 min., col. – *p*: Ima Films/Les Films Alain Sarde 1994

François Truffaut
Les Mistons
sc: François Truffaut from the short story *Les Virginales* by Maurice Pons
– *c*: Jean Malige – *l.p.*: Gérard Blain, Bernadette Lafont – *r*: 26 min., b/w
– *p*: Les Films du Carrosse 1957

Les 400 coups
sc: François Truffaut, Marcel Moussy – *c*: Henri Decaë – *l.p.*: Jean-Pierre
Léaud, Claire Maurier, Albert Rémy, Patrick Auffay – *r*: 101 min., b/w –
p: Les Films du Carrosse 1959

Tirez sur le pianiste
sc: François Truffaut, Marcel Moussy, from the novel *Down There* by
David Goodis – *c*: Raoul Coutard – *l.p.*: Charles Aznavour, Marie Dubois,
Nicole Berger – *r*: 80 min., b/w – *p*: Les Films de la Pléïade 1960

Jules et Jim
sc: François Truffaut, Jean Gruault, from the novel *Jules et Jim* by Henri-
Pierre Roché – *c*: Raoul Coutard – *l.p.*: Jeanne Moreau, Oskar Werner,
Henri Serre, Marie Dubois, Sabine Haudepin – *r*: 105 min., b/w – *p*: Les
Films du Carrosse 1961

Fahrenheit 451
sc: François Truffaut, from the novel *Fahrenheit 451* by Ray Bradbury –
c: Nicolas Roeg – *l.p.*: Julie Christie, Oskar Werner, Cyril Cusack – *r*:
112 min., col. – *p*: Anglo Enterprise/Vineyard Farms 1966

La Mariée était en noir
sc: François Truffaut, Jean-Louis Richard, from the novel *The Bride wore
Black* by William Irish – *c*: Raoul Coutard – *l.p.*: Jeanne Moreau, Claude
Rich, Jean-Claude Brialy, Michel Bouquet, Michel Lonsdale, Charles
Denner, Daniel Boulanger, Alexandra Stewart – *r*: 107 min., col. – *p*: Les
Films du Carrosse/Artistes Associés/Dino de Laurentis 1967

La Sirène du Mississippi
sc: François Truffaut, from the novel *Waltz into Darkness* by William
Irish – *c*: Denys Clerval – *l.p.*: Jean-Paul Belmondo, Catherine Deneuve,
Michel Bouquet – *r*: 123 min., col. – *p*: Les Films du Carrosse 1969

L'Enfant sauvage
sc: François Truffaut, Jean Gruault, from the *mémoire* by Jean Itard – *c*:
Nestor Almendros – *l.p.*: Jean-Pierre Cargol, François Truffaut – *r*: 84
min., b/w – *p*: Les Films du Carrosse 1969

Les Deux Anglaises et le continent

sc: François Truffaut – *c*: Nestor Almendros – *l.p.*: Jean-Pierre Léaud, Kika Markham, Stacey Tendeter – *r*: 108 min., col. – *p*: Les Films du Carrosse 1971

Une Belle Fille comme moi

sc: Jean-Loup Dabadie, François Truffaut, from the novel *Such a Gorgeous Kid Like Me* by Henri Farrell – *c*: Pierre-William Glenn – *l.p.*: Bernadette Lafont, Claude Brasseur, Charles Denner, Guy Marchand, André Dussolier, Philippe Léotard – *r*: 100 min., col. – *p*: Les Films du Carrosse/Columbia 1972

La Nuit américaine

sc: François Truffaut, Jean-Louis Richard, Suzanne Schiffman – *c*: Pierre-William Glenn – *l.p.*: Jacqueline Bisset, Valentine Cortese, Alexandra Stewart, Jean-Pierre Aumont, Jean-Pierre Léaud, François Truffaut, Nathalie Baye – *r*: 120 min., col. – *p*: Les Films du Carrosse 1973

L'Histoire d'Adèle H.

sc: François Truffaut, Jean Gruault, from the diary of Adèle Hugo – *c*: Nestor Almendros – *l.p.*: Isabelle Adjani, Bruce Robinson, Sylvia Marriott – *r*: 95 min., col. – *p*: Les Films du Carrosse 1975

L'Homme qui aimait les femmes

sc: François Truffaut, Michel Fermaud, Suzanne Schiffman – *c*: Nestor Almendros – *l.p.*: Charles Denner, Lesley Caron, Brigitte Fossey – *r*: 119 min., col. – *p*: Les Films du Carrosse 1977

La Chambre verte

sc: François Truffaut, Jean Gruault, from *The Altar of the Dead*, *Friends of Friends* and *The Beast in the Jungle* by Henry James – *c*: Nestor Almendros – *l.p.*: François Truffaut, Nathalie Baye, Jean Dasté – *r*: 94 min., col. – *p*: Les Films du Carrosse 1978

Vivement dimanche

sc: François Truffaut, Suzanne Schiffman, Jean Aurel, from the novel *The Long Saturday Night* by Charles Williams – *c*: Nestor Almendros – *l.p.*: Fanny Ardant, Jean-Louis Trintignant, Jean-Pierre Kalfon – *r*: 111 min., b/w – *p*: Les Films du Carrosse/Films A2/Soprofilms 1983

Agnès Varda
Cléo de 5 à 7
sc: Agnès Varda – *c*: Jean Rabier – *l.p.*: Corrine Marchand, Antoine Bousseiller, Dorothy Blank, Michel Legrand, Dominique Davray – *r*: 90 min., b/w (brief colour) – *p*: Rome-Paris Films 1962

L'Une chante l'autre pas
sc: Agnès Varda – *c*: Charlie van Damm, Nurith Aviv – *l.p.*: Valérie Mairesse, Robert Dadiès, Thérèse Liotard, Gisèle Halimim, Dominique Ducros, Ali Raffi, Jean-Pierre Pellegrin – *r*: 120 min., col. *p*: Ciné-Tamaris/ SFP/INA 1977

Jean Vigo
Zéro de conduite
sc: Jean Vigo – *c*: Boris Kaufman – *l.p.*: Jean Dasté, Louis Lefebvre, Gilbert Pruchon, Robert le Flon, Delphin – *r*: 44 min., b/w – *p*: Nounez/ Gaumont 1933

Bibliography

Abel, Richard (1995), 'The Perils of Pathé, or the Americanization of Early American Cinema', in L. Charney and V. R. Schwartz (eds), *Cinema and the Invention of Modern Life*, Berkeley, CA, University of California Press.

Aitkin, Ian (1996), 'Current Problems in the Study of European Cinema and the Role of Questions on Cultural Identity', in Wendy Everett (ed.), *European Identity in Cinema*, pp. 75–82, Exeter, Intellect.

Anderson, Benedict (1991), *Imagined Communities*, revised edition, New York, Verso.

Andrew, Dudley (1976), *The Major Film Theories: An Introduction*, Oxford, Oxford University Press.

Ardagh, John (1966), 'An Alpha for Godard?', *The Guardian* (12 December): 7.

Austin, Guy (1996), *Contemporary French Cinema, An Introduction*, Manchester University Press.

Auty, Martin (1982), 'Breathless: *Diva*,' *Sight and Sound,* 51 (4): 302.

Baecque, Antoine de (1998), *La Nouvelle Vague*, Paris, Flammarion.

Balio, Tino (1996), 'Adjusting to the New Global Economy: Hollywood in the 1990s', in A. Moran (ed.), *Film Policy: International, National and Regional Perspectives*, London and New York, Routledge.

Barthes, Roland (1957), *Mythologies*, Paris, Editions du Seuil.

—— (1994), *Camera Lucida*, trans. Richard Howard, New York, Hill and Wang.

Bazin, André (1984), *What is Cinema?* Vol. I, trans. Hugh Gray, Berkeley, CA, University of California Press.

—— (1989), *Jean Renoir*, Paris, Lebovici.

Beebe, John (1992), 'The Anima in Film,' on Don Williams's web site 'C. G. Jung, Analytical Psychology, and Culture,' http://www.cgjung.com/films.

Benjamin, Walter (1989), 'The Work of Art in the Age of Mechanical Reproduction', in *Illuminations*, trans. Harry Zohn, pp. 217–51, New York, Schocken Books.

Bergstrom, Janet (1996), unpublished paper delivered at Rutgers University.

Bessie, Maurice and Beylie, Claude (1989), *Jean Renoir*, Paris, Gérard Watelet.

Bhabha, Homi (1990), *Nation and Narration*, London and New York, Routledge.

Borde, Raymond (1959), 'Critique et marxisme vivant', *Cinéma 59*, no. 33: 104–6.

—— (1962a), 'Dictionnaire partiel et partial d'un nouveau cinéma français', *Positif*, no. 46 (June): 19–38.

—— (1962b), 'L'hypothèque Sadoul', *Positif*, no. 46 (June): 70–7.

Bordwell, David (1995), *Narration in the Fiction Film*, London, Routledge.

Bresson, Robert (1975), *Notes sur le cinématographe*, Paris, Gallimard.

Buchsbaum, Jonathon (1988), *Cinéma Engagé. Film in the Popular Front*, Chicago, University of Chicago.

Buck-Morss, Susan (1989), *The Dialectics of Seeing*, Cambridge, MA, MIT Press.

Buss, Robin (1994), *French Film Noir*, London, Marion Boyars.

Butler, Judith (1993), *Bodies that Matter*, London and New York, Routledge.

Capdenac, Michel (1960), 'Non, Monsieur Chabrol!', *Les Lettres françaises*, no. 822 (28 April): 1, 7.

Casanova, Laurent (1949), *Responsabilité de l'intellectuel communiste*, Paris, Éditions de la Nouvelle Critique.

Cellule des Cinéastes (1959), 'Ordre du jour du 3 février 1959', Paris, BIFI, Fonds Jean-Paul Le Chanois, 163-B 35.

—— (No date), 'Rapport de la commission chargée d'étudier les problèmes nouveaux et les méthodes de travail ou la structure de l'industrie cinématographique', Paris, BIFI, Fonds Jean-Paul Le Chanois, 163-B 35.

Cervoni, Albert (1959a), 'Les points sur les « i » de *Hiroshima mon amour*', *France nouvelle*, no. 714 (2 July): 28-9.

—— (1959b), '*Les 400 coups* . . . une vérité qui n'est pas sans limite', *France nouvelle*, no. 716 (16 July): 28–9.

—— (1959c), 'Citizen Welles', *France nouvelle*, no. 735 (26 November): 24–5.

—— (1965), Paris, BIFI, archives Sadoul, GS-D 10.

Commission of the EC (1992), *Treaty on European Union Signed at Maastricht on 7 February*, Luxembourg, Office for Official Publications of the EC.

Conseil Supérieur de la Langue française (1994), 'Le CSA et l'application de la directive « Télévision sans frontières »', *La Lettre du CSA*, January.

De Certeau, Michel (1975), *L'Ecriture de l'histoire*, Paris, Gallimard.

Deleuze, Gilles (1983), *Cinéma 1: L'Image-Mouvement*, Paris, Les Editions de Minuit.

Denis, Claire (1994), Interview, *Cahiers du cinéma* no. 479 (April).

Denzin, Norman K. (1991), *Images of Postmodern Society: Social Theory and Contemporary Cinema*, London, Sage.

Derrida, Jacques (1976), *Of Grammatology*, trans. Gayatri Chakravorti Spivak, Baltimore, MD, Johns Hopkins University Press.

Deslandes, Jacques (1963), *Le Boulevard du cinéma à l'époque de Georges Méliès*, Paris, Editions du Cerf.

Docherty, Thomas (1996), *Alterities*, Oxford, Clarendon Press.

Douchet, Jean (1994), 'D'un réalisme l'autre', *Retour vers le réel*, [?], Conseil Général de Seine Saint-Denis.

—— (1998), *La Nouvelle Vague*, Paris, Hazan.

Drake, Helen (1994), 'François Mitterrand, France and European Integration', in G. Raymond (ed.), *France During the Socialist Years*, Aldershot, Dartmouth.

Dreyfus, Alfred (1994), *Cinq Années de ma vie*, Paris, La Découverte.

Drouin, Michel (ed.) (1994), *L'Affaire Dreyfus de A à Z*, Paris, Flammarion.

Duchen, Claire (1994), *Women's Rights and Women's Lives in France 1944–1968*, London, Routledge.

Dyer, Richard (1990), *Now You See it: Studies on Lesbian and Gay Film*, London, Routledge.

—— (1997), *White*, London, Routledge.

—— and Vincendeau, Ginette (1992), 'Introduction', in Richard Dyer and Ginette Vincendeau (eds), *Popular European Cinema*, pp. 1–14, London and New York, Routledge.

Ehrlich, Evelyn (1985), *Cinema of Paradox*, New York, Columbia University Press.

Elsaesser, Thomas (ed.) (1990), *Early Cinema: Space, Frame, Narrative*, London, British Film Institute.

Englund, Steven (1996), 'History in a Late Age', in *French Politics and Society*, Vol. 14, No. 1.

Esnault, Philippe (1960), 'Une industrie qui pourrait être un art – I. De la nécessité d'une relève', *Les Lettres francaises*, no. 817 (17 March): 10.

Fanon, Frantz (1967), *Black Skin, White Masks*, New York, Grove Press.

Faulkner, Christopher (1986), *The Social Cinema of Jean Renoir*, Princeton, NJ, Princeton University Press.

Featherstone, Mike (1995), *Undoing Culture: Globalization, Culture, Postmodernism*, London, Sage.

Forbes, Jill (1992), *The Cinema in France after the New Wave*, London, Macmillan.

—— (1995a), 'Popular Culture and Cultural Politics', in J. Forbes and M. Kelly (eds), *French Cultural Studies: An Introduction*, Oxford, Oxford University Press.

—— (1995b), 'Conclusion: French Cultural Studies in the Future', in J. Forbes and M. Kelly (eds), *French Cultural Studies: An Introduction*, Oxford, Oxford University Press.

Forest, Philippe (1993), 'Le Concept contemporain de la culture', *Cahiers français*, no. 260 « Culture et société », March–April.

Gaffney, John (1989), *The French Left and the Fifth Republic: The Discourses of Communism and Socialism in Contemporary France*, London, Macmillan.

—— (1991), 'French Political Culture and Republicanism', in J. Gaffney and E. Kolinsky (eds), *Political Culture in France and Germany: A Contemporary Perspective*, London, Routledge.

—— (1993), 'Language and Style in Politics', in C. Sanders (ed.), *French Today: Language in its Social Context*, Cambridge, Cambridge University Press.

Gaillard, Jean-Michel (1994), 'L'Ennemi américain 1944–1994', *L'Histoire*, April.

Garber, Marjorie (1992), 'The Occidental Tourist: *M. Butterfly* and the Scandal of Transvestism', in *Nationalisms and Sexualities*, London and New York, Routledge.

Genette, Gérard (1987), *Seuils*, Paris, Seuil.

Gillain, Anne (1991), *François Truffaut – Le Secret perdu*, Paris, Hatier.

Gledhill, Christine (1980), '*Klute* 1: A Contemporary Film Noir and Feminist Criticism', in E. A. Kaplan (ed.), *Women in Film Noir*, London, British Film Institute Publishing.

Godard, Jean-Luc (1980), *Introduction à une véritable histoire du cinéma*, Paris, Albatros.

—— (1982), 'Le chemin vers la parole' (Interview with Alain Bergala, Serge Daney and Serge Toubiana), *Les Cahiers du cinéma*, 336: 8–14, 57–66.

—— (1983), 'Godard à Venise', *Cinématographe*, 95: 3–7 (transcription of Godard's press conference at the 1983 Venice Film Festival).

—— (1984–5), 'Jean-Luc Godard: la curiosité du sujet' (Interview with Dominique Païni and Guy Scarpetta), *art press* (sic), («Spécial Godard»), hors série 4 (December 1984 – January/February 1985): 4–18.

—— (1985 [1958]), 'Désespérant', *Arts*, 680. Also in Godard, Jean-Luc (1985), *Jean-Luc Godard par Jean-Luc Godard*, ed. Alain Bergala, pp. 137–8, Paris, Cahiers du Cinéma/Editions de l'Etoile.

—— (1989), '«Cultivons notre jardin»: Une interview de Jean-Luc Godard' (Interview with François Albéra), *CinémAction* 52, («*Le cinéma selon Godard*»), ed. René Prédal, pp. 81–9.

—— (1988), 'Godard fait des histoires' (Interview with Serge Daney), *Libération* (26 December): 24–7. Reprinted in Godard, Jean-Luc (1988) *Jean-Luc Godard par Jean-Luc Godard* (volume 2, 1984–1988), edited by Alain Bergala, Paris, Cahiers du Cinéma, 161–173. In English as 'Godard makes (hi)stories', in Raymond Bellour and Mary Lea Bandy (eds) (1992), *Jean-Luc Godard: Son + Image, 1974–1991*, pp. 159–67, New York, The Museum of Modern Art.

—— (1992a), 'Jean-Luc Godard in conversation with Colin MacCabe', in Duncan Petrie (ed.) (1992), *Screening Europe: Image and Identity in Contemporary European Cinema*, pp. 97–105, London, BFI.

—— (1992b), 'Entretien avec Jean-Luc Godard: Le Briquet de Capitaine Cook' (Interview with François Albéra and Mikhaïl Iampolski), *Les Lettres Françaises* (19 April): 17–21.

Gordon, Joëlle (1983), 'Diane Kurys', *Le Matin Magazine,* 1.4.83.

Gozlan, Gérard (1962a), 'Les délices de l'ambiguïté (éloge d'André Bazin)', *Positif*, no. 46 (June): 36–69.

—— (1962b), 'Éloge d'André Bazin (suite et fin)', *Positif*, no. 47 (July): 16–61.

Grewal, Inderpal and Kaplan, Caren (eds) (1994), *Scattered Hegemonies: Postmodernity and Transnational Feminist Practices*, Minneapolis and London, University of Minnesota Press.

Haffner, Pierre (1988), *Jean Renoir,* Paris, Rivages.

Hayward, Susan (1993), *French National Cinema*, London, Routledge.

—— (2000), 'Framing National Cinemas', in Mette Hjort and Scott MacKenzie (eds), *Cinema and Nation*, London, Routledge (forthcoming).

Higson, Andrew (1993), 'Re-presenting the National Past; Nostalgia and Pastiche in the Heritage Film', in Lester Friedman (ed.), *British Cinema and Thatcherism: Fires Were Started*, pp.109–29, London, UCL Press.

Hunt, Lynn. (1996) 'The Many Bodies of Marie-Antoinette', in P. Jones (ed.), *The French Revolution in Social and Political Perspective*, pp. 268–84, London, New York, Arnold.

Huret, M. (1984), *Ciné actualités*, Paris, Henri Veyrier.

Insdorf, Annette (1989), *François Truffaut*, New York, Touchstone: Simon and Schuster.

Jameson, Frederic (1981), *The Political Unconscious*, Ithaca, NY, Cornell University Press.

Jeanne, René and Ford, Charles (1961), *Le Cinéma et la presse 1895–1960*, Paris, Armand Colin.

Jenn, Pierre (1984), *Georges Méliès cinéaste*, Paris, Albatros.

Joly, Danièle (1991), *The French Communist Party and the Algerian War*, Paris, Macmillan.

Jung, C.G. (1966 [1931]), 'On the Relation of Analytical Psychology to Poetry', *The Collected Works,* Vol. 15: *The Spirit in Man, Art and Literature*, London, Routledge & Kegan Paul.

—— (1968 [1954]), 'Archetypes of the Collective Unconscious', *The Collected Works,* Vol. 9 (1): *The Archetypes and the Collective Unconscious*, 2nd edn, London, Routledge & Kegan Paul.

—— (1976 [1921]), *The Collected Works,* Vol. 6: *Psychological Types,* rev edn, Princeton NJ, Princeton University Press.

Kelly, Michael (1995), 'Introduction: French Cultural Studies', in J. Forbes and M. Kelly (eds), *French Cultural Studies: An Introduction*, Oxford, Oxford University Press.

Kristeva, Julia (1982), *The Powers of Horror*, New York, Columbia University Press.

Kuisel, Richard (1993), *Seducing the French: The Dilemma of Americanization*, Berkeley, CA, University of California Press.

—— (1996), 'Modernization and Identity', *French Politics and Society*, vol. 14, no.1 (Winter).

Lachize, Samuel (1959), 'Une réussite (où personne n'a triché)', *L'Humanité*, no. 4495 (14 February): 2.

—— (1960), '*A bout de souffle.* . . (mais avec espérances!)', *L'Humanité*, no. 4836 (19 March): 2.

La Lettre de Matignon (1992), supplement 'La France au coeur de l'Europe', July.

—— (1995), supplement 'La Présidence française de l'Union européenne 1995', January.

Lebovics, Herman (1992), *True France: The Wars Over Cultural Identity, 1900–1945*, Ithaca, NY, Cornell University Press.

Libération 22 September 1993.

Liebman *et al.* (1996), 'Politics and the Cinema of Jean Renoir', *Persistence of Vision*, 12/13 (Special number of the periodical largely focusing on Renoir's Popular Front films).

Looseley, David (1994), 'Cultural Policy and Democratization under Mitterrand' in G. Raymond (ed.), *France During the Socialist Years*, Aldershot, Dartmouth.

—— (1995), *The Politics of Fun: Cultural Policy and Debate in Contemporary France*, Oxford, Berg.

Lurçat, Liliane (1960), 'Du cinéma, école de psychologie et des *Bonnes femmes*', *L'Humanité*, no. 5031 (2 November): 2.

Maccoby, Hyam (1992), *Judas Iscariot and the Myth of Jewish Evil*, London, Peter Halban.

Maillot, Pierre (1997), *Les Fiancés de Marianne*, Paris, Nathan.

Malthête, Jacques (1981), *Essai de Reconstitution du catalogue français de la Star-Film*, Paris, Centre Nationale de la Cinématographie.

—— (1982), 'L'Affaire Dreyfus de Georges Méliès', *Les Cahiers de la Cinémathèque* 35/36, automne, special issue: 'Cinéma et histoire, histoire du cinéma'.

—— (1989), 'Les Actualités reconstituées de Georges Méliès', *Archives* 21, mars, Institut Jean Vigo-Cinémathèque Toulouse.

—— (1995), 'Georges Méliès, de la non-fiction à la fiction', *1895* 18, été, special issue: 'Images du réel: la non-fiction en France (1890–1930)'.

Malthête-Méliès, Madeleine (1995), *Méliès l'enchanteur*, Paris, Ramsay.

Marest, Lucien (1994), 'GATT: quand le bras droit de Balladur se met à table', *Libération,* 4 January.

Marie, Michel (1998), *La Nouvelle Vague*, Paris, Nathan.

Mégret, Bruno (1993) 'Pour un protectionnisme culturel', speech at 'Colloque du conseil scientifique du Front National', 30 October.

Metz, Christian (1968), *Essai sur la signification au cinéma*, Vol. 2, Paris, Klincksieck.

Mitterrand, François (1993), 'Allocution prononcée par le Président de la République à l'occasion de la remise du diplôme de docteur Honoris Causa', 21 September.

Monjo, Armand (1959), 'J'attendais beaucoup plus', in 'Le film le plus discuté de l'année divise aussi nos critiques', *L'Humanité*, no. 4596 (13 June): 2.

Morin, E. (1956), *Le Cinéma ou l'homme imaginaire*, Paris, Les Editions de Minuit.

Morley, David (1996), 'EurAm, Modernity, Reason and Alterity: Or Postmodernism, the Highest Stage of Cultural Imperialism', in D. Morley and K. H. Chen (eds), *Stuart Hall – Critical Dialogues in Cultural Studies*, London, Routledge.

Mosse, Georges (1985), *Nationalism and Sexuality*, University of Wisconsin.

Mouffe, Chantal (1992), 'Feminism, Citizenship and Radical Democratic Politics', in J. Butler and J. W. Scott, *Feminists Theorize the Political*, pp. 369–84, New York, Routledge.

Moussinac, Léon (no date), 'Une Nouvelle Vague ?', original manuscript, Paris, Bibliothèque de l'Arsenal, fonds Léon Moussinac, 114 (13) 4340.

Muchembled, Robert (1989), 'L'Etat et l'image du roi/président: héritages de l'ancien régime', in *L'Identité Française, Colloque à l'Université de Copenhague*, Copenhagen, Akademisk Forlag.

Oms, Marcel (1962), 'Le grand mensonge', *Positif*, no. 47 (July): 5–11.

O'Regan, Tom (1996), *Australian National Cinema*, London and New York, Routledge.

Pateman, Carole (1988), *The Sexual Contract*, Cambridge, Polity.

Pivasset, Jean (1970), *Essai sur la signification politique du cinéma ; l'exemple français, de la libération aux événements de Mai 1968*, Paris, Cujas, 1971.

Proust, Marcel (1956), *A la Recherche du temps perdu*, Paris, Gallimard.

Radhakrishnan, R. (1992), 'Nationalism, Gender, and the Narrative of Identity', in A. Parker, M. Russo, D. Sommer and P. Yaeger (eds), *Nationalisms and Sexualities*, London and New York, Routledge.

Ralite, Jack (1993) 'Laissons la culture hors des conséquences du GATT', *Libération,* 20 April.

Roberts, Mary Louise (1994), *Civilization without Sexes. Reconstructing Gender in Postwar France, 1917–1927*, Chicago, University of Chicago Press.

Rochereau, Jean (1959), '*Hiroshima mon amour*', *La Croix*, no. 23257 (24 June): 6.

Rosenbaum, Jonathan (1996), 'International Harvest', *Chicago Reader* (22 November): 38–41.

—— (1997), 'Trailer for Godard's *Histoire(s) du cinéma*', *Vertigo*, 7, 13–20. First published as Rosenbaum, Jonathan (1997), 'Bande-annonce pour les *Histoire(s) du cinéma* de Godard', *Trafic*, 21: 5–18.

Ross, Kristin (1995), *Fast Cars, Clean Bodies. Decolonization and the Reordering of French Culture*, Cambridge, MA, MIT Press.

Ruby, Christian, Nouvel, Kevin and Simonet, Julie (1993), 'La Bataille du culturel', *Regards sur l'actualité*, no.189 (March 1993).

Rushing, Janice Hocker and Frentz, Thomas S. (1991), 'Integrating Ideology and Archetype in Rhetorical Criticism', *Quarterly Journal of Speech* 77 (3) (November): 385–406.

Sadoul, Georges (1946), 'Hypertrophie du cerveau', *Les Lettres françaises*, no. 115 (5 July): 9.

—— (1947a), 'Georges Méliès et la première élaboration du langage cinématographique', *Revue Internationale de la Filmologie* 1 (juillet–août): 23–30.

—— (ed.) (1947b), Special Supplement to *Sight and Sound*, August.

—— (1958a), 'Depuis Octobre, le cinéma français connait une crise . . .', January, Paris, BIFI, archives Sadoul, GS-A 137.

—— (1958b), 'André Bazin', November, Paris, BIFI, archives Sadoul, GS-A 143.

—— (1958c), 'Enfin un film d'amour', *Les Lettres françaises*, no. 747 (13 November): 6.

—— (1958d), 'Sur le plan de l'art, le dernier semestre 1958 a été bénéfique pour le cinéma français', December, Paris, BIFI, archives Sadoul, GS-A 147.

—— (1959a), 'Livres de cinéma', *Les Lettres françaises*, no. 757 (22 January): 7.

—— (1959b), 'Un jeune auteur complet', *Les Lettres françaises*, no. 761 (19 February): 6.

—— (1959c), 'Naissance d'un néo-romantisme', *Les Lettres françaises*, no. 768 (9 April): 11.

—— (1959d), 'L'univers et la rosée', *Les Lettres françaises*, no. 778, (18 June): 6.

—— (1959e), 'Notes on a New Generation', *Sight and Sound*, vol. 28, no. 3/4 (Summer/Autumn): 111–17, originally in 'Nouveaux réalisateurs et nouveaux films français', June, Paris, BIFI, archives Sadoul, GS-A 149.

—— (1960a), 'Le cinéma français au début de 1960', March, Paris, BIFI, archives Sadoul, GS-A 159.

—— (1960b), 'Quelques sources du nouveau cinéma français', *Esprit*, no. 6 (1 June): 968–78.

—— (1960c), 'Le néoréalisme est mort, vive le néoromantisme . . .', Paris, BIFI, archives Sadoul, GS-A 165.

—— (1960d), 'Le cinéma et l'homme de 1960', *Les Lettres françaises*, no. 837 (18 August): 6.

—— (1962a), '*Entrevista con Georges Sadoul, el Papa de la Critica Cinematographica*, in *Novedades*, Mexico, 29 June, Paris, BIFI, archives Sadoul, GS-E 26.

—— (1962b), *Le Cinéma français*, Paris, Flammarion.

—— (1963), 'Euthanasie du cinéma français', *Les Lettres françaises*, no. 961 (17 January): 1, 7.

—— (1965a), 'Le cinéma français est-il un luxe ?', *Les Lettres françaises*, no. 1062 (7 January): 1, 10.

—— (1965b), 'Les films à gros budgets tuent-ils le cinéma ?', *Les Lettres françaises*, no. 1065 (28 January): 8.

—— (1966), 'Comme l'as de pique', *Les Lettres françaises*, no. 1161 (15 December): 36.

—— (1970), *Georges Méliès*, Paris, Seghers.

Saïd, Edward (1993), *Culture and Imperialism*, New York, Knopf.

Samuels, Andrew (1993), *The Political Psyche,* London, Routledge.

Sand, S. (1994), 'Les sosies cinématographiques de Dreyfus', in L. Gervereau and C. Prochasson (eds), *L'Affaire Dreyfus et le tournant du siècle*, pp. 224–7, Paris, BDIC.

Sartre, Jean-Paul (1947), *Réflexions sur la question juive*, Paris, Gallimard.

Shore, Chris (1993) 'Inventing the "People's Europe": Critical Approaches to European Community "Cultural Policy"', *Man*, Vol. 28, no.4.

Smith, Murray (1995), *Engaging Characters: Fiction, Emotion, and the Cinema*, Oxford, Clarendon Press.

Sontag, Susan (1996), 'The Decay of Cinema', *New York Times Magazine* (25 February): 60–1.

Sorlin, Pierre (1980), 'Présence des Juifs dans le cinéma français à la veille de la Seconde Guerre Mondiale,' in Myriam Yardeni (ed.), *Le Juif dans l'histoire de France*, Leiden, E. J. Brill.

—— (1981). 'Jewish Images in the French Cinema of the 1930s,' *Historical Journal of Film, Radio and Television,* 1 (2): 139–50.

Strauss, Frédéric (1995), 'Lesdits commandements', *Cahiers du cinéma* no. 494 (September).

Taylor, Peter (1997), 'Historical Geography of Modernities', inaugural lecture given at Loughborough University, 30 April 1997.

Terzian, Alain (1993), 'Il n'y a rien à négocier au GATT', *Le Nouvel Economiste*, 3 September.

Toubon, Jacques (1993a), speech at 'Assemblée des Réalisateurs à Vénise', 6 September.

—— (1993b) speech at 'Rencontres cinématographiques de Beaune', 30 October.

Truffaut, François (1975), *Les Films de ma Vie*, Paris, Flammarion.

—— (1986), *Hitchcock*, revised edition, Paris, Paladin.

—— (1987), *Le Plaisir des Yeux*, Paris, Flammarion.

—— (1988), *Le Cinéma selon François Truffaut,* ed. Anne Gillain, Paris, Flammarion.

Turk, Edward Baron (1989), *Child of Paradise: Marcel Carné and the Golden Age of French Cinema*, Cambridge, MA, Harvard University Press.

Turner, Graeme (1993), *Film as Social Practice*, London, Routledge.

Ulanov, Ann Belford (1971), *The Feminine in Jungian Psychology and in Christian Theology,* Evanston, IL, Northwestern University Press.

—— and Ulanov, Barry (1994), *Transforming Sexuality: The Archetypal World of Anima and Animus*, London, Shambhala.

Vautier, René (1998), *Caméra citoyenne*, Paris, Éditions Apogée.

Vincendeau, Ginette (1991), 'Like Eating a Lot of Madeleines', *Monthly Film Bulletin*, March, Vol. 58, no. 686: 69–70.

—— (1995), 'Unsettling Memories', *Sight and Sound*, Vol. 5, Issue 7 (July): 30–2.

—— and Gauteur, Claude (1993), *Jean Gabin. Anatomie d'un mythe*, Paris, Nathan.

Wall, Irwin M. (1983), *French Communism in the Era of Stalin*, Westport, CT, Greenwood Press.

Wallerstein, Immanuel (1983), *Historical Capitalism*, London, Verso.

Wehr, Demaris S. (1987), *Jung and Feminism: Liberating Archetypes*, Boston, Beacon Press.

White, Hayden (1973), *Metahistory: The Historical Imagination in Nineteenth-Century Europe*, Baltimore, MD, Johns Hopkins University Press.

Wild, Florianne (1996), 'L'Histoire ressuscitée: Jewishness and Scapegoating in Julien Duvivier's *Panique*,' in Steven Ungar and Tom Conley (eds), *Identity Papers: Contested Nationhood in Twentieth-Century France*, pp. 178–92, Minneapolis, University of Minnesota Press.

Winock, Michel (1995), *Parlez-moi de la France*, Paris, Editions Plon.

Witt, Michael (1999), 'The Death(s) of Cinema According To Godard', *Screen*, 40 (3): 331–46.

Wood, Robin (1986), *Hollywood from Vietnam to Reagan*, New York, Columbia University Press.

Yonnet, Paul (1993), *Voyage au centre du mal français; l'antiracisme et le roman national*, Paris, Gallimard.

Zavarsadeh, Mas'ud (1991), *Seeing Films Politically*, Albany, NY, State University of New York Press.

Zeldin, Theodore (1977), *France 1848–1945, Vol.2*, New York, Oxford University Press.

Zhang, Yingjin (1994), 'From "Minority Film" to "Minority Discourse": The Questions of Nationhood and Ethnicity in Chinese Cinema', paper delivered at the East Asian Colloquium at the University of Indiana (September).

Zola, Emile (1968), 'La Féerie et l'Opérette', in *Oeuvres complètes*, Vol. 11, Paris, Cercle du Livre Précieux.

Index

Index

Index

in the films of Julien Duvivier 5, 80, 82–83, 85–86, 89–90
Johnny Guitar 172
Joli mai, Le 19
Joly, Danièle 54
Judex 152
Juge et l'assassin, Le 117
Jules et Jim 46, 171
Jungian psychology
    anima/animus 181–5, 191
    archetypes 181, 187–8
    conjunctio oppositorum 192
    cultural unconscious 187–92
    symbols 187–8, 190

Kassovitz, Mathieu 2
    see also La Haine
Kast, Pierre 51
Kerjean, Germaine 160
King, Rodney 154
Klapisch, Cédric 21
Kracauer, Siegfried 31
Kristeva, Julia 195
Kurosawa, Akira 174
Kurys, Diane 6, 115–125
    authorial presence in films 120
    autobiography 115–6
    critique of male behaviour 124
    female experiences 116–7, 122–5
    funding 119
    nostalgia 116–7, 119–21, 124–5
    period reconstruction 119–21
    use of music 120
    visual motifs 120
    see also *Diabolo menthe, Coup de foudre, Cocktail molotov, La Baule les Pins*
Kyrou Ado 51, 53

Lacan, Jacques 104
Lachize, Samuel 44, 50, 52
Lacombe Lucien 117, 196
Lamartine, Alphonse de 51
Lang, Fritz 27, 174
Langlois, Henri 16, 19, 25, 29
Le Chanois, Jean-Paul
Le Vigan, Robert 90, 159
Léaud, Jean-Pierre 152
Ledoux, Fernand 159
Leiris, Michel 21

Lettres françaises, Les 47, 53, 55
Lois d'aide
    Loi d'aide 1948 15, 19
    Loi d'aide 1953 16, 19
    Loi d'aide 1959 16, 19
Louise l'insoumise 116
Lubitsch, Ernst 174
Lumière brothers 98, 147–8, 151–2
Luna, La 183

Maastricht treaty 61–62, 66, 68
MacCabe, Colin 33–34
Magnificent Ambersons, The 47
May 1968 4, 27, 54, 116–119, 121
Malle, Louis 45, 46, 49, 51, 55, 116–7, 173, 196
    see also *Ascenseur pour l'échafaud, Au revoir les enfants, Les Amants, Lacaome Lucien*
Malraux, André 16, 19
Marcuse, Herbert 137
Marey, Etienne-Jules 9
Maria Braun 37
Marianne 79
Marie, Michel 43
Mariee était en noir, La 171
Marker, Chris 19, 46
Marseillaise, la (anthem) 66, 131
Marseillaise, La (film) 132–6, 139
Marshall, Tonie 21
Martin, Marcel
Marx, Karl 162
masquerade 109–112
Maupassant, Guy de 51
Mazursky, Paul 118
    see also *An Unmarried Woman*
Méliès, Georges 7, 145–156
    and Doublier Affair 149–152
    as actor 147
    censorship 150
    deep staging 147
    see also *L'Affaire Dreyfus*
Metz, Christian 151
Miéville, Anne-Marie 30, 36
Minghella, Anthony 100
    see also *The English Patient*
Miou-Miou 119
Mistons, Les 170, 173
Mitry, Jean 151